D0214460

The Tradition of Women's Autobiography: From Antiquity to the Present

The Tradition of Women's Autobiography: From Antiquity to the Present

Estelle C. Jelinek

Twayne Publishers • Boston
A Division of G. K. Hall & Co.

The Tradition of
Women's Autobiography:
From Antiquity to the Present

Estelle C. Jelinek

Published by Twayne Publishers
A Division of G. K. Hall & Co.
70 Lincoln Street, Boston, Massachusetts 02111

Copyediting supervised by Lewis DeSimone
Designed and produced by Marne B. Sultz
Typeset by Compset, Inc. of Beverly, Massachusetts

Printed on permanent/durable acid-free
paper and bound in the United States of America

First Printing

Library of Congress Cataloging in Publication Data

Jelinek, Estelle C.
The tradition of women's autobiography from antiquity to the present.

Bibliography: p. 212
Includes index.
1. Autobiography—Women authors. I. Title.
CT25.J45 1986 810'.99287 86-9962
ISBN 0-8057-9018-7
ISBN 0-8057-9021-7 (pbk)

To my mother and my sister, and to
the memory of my father

Contents

Preface

In 1976 I first formulated my observation that women and men write different kinds of autobiographies.[1] This difference came to me empirically when, after a decade of reading, teaching, and studying women's autobiographies, I began to read many more men's autobiographies than before. It was underscored when I studied in earnest the many critical works on autobiography and discovered that the theories presented, for the most part, were not applicable to women's autobiographies. And for good reason: All the attempts to define the genre were based exclusively on men's autobiographies (see the Introduction).

In 1980, in my introductory essay to the anthology *Women's Autobiography: Essays in Criticism,*[2] I compared in detail the differences between women's and men's autobiographies that I had found in the most familiar and famous works, especially those written in the last two centuries. But I was not satisfied. I felt the need to read many unfamiliar and unknown works from literary history to see whether the separate women's autobiographical tradition that I had found was a phenomenon of the modern era or had also existed in earlier times. Thus, I undertook the present study.

My continued research supported my theory even more than I had anticipated. It was substantiated in the earliest known self-writings by women—Egyptian inscriptions and tales, a Roman memoir, and three religious confessionals; in autobiographies from the first centuries of literature in England and America; and finally in the nineteenth and twentieth centuries.

Since there is no complete bibliography of women's autobiographies in the English language—in any language for that matter—nor any quantitative data on the types of autobiographies written in given historical periods, most of the works discussed or mentioned here were culled from the bibliographies compiled by William Matthews (British before 1951) and Louis Kaplan (American up to 1945).[3] Thereafter, I made choices from the many published autobiographies found in sources from a variety of disciplines, including contemporary book reviews and personal correspondence.

The reader should understand at the outset that this is not a comparative study. While I sometimes refer to men's autobiographies or the male autobiographical tradition,[4] that tradition is already adequately documented and analyzed in dozens of critical works on autobiography, most of which are cited in the notes or the Bibliography. However, I shall mention differences in various aspects of content and form between women's and men's autobiographies when a comparison seems obvious and appropriate.

My intention is to trace the history of women's autobiographies by focusing on their subject matter and narrative forms and the self-image that is projected. I have chosen to describe these life studies chronologically, rather than thematically, in the interest of historical continuity rather than with some developmental theory in mind, although one cannot help but notice a progression in self-assertion, self-confidence, and literary sophistication. Psychological and political sophistication also changed as women became more active and accepted members of society. But the consistent pattern of similar characteristics that I found from earliest times is there, for the most part irrespective of, indifferent to, or ignorant of what others (female or male) were writing, or even the time, place, occupation, personality, or historical/political events involved.

Most autobiographical criticism today falls into two categories: thematic interpretation and theoretical definition of the genre. At different stages of the preparation of this work, various readers have offered suggestions for a thematic study. Many pointed to psychological themes, such as the relationship between the autobiographer and her mother, her father, siblings, men, and other women; the childhood crises of autobiographers; and their efforts to reconcile their professional and personal lives. Others suggested symbolic themes, such as the ordinary or domestic versus the exotic or eccentric, or woman as mythic heroine. Still others proposed historical themes, such as the course of feminist consciousness or women's cultural history. The themes suggested were as many and as varied as those who offered them.

Some readers have wondered how these autobiographies fit the dicta of theoretical critics who attempt to define the genre by citing only male autobiographies. Again, as with the themes, there are too many studies, too many theories and theorists, to undertake such a task, and it would result in a totally different book from that intended here. However, I do, in places—primarily in the notes—cite appraisals by critics when they mention a woman's autobiography and their interpretations and prejudices shed some light on why so many of these life studies have been ignored.

Thus, this study takes a different tack from such thematic and theoretical considerations. I could have chosen any number of themes and with a selective sample developed an analysis; indeed, it is possible to choose a sample to fit virtually any theory. But I wanted to trace the most salient and basic traits that appeared—in and of themselves—in as representative a sampling as possible of published autobiographies written by women in the English language. I did my research empirically, reading randomly among the unknown autobiographies and gleaning their characteristics from their contents alone. The scant criticism on these and more familiar life studies either substantiated my findings or offered nothing contradictory. (See the Introduction for a discussion of the traits most commonly associated with men's autobiographies.)

The reader should also note that I have not compared information presented in these works with that in respective biographies, for I treat each autobiography as a literary work. Personality and writing skill are what shape an autobiography, and it is the final product that I describe, without judging the accuracy or objectivity of the narrative. I assume that the "self" portrayed in each work is as unified and accurate (or not) as the writer projects and that the self-knowledge provided is as reliable as the author wants or is able to present, just as the protagonist of a novel is as unified and as reliable as the author is able to create. Of course, the novelist has omniscient control of her material, and the autobiographer does not, though she may strive for it.

Moreover, though I am a feminist and often point out the feminist consciousness of many of the autobiographies, this book is not intended as feminist history; however, the evolution of women's history asserts itself in the subjects these writers treat. As a humanist, rather than as a social scientist or a historian, I focus on the literary characteristics of the autobiographies—not on the women as people, which a biographer would analyze, nor on the historical, sociological, or cultural times in which the autobiographers lived and wrote. Indeed, too long a time span is covered to discuss more than the highlights of the political events that figure in the autobiographies—most often in those by nonliterary women. My concern is with the nature of the autobiographies themselves: their content, the narrative forms in which they are shaped, and the self-image that informs them.

I must also mention the nature/nurture issue, which is a point of contention frequently raised with studies such as the present one. I do not claim a hereditary or biological explanation for the consistent pattern of characteristics I find in these female autobiographies. Freud, Jung, and Erikson, among others, have offered theories that the differences between women and men seem predominantly "natural," or at least "inevitable"; other psychologists, sociologists, and students of human nature and society are persuaded that it is the "nurturing" socialization processes of civilizations—where physical and material resources constitute power—that are responsible for these differences. Surely, both nature and nurture are involved in an interactive way, and at this point, it would be presumptuous to postulate a definitive explanation.[5]

Many critics seem to feel threatened by the notion of a "women's autobiographical tradition" because it conjures up a relativism that negates conventional valuation. However, in what follows I am not arguing for "better" (or "worse"), but for "different." An autobiography may be "good" or "great" independent of whether it has the characteristics usually associated with men's or women's autobiographies. My argument is with critics who ignore women's autobiographies because they do not fit their criteria of a "proper" autobiography, one that has the characteristics found in men's autobiographies.

Thus, this study seeks to accomplish for women's autobiography what Wayne Shumaker's *English Autobiography* did for men's autobiography thirty years ago: It documents the literary history of the characteristics in women's self-writings, which contemporary autobiographers continue. My title could easily have been a variant of Shumaker's: *Women's Autobiography: Its Emergence, Materials, and Forms,* because that describes my effort precisely. Although this is not a definitive literary history or study of all the types of autobiographies written by women, it does attempt to fill the gap between a wasteland of criticism on women's autobiography and the critical plunge feminist scholarship has taken in the past ten years or so without benefit of a solid background in women's autobiographical works.

I consider an autobiography as that work each autobiographer writes with the intention of its being her life story—whatever form, content, or style it takes. Though I occasionally refer to diaries, letters, and journals (to place them in historical context), I rarely discuss them because I do not consider them autobiographies. I do consider works entitled "recollections," "reminiscences," "memoirs," and the like as autobiographies if the author's intent was to write a life study, to look back over her life or a portion of it. Autobiography is an amalgam of one's self-image, one's process of thinking and feeling, and one's talent as a formal writer. Each autobiography, therefore, is unique and defies a formal definition that subsumes all autobiography.

Because many of the autobiographers I discuss here are not generally known, I include birth and death dates where available, single and married names, and pertinent information about their lives and/or their other published works. I also include summaries of autobiographies not easily accessible to the public and whose content seems especially interesting or relevant to contemporary readers, for example, their feminist consciousness, their early awareness of medical issues, or their active participation in politics. Because there are so many, I have not been able to read or analyze all the books mentioned, but I do discuss a fair representation of the various types I found during each given period in England and America. Thereafter, I may list similar works to indicate the extent and variety of such life studies.

In brief, the subjects women write about are remarkably similar: family, close friends, domestic activities. While there is a subjective strain in the mode of expression, on the whole it is straightforward and objective. Motives and intentions differ, of course. The catalyst may be a religious purpose or a specific event, such as Indian captivity, the Civil War, women's suffrage, or birth control. But the emphasis remains on personal matters—not the professional, philosophical, or historical events that are more often the subject of men's autobiographies.

Likewise, the identity image is similar throughout women's autobiographies. In contrast to the self-confident, one-dimensional self-image that men usually project, women often depict a multidimensional, fragmented self-image colored by a sense of inadequacy and alienation, of being outsiders or "other"; they feel the need for authentication, to prove their self-worth. At the same time, and paradoxically, they project self-confidence and a positive sense of accomplishment in having overcome many obstacles to their success—whether it be personal or professional.

Perhaps not surprisingly, the style of these autobiographies is, for the most part, also similar, and it is integral with such a paradoxical self-image: episodic and anecdotal, nonchronological and disjunctive. Although there are a fair number of exceptions—women writing in typically male progressive and linear narratives and men writing anecdotally and disjunctively, especially in recent decades—the pattern does persist. Whether or not there is a direct connection between the disjunctive style of women's autobiographies and the fragmentation of their lives may be speculative, but it is a reasonable conjecture.

• • •

The plan of this work is as follows. To accomplish my first objective of documenting the tradition out of which contemporary American female autobiographers write, I offer in the Introduction a retrospective summary of the critical literature on male autobiography to provide a context for my own criticism of female autobiographers. I then sketch in Part I the beginnings of women's autobiographical writings from antiquity through the Renaissance, and then British autobiography to the end of the nineteenth century. Most of the works I discuss here are recognized by critics, though their treatment has often been scanty or shortsighted. I fill in the picture with an analysis of similar but unknown autobiographies culled primarily from Matthews's bibliography.

In Part II my survey of American autobiographies from the early seventeenth century through the nineteenth includes works recognized by critics, as well as many more that have not been treated before. Some of these were selected from Kaplan's bibliography, but I also draw my examples from various other sources.

From this review of the tradition of women's autobiographies—including its contribution to the autobiographical tradition as a whole—I proceed in Part III with my second major objective: to demonstrate with case studies my thesis of a separate tradition. Here I analyze four modern American autobiographers—two political figures and two literary ones—who continue the female tradition and also make their own personal contributions to it. They are Elizabeth Cady Stanton (*Eighty Years and More: Reminiscences, 1815–1897,* 1898), Gertrude Stein (*The Autobiography of Alice B. Toklas,* 1933, and *Everybody's Autobiography,* 1937), Lillian Hellman (*An Unfinished Woman,* 1969, *Pentimento,* 1973, and *Scoundrel Time,* 1976), and Kate Millett (*Flying,* 1974).

Stanton's *Reminiscences* is never considered in critical studies of autobiography. Yet in women's history, she was the major intellectual figure of her time, a leader in the first important movement for women's rights. Stanton's life spanned the nineteenth century (1815–1902), and as such her life study has many of the characteristics of historical and progressive autobiographies of the time, but it is also shaped by the female tradition with its personal emphasis and digressive style. Stanton consciously manipulated her narrative in order to avoid unpleasantness and to achieve her twofold intention: to gain personal and professional acceptance as both an ordinary *and* an exceptional woman, and to propagandize for the cause of women's suffrage.

Gertrude Stein (1874–1946) was also in many ways a nineteenth-century woman. Though she benefited from the first wave of feminism and led a life of expatriation and literary independence, she was still a product of American Puritanism. In transforming the exotic strain in women's autobiographies from a subjective mode to an intellectual exercise, Stein is able to protect her intimate life from public scrutiny. This considerably more male than female treatment may explain why her autobiography has been given such extensive attention in studies of the genre. It is important then to consider how her two life studies fit into the female tradition.

Lillian Hellman (1905–84) was a product of the upheaval of American society after World War I. An emancipated adult in a society liberated from Victorianism, she nonetheless represents the generation of women who still needed to prove themselves the equals of men. Her psychological sophistication and dramatic skills combine in autobiographies that emphasize the personal and gradually discard imitation of the progressive mode for the disjunctive one.

Kate Millett (1934–) represents the struggles of the twentieth-century New Woman, a feminist who is more liberated than her nineteenth-century sisters but who is still part of the ongoing movement for a freer society for both men and women. Heir to Stanton's political activism, Millett integrates the personal and the political in the story of her life and extends the stylistic characteristics of the female tradition to its outer limits.

Each of these women is an important representative of her generation, and her autobiography represents one moment in the history of the progressive articulation of the women's autobiographical tradition. No matter how different the objective facts of their lives, the characteristics of their autobiographies demonstrate the continuation of a discrete women's autobiographical tradition, a literary tradition of their own.

Acknowledgments

Many people have lent their support to this project, from its earliest stages through the many years since, as the manuscript went through several drafts and revisions. For earlier help, my special thanks to Leslie Fiedler, my dissertation supervisor, who offered his enthusiasm and invaluable insights; to Claire Kahane, who helped to sharpen my perceptions; to Ellen DuBois, whose finely tuned feminist consciousness brought clarity to many of the conflicts in my own mind as well as some in my authors', especially Elizabeth Cady Stanton; and to Howard Wolf, who was the first to take my writing seriously.

Since those days, many others have lent much needed emotional, intellectual, and/or practical support. They include Joey D. Botti, Brad Bunnin, Denis Clifford, Zippie Collins, Miriam DeVries, Clifford Fred, Judith Lerner, Sheila Levine, Celeste MacLeod, Naomi Puro, Lisa Smith, Harriet Ziskin, my diligent typist Barbara Gunderson, and the fine staff of the Interlibrary Borrowing Service of the University of California at Berkeley. I also want to thank Anne M. Jones, my editor at G. K. Hall, and Josephine Donovan for her excellent job of copyediting the book at its final stage.

Finally, although few critical studies of autobiography were relevant to my study, nonetheless, I am indebted to Wayne Shumaker, James Olney, Albert E. Stone, and Patricia Meyer Spacks, whose intelligent and sensitive studies enriched my reading of autobiography in general.

I also wish to acknowledge that parts of the Introduction and of the chapter on Elizabeth Cady Stanton appeared in *Women's Autobiography: Essays in Criticism* (Indiana University Press, 1980).

Introduction

Autobiographical Criticism: An Overview

The Question of Genre: Legitimacy

Before beginning our study of women's autobiography, it will be useful to summarize the criticism that has set the standards for judging autobiographies by both men and women. It is only since World War II that autobiography has been considered a legitimate genre worthy of formal study. Before then, autobiographies were considered of interest almost exclusively for the information they provided about the lives of their authors; there was virtually no interest in the style or form of the life studies. Most criticism concentrated on British and Continental autobiographies of famous men whose private lives were a source of curiosity. Even today, with increasing interest in American autobiographies, British life studies still garner the most critical attention. Although there are quite a number of articles and books on American autobiography, they deal with only a fraction of the total: There is as yet no full-scale critical study of American autobiography.[1]

The first decade of the twentieth century witnessed two pioneering historical studies of autobiography. Georg Misch's 1907 two-volume *History of Autobiography in Antiquity* traces the growth of the concept of individuality from the self-presentations seen in Egyptian inscriptions, through Greek love lyrics and Roman orations, to Augustine's *Confessions.* Anna Robeson Burr's 1909 *Autobiography: A Critical and Comparative Study* concentrates on French memoirs and British Quaker journals of the seventeenth and eighteenth centuries, largely in terms of their authors' occupations and personalities. Burr's concern with the seriousness, sincerity, and high moral character of autobiographers leads her to deplore the only American autobiography she mentions, Benjamin Franklin's, for its typically American materialism.

During the next twenty years no studies of autobiography appeared. However, in the 1930s, publication of a larger number of autobiographies revived interest in their critical analysis. These critics, in the Misch-Burr tradition, discuss only the subject matter of the autobiographies and share a propensity for making moral judgments about the authors.[2] They rarely see any distinction between autobiography and biography, considering both merely the story of a person's life.[3] Edgar Johnson's definition of biography best sums up this thirties view. It includes "not only formal biography, but all kinds of autobiography—letters, journals, reminiscences—for all biography is ultimately founded in a kind of autobiography."[4]

The critical study of autobiography began to come into its own after World War II, when the formal analysis of all types of literature burgeoned. The publication of two bibliographies of autobiographies—William Matthews's *British Autobiographies: An Annotated Bibliography of British Autobiographies Published or Written before 1951* (1955) and Louis Kaplan's *A Bibliography of American Autobiographies* (1961) up to 1945[5]—contributed to the study of the genre.

During the fifties and sixties, critics of autobiography turned their attention primarily to questions of legitimacy: whether or not autobiography was, indeed, a genuine literary genre or merely a branch of history. A particular concern was to distinguish autobiography from letters, journals, reminiscences, biographies, and the like, that is, the forms the thirties critics lumped together. Wayne Shumaker was the first to come out clearly on the literary side of the debate, advancing the claim that autobiography was a genre distinct from biography.[6] Barrett John Mandel agrees, arguing that autobiography is a "conscious shaping of the selected events of one's life into a coherent whole." Other forms may be unified, he writes, but they are not centered "on the life of the author as it was lived."[7] Georges Gusdorf argues that "the literary, artistic function is . . . of greater importance than the historical and objective function."[8]

Roy Pascal's *Design and Truth in Autobiography* (1960) decisively opts for a formal distinction. He maintains that memoirs and reminiscences are works about others whereas autobiography is a retrospective, coherent, and holistic shaping, the imposition of a pattern upon a life.[9] Robert Sayre's *The Examined Self* (1964) similarly rejects the equation of autobiography with biography and history, suggesting themes and techniques shared by novels and autobiographies.[10]

Some critics, however, were uncomfortable with the limitations imposed by formal definitions and argued for more flexibility in defining the genre. Thus, Stephen Spender, in "Confessions and Autobiography" (1955), urges the acceptance of subjective revelations, albeit recognizing that the effort to integrate the public and the private selves sometimes results in autobiographies ungainly in form.[11] Richard Lillard (*American Life in Autobiography,* 1956), contending that an autobiography always has a historical frame of reference, finds merit in life studies that exemplify the American theme of progress.[12] A decade later Stephen Shapiro considered autobiography as straddling the realms of both literature and history. Autobiography's "aesthetic function," he writes, "is not its major function: education or reality testing is its reason for being. Autobiography is a mixed form, less delightful than poetry but more useful."[13] James Cox goes so far as to describe autobiography as "not a genre at all in the sense that poetry, fiction, and drama are. It is a term designating a subclass of that hopelessly confusing variety of writing we place under the heading of nonfiction prose."[14] And Albert Stone defines it as "a content not a form."[15]

The seventies saw a few formal critics shifting ground somewhat from the earlier purist position, perhaps because of the waning influence of New Criticism, perhaps because of the appearance of so many and varied autobiographies during the second half of the twentieth century, perhaps because of a relativism engendered by the sixties' cultural revolution—most likely because of a combination of factors. Then, it was not unusual to find critics arguing that in autobiography content and form may be indistinguishable, an opinion current today.

For example, Francis Hart, in "Notes for an Anatomy of Modern Autobiography" (1970), asserts that as a genre of self-discovery autobiography is capable of any combination of truth and fiction. Of its form, Hart writes: "The paradox of continuity in discontinuity is itself a problem to be experimented with, and it is a problem both of truth and form."[16] In *Metaphors of Self* (1972), James Olney contends that all autobiography is a process, neither a form nor a content. It is neither fiction nor history, but each man's metaphor of his self—the predetermined self-image that shapes both the content and form of his life and his life study.[17] (When I use "men" or "his," I do so intentionally; these critics are speaking of *men's* autobiographies. See below, "Subjects of the Search.") Elizabeth Bruss (*Autobiographical Acts,* 1976) argues, in a similar vein, that each autobiography's form varies according to the person writing it. But despite variations in the genre, there "are certain common tendencies . . . a leaning toward discontinuous structures, for instance, with disrupted narrative sequences and competing foci of attention. The 'story' the autobiography tells is never seamless, and often is not a story at all but a string of meditations and vignettes."[18]

In *The Value of the Individual* (1978) Karl Weintraub analyzes autobiographical forms as having evolved from stereotypical personality modes to the modern expression of each author's unique personality.[19] William Spengemann (*The Forms of Autobiography,* 1980) traces the evolution of autobiographical form from its historical origins to its kinship with poetic and fictional modes, in which each author invents a self in the process of writing.[20]

In *Figures of Autobiography* (1983) Avrom Fleishman argues that autobiography may not be a genre at all—as did Paul deMan several years earlier—because it takes so many different forms. Fleishman "doubts that a continuous history of autobiography can be written," but he does trace "continuities in the language" that persist from Augustine to nineteenth-century British autobiographers and novelists. Paul John Eakin, in *Fictions in Autobiography: Studies in the Art of Self-Invention* (1985), claims that autobiographical truth is not a fixed but an evolving constant in a process of self-creation.[21]

The varieties of definitions—that is, the lack of definition, which, after all, implies consensus—of the genre may be an occupational hazard of critics still defensive about the legitimacy of autobiography as a *literary* genre. Antihistoricists, such as linguists, deconstructionists, and post-structuralists, believe that no literary history can be written about autobiography because its characteristics have not been defined. However, most critics today tend to accept autobiography as a content, not a strictly defined form, and get on with the interpretative function of literary criticism. That has been the case with most contemporary female critics—Patricia Meyer Spacks, Mary Mason, and Lynn Z. Bloom, among others.[22] There is less concern now with prescriptive definitions of a "true" or "good" autobiography, less interest, by and large, in the philosophical or abstract, more with the concrete and the personal.

Despite this egalitarianism, critics by and large still have certain expectations of a "good" autobiography. It must center exclusively or mostly on their authors, not on others; otherwise, it becomes memoir or reminiscence. It should be representative of its times, a mirror of the predominant zeitgeist. The autobiographer should be self-aware, a seeker after self-knowledge. He must aim to explore, not to exhort. His autobiography should be an effort to give meaning to some personal mythos.

Such expectations or assumptions about the "ideal" autobiography are frequently grander than the achievements. Critics, especially in reviewing new autobiographies, often complain that they merely describe a profession or a calling, rarely attempting to integrate the public image with the inner life. Autobiographers are frequently faulted for excluding the personal and intimate, the very details most readers want to know. This is, perhaps, an unrealistic expectation for reasons expressed by William Matthews three decades ago:

> Few autobiographers put into their books very much of that private, intimate knowledge of themselves that only they can have. Oftener than not, they shun their own inner peculiarities and fit themselves into patterns of behavior and character suggested by the ideas and ideals of their period and by the fashions in autobiography with which they associate themselves. The laws of literature and the human reluctance to stand individually naked combine to cheat the expectations of readers who hope to find in autobiographies many revelations of men's true selves.[23]

Although intimacy is rare in autobiography—by men or women—certain personal details are considered extraneous to a reflective, artistically selective life study. These include one's domestic life, minor illnesses, and other matters considered trivial and mundane. Although most critics no longer expect autobiographies to adhere stylistically to a precise progressive narrative, nonetheless a unified shaping is considered ideal. That unity should be achieved by concentrating on one period of the autobiographer's life, the development of his life according to one theme, or the analysis of his character in terms of an important aspect of it. The autobiographer is expected to "gather the different elements of his personal life and organize them into a single whole," to begin his life study "with the problem already solved."[24]

These expectations and assumptions figure significantly in explaining the neglect and disparagement of women's autobiographies from earliest times to the present. It will be valuable for the reader to keep them in mind as we describe women's autobiographies in the chapters that follow.

Subjects of the Search

The reader should also be aware that such expectations or definitions of autobiography are based on the reading—almost exclusively—of men's autobiographies. This section reveals which autobiographies critics have analyzed, in order to shed more light on why the characteristics of the women's autobiographical tradition have been ignored or are unknown.

Shumaker covers all the major autobiographies by men from Augustine through Yeats—with special chapters on Mill, Trollope, and George Moore. His is the only study to pay respectable attention to British female autobiographers in the context of the male autobiographies he analyzes, crediting several women in the eighteenth century with major innovations in the genre (see chapter 3). But though he considers male autobiographers up to World War II, he treats no twentieth-century women (and only three in the nineteenth century: Margaret Oliphant, Harriet Martineau, and Annie Besant).

Spender discusses the autobiographies of Augustine, Rousseau, and Henry Miller; and Gusdorf those by Augustine, Cellini, Montaigne, Cardinal de Retz, Goethe, Chateaubriand, Newman, and Mill. Neither critic mentions a single woman's autobiography. Though Pascal gives some attention to Teresa's *Life* in his discussion of classical and early post-Christian autobiographies, for the modern period he discusses only famous male autobiographies, including those by Freud, Trotsky, Yeats, O'Casey, Collingwood, Gosse, Churchill, and Gandhi, but mentions only briefly those by Martineau and Beatrice Webb.

Sayre's work on American autobiography treats Franklin, Adams, and James. Mandel considers Augustine, Rousseau, Goethe, Cowper, Wordsworth, George Anne Bellamy, Franklin, Twain, Adams, and Gertrude Stein. Shapiro refers to Rousseau, Goethe, Gibbon, Collingwood, Freud, Darwin, and Trotsky, many other British and Continental autobiographers, and Americans Franklin, Adams, and Henry Miller. Hart refers to the life studies of Gibbon, Wordsworth, George Moore, Gosse, O'Casey, Wells, T. E. Lawrence, Basil Willey, C. Day Lewis, Goethe, Gide, Sartre, and Malraux, plus a number of Americans—Hemingway, Nabokov, Dahlberg, Mailer, Claude Brown, Richard Wright, Podhoretz, Cleaver, and Anaïs Nin.

Cox examines the autobiographies of Franklin, Thoreau, Whitman, and Adams, with brief remarks on Stein. In *Metaphors of Self* Olney devotes whole chapters to Montaigne, Fox, Darwin, Newman, Mill, and T. S. Eliot with not a single mention, even in passing, of a female autobiographer. Almost a decade later, despite the women's movement, Olney remains ignorant of or indifferent to women's autobiographies both in the introduction to his 1980 edited collection of essays and even in the selections themselves: Only a single essay (Mary Mason's) deals with women's autobiographies.[25]

Nor is Olney exceptional in this respect. Despite the second women's movement of the late sixties and seventies, critics still exclude women's autobiographies from their theoretical analyses. Weintraub's study includes an almost entirely male cast of classic Continental authors, from Augustine, Abélard, and Petrarch to Bunyan, Vico, Gibbon, and Goethe, among others. Spengemann encompasses an international list of classic authors (all male): Augustine—whom he considers the ancestor of all autobiographers—Dante, Bunyan, Franklin, Rousseau, Wordsworth, De Quincey, Carlyle, Dickens, and Hawthorne. Fleishman, too, includes only male autobiographers, though he analyzes the works of several female novelists—Charlotte Brontë, George Eliot, Virginia Woolf, and Dorothy Richardson—for the way in which these reflect their authors' lives.

Thematic and nontheoretical critical studies and those that specialize in a particular historical period are only slightly more likely to include women. In British studies, Paul Delany's work on seventeenth-century autobiography segregates female autobiographers in a separate chapter, out of chronology and context, even though he credits the women with major innovations in the development of the genre and even considers them far superior to the male autobiographers discussed in the rest of his critique. Another study of seventeenth-century British autobiographies, by Dean Ebner, which investigates the theological influence on the shaping of the self, gives scant attention to several women, most of whom are treated in footnotes. In *The Art of Autobiography in Nineteenth- and Twentieth-Century England* (1984), A. O. J. Cockshut analyzes the relation of autobiography to truth and imaginative literature, stressing the childhood of autobiographers and how they come to reject its values and social mores. Although Cockshut discusses in great detail the works of many men, such as Victor Gollancz, Stephen Spender, W. H. Hudson, Edmund Gosse, John Cowper Powys, and a number of lesser known male autobiographers, the only female writers to which he devotes respectable attention are Beatrice Webb, Kathleen Raine, and Harriette Wilson. He barely touches on several obscure female autobiographers and does not even mention Harriet Martineau or Margaret Oliphant.[26]

This is also the case with most critical studies of American autobiographies. Daniel Shea's work on spiritual autobiography does give attention to the three most famous colonial women's autobiographies, those by Elizabeth Ashbridge, Anne Bradstreet, and Elizabeth White. Mutlu K. Blasing's *The Art of Life* (1977) treats only men; Thomas Cooley, in his *Educated Lives* (1976), discusses Adams, Twain, Howells, James, Stephens, Anderson, and Stein. G. Thomas Couser's tracing of the prophetic tradition in American literature from Thomas Shepard to Robert Pirsig makes a weak case for the only woman he includes—of course, Gertrude Stein. Standing almost alone, Albert Stone (*Autobiographical Occasions*, 1982) devotes credible attention to Margaret Mead, Lillian Hellman, and Anaïs Nin and discusses briefly, in context, many other female autobiographers.[27]

The fact that a critic is female does not guarantee that she has caught up with history, as Elizabeth Bruss's *Autobiographical Acts* (1976) demonstrates; her four chapters on Bunyan, Boswell, De Quincey, and Nabokov reveal an international egalitarianism but not a gender one. This is also the case with Janet Varner Gunn's *Autobiography: Toward a Poetics of Experience* (1982); four chapters analyze the autobiographical works of Thoreau, Wordsworth, Proust, and Augustine and Black Elk.[28]

Clearly, women's autobiographies are not discussed or analyzed nearly as much as men's. What would happen if critics as a matter of course included representative women's autobiographies in their studies? Would they modify their definitions, their theories, their ideas about the major characteristics of the genre? It is an open question. However, they could not escape the conclusion that contemporary women are writing out of and continuing to create a wholly different autobiographical tradition from that delineated in studies of male autobiography. Perhaps, if evaluated in light of the female tradition, women's autobiographies might earn more attention and respect than they have previously been granted.

We turn now to our primary concern, the study of women's autobiographies from antiquity to the present, with an eye to ascertaining what characteristics, definitions, and criteria emerge from an analysis of their content and style, their form and organization, and the self-image that informs their work.

PART I:
From Antiquity to Nineteenth-Century British Autobiography

· 1 ·

Earliest Stirrings:
The Mystical Voice

Autobiographical works are rare in antiquity before the Roman and Christian eras, beginning about A.D. 100. However, the earliest known first-person records come from Egyptian inscriptions to gods on tombs and pillars. The only known inscriptions to a goddess concern Isis; one typical pillar inscription reads: "What I have made law can be dissolved by no man."[1] The earliest secular inscriptions consisted of prayers for offerings and for a good reception in the land of the dead, the ancient Egyptians being firm believers in an afterlife. Most of these tomb inscriptions glorify the careers and heroic deeds of statesmen, generals, and emperors. In Assyria and Babylonia as well as Egypt, it was customary to record the deeds of kings in the form of chronicles in the first person, making it appear that the king was telling his own story, but it is highly unlikely that they were autobiographical. These inscriptions and chronicles were neither elaborate nor introspective, but, befitting epitaphs for immortals, were self-laudatory catalogs of virtues.[2]

The earliest known tomb inscription by a woman occurs in the Old Kingdom, during the Fifth Dynasty, ca. 2450–2300 B.C., that by Princess Nj-sedjer-kai, which typically and briefly lists prayers for offerings and for a good reception in the afterlife. In the Sixth Dynasty (ca. 2300–2150 B.C.) such prayers gradually gave way to longer, more autobiographical portraits, two of which by men are extant—by Weni and by Harkhuf—but none by a woman. They provide elaborate listings of their deeds as statesmen and military leaders, are chronological and self-congratulatory, and make no mention of personal matters.[3]

The earliest known first-person narratives, as distinct from inscriptions or biographical listings, come from the Middle Kingdom (ca. 2000–1786 B.C.). None is by a woman. During the Eighteenth and Nineteenth Dynasties of the New Kingdom (ca. 1570–1085 B.C.), these narratives became increasingly imaginative. Generally tales of magic and fantasy, they probably existed during the earlier kingdoms and in the Orient; however the extant papyri are from this later Egyptian period. Because the protagonists are usually gods and because the worlds of myth, religion, and folk history intermingle, first-person narrators serve to make the tales more credible. Only one such tale narrated by a woman is extant, the first-person "Tale of Ahuri," from the Nineteenth Dynasty,[4] which occurs within a longer tale, "Setna and the Magic Book."

Unlike the tales narrated by men, such as the "Life of Sinuhe," which begins with a crisis in his fortunes, Ahuri (or Ahura) describes her whole life, from childhood to death. The daughter of a pharaoh, she tells of her courtship by her brother, her "getting around" her father, the pharaoh, to elicit his agreement to the marriage—a common practice to ensure royal blood for heirs—the birth of her son, her marital difficulties, and her burial arrangements. It seems likely that a real female author dictated this tale because the focus on personal and familial matters is uncharacteristic of the tales narrated from the male perspective. Ahuri also notes that she can read but not write, which would mean that she had to dictate her tale. Women, even queens and their daughters, did not hold a high place in Egyptian society and were usually uneducated, even illiterate. Another bit of speculative evidence for a possible female author is the frequent interruption of the narrative with flashbacks—Ahuri tells her story as though from the grave. All the tales narrated from the male perspective that I read were written in strictly chronological order. As we shall see, Ahuri's disjunctiveness is characteristic of women's autobiographies.

Not until the Hellenistic age does the history of self-portraits resume. The Greeks, however, were interested in a collective ideal, not in the lives of individuals per se. Nor were they concerned with a person's reputation after death or in immortality, unlike the Egyptians, but rather with "the idea of man's helplessness before the mysterious forces of Fate."[5] Nonetheless, the Hellenic concept of the self to which many of the lyric poets of the sixth century B.C. gave voice was a major contribution to autobiography. One of these poets was Sappho, whom Plato called the Tenth Muse. Misch, in his discussion of the beginning of self-reflection in Greek lyric poetry—in contrast to mere self-presentation—credits two of Sappho's male contemporaries with originating this perspective. But whereas Archilochus's poetry emphasized his warrior activities and Solon's elegiac poems to himself recorded his great work of political reform, Sappho's poems are personal love lyrics and constitute a self-portrait. Plato characterized them as passionately direct and simple. Misch dismisses Sappho's verses with the following cryptic assessment of her contribution to the autobiographical mode:

Among the new fragments of Sappho yielded to us by the papyri is one in which experts find "some trace of the poem of reflection," in which the audience is, as it were, the writer herself. But the broad fact that at that time individual situations and states of mind had become the subject of poetry is hardly likely to have arisen from such introspection.[6]

It is in Roman times that we have the first solid example of a woman's autobiographical work. There were a number of women writers married to men associated with artistic circles, but what remains are only references in other works to the writings of such women as Sulpicia, Lesbia, and Cassia. The last probably wrote a semiautobiographical poem. Of Agrippina's *Memoirs* we are certain, however. Barely a fragment is extant of this intimate family history by Agrippina II (A.D. 15–59), daughter of Agrippina I and Germanicus, and the mother of Nero; it is Tacitus who cites this work as the source for his history of the reign of Tiberius in Book 4 of his *Annals*: "This, not reported by the writers of histories, I found in the writings of Agrippina's daughter, the mother of the emperor Nero, who related for posterity her life and the fate of her family."[7] Misch credits this memoir with introducing the new element of family history into autobiography. Among the very personal scenes that Agrippina depicts, including her son's breech birth, is a particularly dramatic one in which Agrippina's mother weeps bitterly and implores Tiberius to grant her daughter a second husband.[8]

It is from women also that we have the earliest extant diaries, an ancient tradition that Alexander the Great (356–323 B.C.) introduced to the Roman Empire after his Persian conquests. Diaries became a highly cultivated form written by women of the sophisticated courts of Japan during the tenth and eleventh centuries A.D. These women, educated and keenly observant, commented on the aristocratic intrigues and splendors around them. Among the extant diaries from that time are *The Sarashina Diary* (1008–?), actually a consecutive narrative full of appreciations of nature and detailed descriptions of dreams; *The Diary of Murasaki Shikibu* (970?–1014?), by the famous author of the autobiographical novel *The Tale of Genji;* and *The Pillow Book of Sei Shonagon* (963?), which contains descriptions of the author's daily life, reflective reminiscences, and poetry. Even these tenth-century diaries from Japanese women evidence clear differences from those by their male counterparts. The men wrote in a wholly different language, one appropriate for recording events and objective records, whereas the women wrote in a language appropriate for recording personal experiences, often retrospectively years afterward and at various sittings.[9]

In the West, with the advent of Christianity, the more personal exploration of the self as a means of relating to a heavenly source—rather than an external one—began finding literary shape. Plutarch (A.D. 100) was responsible for the initial development of the form in his personal letters, autobiographical fragments, and the *Lives.* Whereas Misch sees Augustine's *Confessions* (A.D. 400) as the culmination of the evolving concept of self-expression, autobiographical critics since 1950 see that work as the inception of a genre that came into its own with Renaissance individualism.

We have no record of autobiographical works by a woman during the early Christian period, probably because women did not hold positions in the church and thus their records would not have been preserved—and because, had they admitted to sins similar to Augustine's, they probably would have been stoned to death. When one reflects on the persecution of women during the later Christian era and even in more modern times—Joan of Arc (1412–31) and Saint Bernadette (1844–79)—it is not surprising that few women left traces of their conversion to Christianity during its earliest times or wrote of their religious struggles.

The three major exceptions were all born Catholics; all experienced unusual visions, and all endured, at the least, indifference and, at the most, persecution in their efforts to convince the authorities of the authenticity of their visions. Finally, each wrote her autobiographical work for the purpose of self-vindication of her extraordinary experiences.

The earliest, from the late Middle Ages, *Revelations of Divine Love* (ca. 1373; 1393) is by Dame Julian (or Juliana) of Norwich (1343–1416?). Little is known about Julian, the first English woman of letters, except for what she tells us of herself in *Revelations,* which is more an intellectual treatise than a personal narrative. The work does contain, however, details of Julian's life, especially those relating to her mystical experience, which occurred when she was thirty, while suffering from an acute illness that left her paralyzed from the waist down. Her condition became so severe that a priest was called in to administer the last rites, after which she witnessed blood dripping from the crucifix in front of her bed and experienced the passion of Christ. During five hours of gazing at the crucifix, she tells us, she saw Christ appear in "shewings," which convinced her to become an anchoress and live in solitary confinement for the rest of her long life.

Julian wrote two versions of this mystical experience, one a more autobiographical account shortly after the event, the other twenty years later,[10] after a life of seclusion spent contemplating the meaning of these "shewings." Though self-conscious of her sex, she felt compelled to write about her experience: "Because I am a woman, ought I therefore to believe that I should not tell you of the goodness of God?" Julian dictated *Revelations,* but there is no question that the words are hers. Though she can be self-effacing, her language is forthright in asserting the authenticity of her experience at death's door; and her psychologically and spiritually astute observations are extraordinarily sensitive. In describing and analyzing Christ's showings, Julian demonstrates high intelligence and theological sophistication. Unusual for her time, she saw a feminine principle in divine nature and incorporated this original idea into the more traditional perception of the "motherhood" of Christ.[11]

Nonetheless, the work has been criticized for its seeming disorganization. In eighty-five chapters—some short revelations are discussed together in a single chapter, others extend through many—she writes about the revelations nonsequentially. For example, the first revelation is discussed in chapter 60, the fifteenth in chapter 41, the ninth in chapter 55, and so on. Interjected allusions—backward and forward—refer to previous and forthcoming revelations. Such disjunctiveness is further proof that Julian dictated the work, for any amanuensis (who would, of course, be a literate male) would have rearranged the chapters chronologically. P. Franklin Chambers concurs:

> She knew what she intended to write, or, having written, remembered it and rewrote earlier chapters to prepare her readers for what was to come. Her mind moves forwards and backwards as she unfolds the process of the revealings during the long years of her writing. . . . These interjections are not the marks of unplanned and undisciplined writing.[12]

This apparent disjointed or fragmented style also appears in the first extant prose autobiography proper in English, *The Book of Margery Kempe* (1436–38),[13] which, unlike Julian's work and other lives of mystics from the medieval period, includes many secular experiences. Margery Burnham Kempe (ca. 1373–1438?) was different from Julian in a number of ways. For one, she was uneducated as well as illiterate, though the daughter of the mayor of Lynn. For another, she was not a recluse but a religious enthusiast who engaged in the real world. Kempe's autobiography begins not with the circumstances of her visions but with her marriage at the age of twenty to John Kempe. A pious woman, she was nonetheless a maverick for her time and circumstances; she loved clothes and fine jewelry, and she tried her hand at various business ventures. Such vanity and industriousness were considered unfitting in a virtuous woman and earned her society's criticism, even before she chose her religious vocation. When Christ first comes to her and urges her to live for him, she describes the difficulties in restraining herself and her husband from sexual intercourse. Kempe struggles to reconcile her obligations as the wife of a loving husband and the mother of fourteen children with her religious calling of pilgrimage. However, when she can no longer ignore the many visitations by Christ, she abandons all worldly pleasures and at the age of thirty-nine takes a vow of poverty.

Once committed to the service of God, Kempe sets out on religious pilgrimages to Jerusalem, Rome, Spain, and Germany, entirely dependent on others' generosity. Although she visits bishops, priests, and mystics and has numerous encounters with local officials, hers is not the typically male historical or political chronicle. Instead, in emotionally charged descriptions, she focuses on the people she encounters, both the few religious and secular ones who befriend her and the many more civil authorities and local clergy who ridicule and persecute her, accusing her of being a whore or heretic and often imprisoning her.

Despite her trials and doubts, for which she needs reassurance from numerous confessors, Kempe is never self-abnegating in descriptions of herself. She is a model of human compassion and, with an observant eye, describes what are generally considered mundane matters: childbirth and postpartum depression (considered fits of insanity then); various customs of dress by class, occupation, and country; the difficulties of sea travel; and many frightening experiences she encounters as a woman walking alone across Europe. Even if read not as a mystical or even as an autobiographical work, it is a remarkable record of life and travel in the early fifteenth century from a woman's point of view.

Kempe dictated her autobiography to a townsman in 1432, at the age of fifty-nine, twenty years after taking the vow of poverty and shortly before her death. Four years later a priest transcribed those notes into a third-person narrative. Her *Book* is unusual for its simple, personal style; unencumbered by intellectual or abstract theorizing, it is filled with novelistic detail. It has the distinction of being not only the first prose autobiography in English but the first subjective life study and the first to exhibit a self-consciousness about the author's life as well as her method of writing. The priest who wrote from Kempe's dictation, aware of its disjunctive style, explains in the proem:

> This book is not written in order, each thing after another as it was done, but like as the matter came to the creature in mind when it should be written; for it was so long ere it was written that she had forgotten the time and the order when things befell. And therefore she had nothing written but what she knew right well for very truth.[14]

Not only is the narrative nonchronological, but it is also interrupted by many revelations of, visions of, and dialogues with Christ, as well as by long sections in which Kempe describes her weeping fits. Some editions of the autobiography relegate the religious evocations to an appendix, but in their original placement, both these and the weeping sections serve as narrative relief and also function internally as support for Kempe's many trials of persecution by friends, priests, and strangers.

Hope Emily Allen describes Kempe as part of a movement of feminine spirituality in Europe from the twelfth to the fifteenth centuries,[15] but it is extremely doubtful that Kempe had any awareness of the movement or its practitioners. Except for *A Shorte Treatyse of Contemplacyon . . . Taken Out of the Boke of Margerie Kempe of Lynn* by Wynken de Worde and printed in 1501, Kempe's *Book* was virtually unknown until the nineteenth century, by which time the same personal subject matter and disjunctive style had appeared in women's autobiographies independent of any direct influence. Although critics of autobiography have had mixed responses to Kempe's work, most praise it. Margaret Bottrall finds it "odd" that the first extant autobiography in English was written by a woman, but she believes that Kempe's life study "combines two types of autobiography, the factual narrative and the spiritual chronicle, which would make it remarkable even if it had been composed at a much later date. Its isolation gives it an almost freakish air."[16]

In comparing Julian and Kempe, whose disjointed writing styles are similar but whose personalities are not, Robert Stone writes:

> The work of Julian is strikingly intellectual. She is an *analytical* mystic, carefully examining her visions, her conclusions, and her questions about the conclusions. . . . The work of Margery Kempe, on the other hand, is basically nonintellectual. There is little or no analysis, little or no examination of philosophical causes, effects, or questions. Instead, we find a primarily emotional reaction, personalized, focusing on Margery herself: *her* feelings, reassurances from God about

> *her* own worth, *her* involvements with the most sacred personages of Christian theology. . . . What we get from her, therefore, is mainly emotional autobiography.[17]

Stone credits Julian's *Revelations* and Kempe's *Book* with making major contributions to English literature. It was these two women's

> type of homiletic and devotional writing that kept English prose alive during the years following the Norman Conquest, when French became the official language and, with Latin, threatened to squeeze out English entirely. Furthermore, the devotional prose of the thirteenth and fourteenth centuries contained a body of writing addressed particularly to women. . . . Julian and Margery go one step farther: they are the most prominent female *writers* of Middle English devotional prose, women who "break a long tradition of feminine silence in England."[18]

Among the various autobiographers of the Middle Ages, Kempe has the distinction of breaking new ground with her emphasis on the personal and the concrete. Previous poetic narratives distanced their readers with various literary conventions, such as the dream vision in Chaucer's *House of Fame* and the allegorical periphrasis of *Piers Plowman* and *The Pearl.* Journalistic military or historical memoirs, such as Bede's eighth-century *Historia ecclesiastica gentis Anglorum,* Asser's tenth-century *Annales rerum gestarum Æfredi Magni,* and Joinville's fourteenth-century *Histoire de Saint Louis,* also obscured the personal details of their authors. With the exceptions of the apologies of Abélard, *Historia calamitatum* (twelfth century), and Giraldus, *De rebus a se gestis* (early thirteenth century), few works of the Middle Ages concentrated on the individual. Instead, as Wayne Shumaker writes: "The impulse to subsume discrete facts under general principles and individual human beings under types seems to have been almost universal"[19]—for men, he might have added, because even before Kempe we have seen evidence of other characteristics in the works of women.

Nonetheless, neither Kempe's concrete and emotional narrative nor those by Abélard and Giraldus reflect the self-awareness that was to become apparent in the Renaissance. There is, however, among Kempe's "disparate adventures" and "hysterical urgings and visions . . . a self-consciousness which belongs to good autobiography," according to Pascal.[20] Indeed, her autobiography is unique in a tradition of medieval indifference to secular experiences.

• • •

After Kempe's autobiography, there are no extant life studies by women until the seventeenth century. The Renaissance concept of autobiography as a secular genre—with an emphasis on the unique, complex individual—did not affect women until a century later. Some letters survive from the fifteenth century, most by Elizabeth Paston to her husband, who spent most of the year at his legal practice in London while she stayed at home managing the country estate; Paston's letters are impersonal and businesslike, describing everything from milking cows to selling lands and combatting invading marauders.[21] From the sixteenth century, we have only one extant diary, kept by Lady Margaret Hoby (1571–1633) during the period 1599–1605; it may be the earliest personal diary in English.[22]

Among the classic autobiographies of the sixteenth century, St. Teresa's *Life* (1562–65) warrants attention here even though our concern is with English-language autobiography. It occupies an important place in the history of autobiography in general and is a significant contribution to the tradition of women's autobiography in particular. It should be noted, however, that neither Teresa's life study nor the two other classic sixteenth-century autobiographies—Benvenuto Cellini's *Autobiography* (1558–62) and Girolamo Cardano's *Book of My Life* (1576)—had any influence on the history of English autobiography. Most autobiographers—especially women—wrote without any awareness of an autobiographical tradition until the nineteenth century.[23]

Teresa's autobiography was originally written in Castilian Spanish but in common speech rich in imagery; it was first translated into English in 1611. Like Kempe's work, it is not an intellectual treatise, but Teresa was a more complex person than Kempe, and her autobiography is a relentless self-examination of the saint's inner life. Teresa (1515–82) divided her *Life* into three parts. First, she describes in personal detail her secure childhood in a well-to-do noble family before the age of sixteen, when she disobeyed her father and ran away from home to become a nun. The more metaphorical and poetical second part interrupts the narrative of her life story with a long dissertation on the four states of prayer that she wishes to teach her readers. The third part resumes her narrative and documents her discontent with the laxity in her convent. This disapproval leads to her clandestine escape from the convent and the secret establishment, in her late forties, of her own order of nuns at a time when only men founded convents and then only with the approval of Rome. Frequently she interrupts even this narrative with long descriptions of the many raptures or ecstasies that accompanied her visions. She also details the practical problems of establishing her convent, St. Joseph's in Ávila, and a more rigorous Carmelite order than had previously existed, the Discalced, or Barefoot, Carmelite. Anna Burr writes: "The unusual fact about Teresa is that she continues to preserve so high a degree of practical energy and executive ability. Apart from her mysticism, she is a woman of intellect, healthy vigor, and healthy imagination, not without humor; all her actions show practical common sense."[24]

Teresa wrote her autobiography at the command of her superiors. As such, it is an account of her spiritual progress, a guide for her sister nuns. But, much more than an instructional manual, it is a document of her passionate visions and a subjective account of the conflict with her confessors who doubted her visions. She was in her late forties and early fifties when she wrote the *Life*—the five "most restful years of my life," she says. For she had endured twenty years of personal agony and frustration before finding a Jesuit priest who trusted her visions, thus validating her in the eyes of the church.

A major theme in Teresa's autobiography is a consciousness that discrimination against her gender was responsible for the skepticism that greeted her long quest for affirmation. Though employing the traditional religious rhetoric of self-abnegation throughout, she displays unusual self-confidence when describing her visions. Repeatedly she urges the nuns who read her story to trust their visions and to persist until they find a confessor who believes in them and gives them the stamp of authenticity. On the other hand, she feels that women need to live in silence and isolation because they are more easily led into sin than men are.

Teresa's autobiography well earns its reputation as a classic for a number of reasons, not the least of which is the beauty of the imagery she uses in describing her raptures. In addition, she is tenacious in honest self-scrutiny—more like a religious zealot—and a female one at that—than a man of the world eager to tout his virtues and accomplishments. Pascal notes: "What makes this work enthralling is the pertinacity and energy with which she examines herself. . . . She is as much concerned for the quality of her soul as for the actual character of the vision; and in this pertinacious, restless, obstinate self-examination *she adds a new dimension to autobiography*" (emphasis mine).[25]

Another noteworthy dimension of her narrative is the tension and suspense created by the many interruptions—both to the descriptions of her visions and ecstasies and to her dissertation on prayer. The latter in particular, with its analytical, sober style, functions as narrative relief (as in Kempe's *Book*) from the emotionality of the first and third sections. "Vivid, disjointed, elliptical, paradoxical, and gaily ungrammatical" is how

Allison Peers describes her style, adding that Teresa's "methods of exposition are not rigidly logical. . . . Her disconnected observations, her revealing parentheses, her transpositions, ellipses, and sudden suspensions of thought make her in one sense, easier to read. . . . She could never have written impeccable manuals or methodically ordered 'guides' to the ascetic or the mystical life: her genius resembles the rushing torrent, not the scientifically constructed canal."[26]

It is instructive to contrast the spiritual autobiographies by Julian, Kempe, and Teresa with early religious autobiographies by men. When Augustine wrote his *Confessions* (ca. 400), he was an accepted leader and scholar in the new church. From his secure position he could detail with intellectual equanimity the excesses and sins he committed before his conversion to Christianity. He had no need to justify himself or prove his authenticity. As with later spiritual writers, he envisioned himself dueling with contrary but abstract forces that were eventually resolved in God. But these women lived at a time when women had no status in the Catholic hierarchy, and therefore any eccentric behavior, any "excesses," on their part was suspect. They accepted their otherness and humbly sought acceptance.[27] They thus took greater risks than Augustine in presenting their experiences.

Their life studies also share an intention very different from Augustine's: to prove their authenticity, especially because they were women. As outcasts or, at least, as nonconformists, they present self-images that lack the assertive confidence of their male counterparts, though they are positive and intact. Dame Julian, having removed herself from controversy, exposed her heart and soul in the protection of her isolation. Kempe always bore the onus of her unsanctioned fits. And Teresa waited for twenty years—when she was in her forties and had written five of her twelve books—for validation. Martin Luther, by contrast, did not lack support from most of his peers and superiors though he was only twenty-one at the time of his celebrated "fit." (The same contrast can be made in America two centuries later, between the ostracism meted to Anne Hutchinson's antinomianism and the acceptance of Jonathan Edwards's visions.)

This difference in acceptance by their respective communities may be a factor in explaining the characteristics we observe in the form and content of these women's autobiographies. The female confessional—intent on authenticity and validation—required a greater emotional outpouring of feelings and less structured forms than its male equivalent. Sexual differences in acceptance and social conditioning seem similarly to affect the content and forms of later women's autobiographies. The criteria by which critics judge autobiographies, whether past or contemporary, still reflect more respect for and acceptance of the sober content and orderly forms of life studies by intellectual achievers such as Augustine, John Stuart Mill, or Henry Adams than for women's more subjective and less tidy renderings, whether of religious experience or of personal transformations.

· 2 ·

The Seventeenth Century:

Psychological Beginnings

Up to the mid-seventeenth century, only about 10 percent of the total number of published autobiographies were by women; actually, very few English autobiographies were published by either sex before 1660.[1] In England, most of these autobiographies (over one hundred of them) were of a religious nature. Prompted by the rivalries among Protestant sects, most were written by Puritan and Quaker ministers for the edification of their congregations. Early in the century, there was Thomas Dempster's *Historia ecclesiastica gentis Scotorum* (1627), but more famous today are John Bunyan's *Grace Abounding to the Chief of Sinners* (1666) and George Fox's *Journal* (written after 1674–75; first published in 1694), which was widely imitated in England, on the Continent, and in America.

From earliest times, the Quaker concept of sexual equality encouraged women to write diaries, journals, and autobiographies that recorded their spiritual progress.[2] Some of these were also emotional outlets for unsatisfactory marriages. This was the motive behind Joan Vokins's (d. 1690) *Some Account Given Forth: God's Mighty Power Magnified* (1691) and Alice Hayes's (1657–1720) *A Short Account of Alice Hayes*, also called *A Legacy, or Widow's Mite* (1723). An exception was *A Brief Account of My Exercises from My Childhood*[3] by the twice happily married Mary Penington (ca. 1625–82), who describes how she resisted family pressures and, with an independent and open mind, struggled to find a religion she respected, finally becoming—after much soul-searching—a Quaker. Unlike other Quaker life studies, which are often tediously abstract and long-winded, Penington's narrative is refreshing in its concreteness, succinctness, and simplicity.

Other confessionals from this period were written by lower middle-class women of various Protestant sects, who retreated to religion as an escape from the hardships of their daily lives. Some examples are Elizabeth Warren of Woodbridge's *Spiritual Thrift . . .* (1647); Jane Turner's *Choice Experiences of the Kind Dealings of God* (1653); Anna Trapnel's *A Legacy for Saints* (1654); Alice Curwen's (d. 1679) *A Relation of the Labour, Travail, and Suffering of . . .* (1680); Hannah Allen's *Satan His Methods and Malice Baffled: A Narrative of God's Gracious Dealings with . . .* (1683); Barbara Blaugdone's *An Account of the Travels, Sufferings, and Persecutions of . . .* (1691); Margaret Fell Fox's (1614–1702) *A Brief Collection of Remarkable Passages* (1710); the *Life* of Elizabeth Stirredge (1634–1706), originally called *Strength in Weakness Manifest* (1711); and *An Account of Anne Jackson* (first published in 1832), which, besides her spiritual life, describes life in seventeenth-century London, including the great plague in 1665 and the great fire in 1666.

When we turn to secular autobiographies, we find that during this period men were writing, for the most part, military, travel, and political memoirs—*res gestae*—progressive and orderly chronicles of their careers, more about deeds (often exaggerated) than about themselves, with little or no mention of their domestic lives—their wives and children—and little in the way of subjective or introspective analysis. For men, self-reflection was more acceptable in poetic or philosophical forms, for example, Donne's Holy Sonnets and Browne's *Religio Medici.*

By contrast, secular autobiographies by women at this time are notable for their emphasis on the personal and even for an incipient self-analysis. Paul Delany, in his study of seventeenth-century British autobiography, notes that as a result of women's lack of participation in vocational activities, "female autobiographers strike the modern reader as having a more 'unified sensibility' than their male counterparts; their lives seem less compartmentalized, they have a wider range of emotional responses to everyday events and more awareness of concrete reality." Seventeenth-century women exposed their emotional lives in print to a much greater extent than their spiritual predecessors or their male contemporaries. Indeed, their life studies may have stimulated the development of the novel in the eighteenth century. Again, Delany writes: "The female autobiographer, being more concerned with intimate feelings than her male counterpart, was less likely to be satisfied with a simple record of *res gestae.*"[4] The very idea that one's domestic and emotional life constituted appropriate subject matter for autobiography was, at least in the English tradition, essentially a female notion.[5]

The journal by Jane Lead (1624–1704), *A Fountain of Gardens,*[6] published in four volumes between 1697 and 1701, provides a bridge between the spiritual autobiographies and the secular ones that began to appear during the late seventeenth and early eighteenth centuries. A poet and visionary, Lead was one of a small group of sectarians who wrote spiritual autobiographies for a lay audience. A pastiche of visions, interpretations, dreams, conversations and arguments, symbolic narratives, and poetry, the journal conveys a distinctively female perception of the self.[7]

Highly unusual for this time was a secular autobiography by neither a particularly religious nor a noble woman, *The Autobiography of Mrs. Alice Thornton* (written after 1669; first published in 1875 in Edinburgh), which spans almost the whole of Alice Wandesford Thornton's long life (1627–1707). Without embellishment, Thornton narrates the trials of her personal life in a straightforward, almost detached style. Objectively, as in a medical history, she recounts her many illnesses from pregnancy, childbirth, and postpartum depression, the indifference of her husband, the deaths of many of her children, and finally, how, as a destitute widow, she handled her financial difficulties in a businesslike manner. Interspersed throughout the narrative are religious digressions, apostrophes to Christ, to whom she looks for sustenance during her sufferings. Thornton's story reveals the life of an ordinary woman, rarely the subject of seventeenth-century autobiography.[8]

More common were autobiographical works by women (and men) of the privileged classes. As opportunities for publication expanded, women from the nobility and the rising bourgeoisie, who were generally literate and educated, began to write secular autobiographical works in greater number. Some kept diaries, such as that by Lady Anne Clifford (1590–1676), *The Diary of Isabella, Wife of Sir Roger Twysden . . . 1645–1651*, and *Mrs. Elizabeth Freke: Her Diary: 1671 to 1714*. Others wrote letters that were published long after their death, such as those by Dorothy Osborne (1627–95) and by Lady Brilliana Harley (1600?–43). These privileged seventeenth-century women were socially and financially secure and often content with their submissive roles in rather flexible marriages. In fact, it was a common practice for women to write portraits of their esteemed husbands or other male relatives of stature, to which they then appended, with appropriate modesty, a briefer portrait of themselves.[9] Both Mary Astell's (1666–1731) acerbic *Reflections upon Marriage* (1706) and Lady Margaret Hamilton's *A Pairt of My Life* (first published in 1833) were unusual for their descriptions of unhappy marriages. More typical were positive portraits of husbands and the marriage state.

Lucy Apsley Hutchinson (1620–71) writes lovingly, even rapturously, of her husband in *Memoirs of the Life of Colonel Hutchinson* (written about 1670–75; first published in 1806). Her "Life of Mrs. Lucy Hutchinson, Written by Herself"[10] is, unfortunately, a fragment added to the more ambitious biography of her husband.

It was also common practice during the seventeenth century to begin one's autobiography with ancestral history; women, however, tended to write more briefly than men of their family's past. (Lord Herbert of Cherbury's *Autobiography* [ca. 1645] is a case in point, covering over two hundred years of family history.) Hutchinson focuses most of her brief "Life" equally on the history and virtues of her parents and her native land. Written for the purpose of "glorifying God's goodness," it is frequently interrupted with religious apostrophes. Unfortunately, the fragment devotes only a few pages to her girlhood, passed in a stimulating and loving environment where as a precocious child she preferred reading and studying to the usual accomplishments expected of women—music and dancing. Hutchinson makes us wish she had "perfectly sett downe" more of her own life as she has the intelligent and sensitive portrait of her husband.

More inclusive though still brief is the *Memoirs* of Ann Fanshawe (1625–80), written a few years after Hutchinson's, in 1676.[11] Addressed to her only surviving son, it focuses primarily on her devoted and adored husband, Sir Richard Fanshawe, who died ten years earlier, when she was only forty-one. Unlike Hutchinson's fragment, Fanshawe's autobiography covers almost her entire life and is narrated with the meticulous detail reminiscent of a diary. Almost daily, she records dates when persons visited and were visited; finances calculated and borrowed (an apparently constant worry); food purchased and eaten; gifts given and received; ceremonies attended with full accounts of the noble personages present and the pomp displayed; encounters with pirates while aboard ship and with ruffians while traveling by coach; the almost yearly birth of a child during some twenty years of a happy marriage; and much more.

Fanshawe was a woman with a sense of humor, a prodigious capacity for business affairs, indefatigable grace and confidence in diplomatic and social events, and extraordinary courage and spunk, displayed during arduous travels and the bearing and burying of children. However, it is only on the occasion of the deaths of ten of her children and especially on her husband's death that she reveals any personal feelings. On the whole the work provides little self-analysis. The value of the *Memoirs* is principally as a social and historical document of the mores of the English court before and after the Civil Wars and of the courts of Portugal and Spain where her husband served as ambassador. However, despite its subject matter, it is neither dull nor insensitive, the usual characteristics of male autobiographies with a similar focus.[12] The narrative has literary skill and is quite readable, notwithstanding the profuse details.

Fanshawe's *Memoirs* is also important for introducing a new organizing principle to autobiography, a unifying personal theme: the mutual love between herself and her husband.[13] The book benefits from this unifying element because its chronological framework is often interrupted by lively anecdotes on politics and society, accounts of sightseeing and ceremonies, or out-of-order events and persons the author suddenly remembers to tell her son.[14]

Fanshawe obviously wants her son to remember his father as she does. Her adoration of her husband and their marriage is exemplified in the following passage: "Glory be to God, we never had but one mind throughout our lives. Our souls were wrapt up in each others; our aims and designs one, our loves one, and our resentments one. We so studied the other, that we knew each others minds by our looks." Such laudatory comments are a frequent and integral part of the narrative.

The *Autobiography* by Mary Boyle Rich, the countess of Warwick (1625–78), written during the years 1671–74, is brief—some forty pages—but like Fanshawe's, it recounts a complete life.[15] Following the example of her father and brother, who also wrote autobiographies,[16] Rich improved on their writings and advanced autobiographical intention by neither focusing on her beloved husband (whom she survived) nor writing for her children (whom she also survived) but rather for posterity, considering her life of value in and of itself. Her *Autobiography* is not a spiritual life study, though Rich, a Presbyterian and extremely pious, alludes frequently to her religious feelings; nor is it a history despite its straightforward, factual style. It differs significantly from both forms in its domestic and personal emphasis, focusing on affairs of the heart—first, Rich's resistance to her father's choice of a husband when she was thirteen, then her persistence in her love for the poor earl of Warwick (the youngest of three sons), whom she married when she was only fifteen. Rich's independent spirit is captured in a statement she made before meeting her husband: "I still continued to have an aversion to marriage, living so much at my ease that I was unwilling to change my condition, and never could bring myself to close with any offered match, but still begged my father to refuse all the most advantageous profers, though I was by him much pressed to settle myself."

After her marriage, the emphasis shifts to the illnesses of Rich's children, herself, and her husband, giving us a glimpse into the details of medical practice in an age when it was based for the most part on herbs and prayers. Except for several long digressions to praise God (amazing, considering her many losses), the autobiography is linear and progressive, with few novelistic embellishments, not even dialogue, which most autobiographies incorporate in varying degrees. Also, unlike most autobiographies of the seventeenth century—by both women and men, but especially by men—Rich refers only peripherally to the Civil War and reveals very little about her husband's work or activities. It is her personal story that takes center stage, not as an accessory to history or to biography.

Although the aforementioned women were extending the personal dimensions of seventeenth-century autobiography, self-analysis and self-revelation were still rarities. Two exceptions were by Margaret Cavendish and Anne Halkett. Cavendish, the duchess of Newcastle (1625–74), was one of the first English women to publish her works—thirteen books in all, including *Poems and Fancies, The World's Olio, Orations of Divers Sorts Accommodated to Divers Places, Plays,* and *Philosophical Letters.* Her autobiography, *A True Relation of My Birth, Breeding, and Life,* first appeared in 1656 and twenty years later was appended to a glowing biography of her husband, William Cavendish.[17]

Cavendish's memoirs are unique in several respects. First, they eschew both the usual religious or moral intentions of her contemporaries and also the historical approach popular in autobiography to the end of the nineteenth century. Instead, Cavendish, advancing beyond even Rich's personal focus, concentrates on her psychological and intellectual development, editing her life story, she tells us, to rid it of insignificant details. Second, in highlighting only those matters she felt were essential to her intention, she rejected a chronological structure and treated her life according to a more radical and original organization than Rich's unifying theme, namely, according to subject categories.[18]

Cavendish begins by summarizing her parents' aristocratic background and personal virtues, her childhood, and her education. Then she describes her intellectual attainments and analyzes her method of writing. Although a professionally successful and sophisticated woman, she alludes only briefly to two of her many publications—*Philosophical Fancies* and *The World's Olio;* she believes that her personality is more interesting and important than her professional accomplishments. Finally, in the last third of the autobiography she conscientiously analyzes her personality, aware that readers are interested not only in the facts of her life but also in "my humor, particular practice, and disposition." This last section is remarkable for its subtle distinctions, exhibiting a rare psychological sensibility and intellectual insight. Cavendish appreciates the influence of her childhood environment,[19] keenly aware of the positive reinforcements that shaped her personality both as a woman and as an intellectual—seven older brothers and sisters "serious and staid in their actions, not given to sport and play" nurtured her childhood addiction "to contemplation rather than conversation, to solitariness rather than society, to melancholy rather than mirth, to write with pen than to work with a needle."

An innocent young woman when she entered her two-year service at court, where she met William Cavendish, thirty years her senior—"the onely person I ever was in love with"—nonetheless she was self-possessed and conscious of court hypocrisy. Proud of her accomplishments, she is critical of the frivolous women she observes there;[20] her high standards of personal excellence account for her dismay at "our sex," who, she asserts, will find "that it is neither words nor place that can advance them, but worth and merit."

Cavendish was a rare woman. She was confident of her worth as a person, a woman, and a writer during an age when learned women were considered social misfits.[21] "My onely trouble," she writes, "is, lest my brain should grow barren, or that the root of my fancies should become insipid, withering into a dull stupidity for want of maturing subjects to write on." She prefers "onely walking a slow pace in my chamber" to dancing and would "rather sit at home and write . . . and contemplate." Cavendish projects a positive self-image and is not ashamed of her ambition, for "'tis neither for beauty, wit, titles, wealth, or power, but as they are steps to raise me to fame's tower, which is to live by remembrance on after-ages." This penetrating psychological self-portrait is rare in autobiography until the twentieth century.[22]

The other exceptional autobiography of the period is by Lady Anne Halkett (1622–99). Written in 1678, when she was in her fifties,[23] Halkett's *Autobiography* was published after her death[24] when it was considered discreet to publish such works. It differs from Cavendish's briefer life study in significant ways. Whereas Cavendish telescopes in broad outline the events of her life, treats them according to subject categories, and devotes a third of her narrative to a detailed self-analysis, Halkett writes chronologically, selectively editing the events of her life and concentrating on complicated amorous and political intrigues in which she figures. Eschewing self-conscious self-analysis, she allows her actions and thoughts, often through dialogue, to reveal her personality.[25] She is not an intellectual like Cavendish but excels in sizing up people and situations and in dissecting her own and others' motives.

Halkett's gift is that of a novelist. She analyzes neither herself nor her characters, the real people she writes about, but allows the narrative to speak for itself. Her intention is always dramatic rather than expository.

Thus, since her interest is in human interaction, she gives us only a brief summary on her parents (the autobiographical convention) and omits her childhood entirely, beginning her autobiography when she was twenty-two and of an age to have suitors and travel. So, the first two-thirds of the book are occupied with two unhappy courtships and an intrigue against her by a chaplain of a noble family with whom she is staying.[26] The last third focuses on her exile in Scotland where, amid efforts to obtain money to support herself and establish a stable living situation—a constant source of anxiety—she describes Royalist meetings and the efforts of the king—also in exile in Scotland—to achieve restoration.

All these events are narrated with sensitivity and insight. New for her time she incorporates, as Delany notes appreciatively,

> minute and serious descriptions of everyday personal relations and domestic scenes . . . [widening] the scope of the genre by showing how minor events, which other autobiographers passed over, had significance for her emotional development and for her moods. . . . Few British autobiographers before had paid such close attention to the household intrigues and drawing-room sentiments that she chronicled.[27]

Halkett is also a master of suspense. Especially gripping are her descriptions of the intrigue with the chaplain; her participation in the escape of the duke of York—later king of Scotland—from St. James Palace, even acquiring and helping to dress him in women's clothing to expedite his departure from England; and especially the mystery surrounding her suitor, Colonel Joseph Bamfield—was his wife actually dead or was he lying and thus compromising her? Halkett informs us at the point in the narrative when she herself learns the truth.

Halkett's novelistic skill can be even more appreciated by noting the fact that she wrote more than twenty devotional meditations, yet her autobiography is not confessional or didactic in the slightest. Delany notes that "though in some respects she anticipated Richardson she wrote without his heavy-handed nonconformist moralizing: she had strong moral principles but, as a devout Anglican, left sermons to the parson."[28]

Like Cavendish, Halkett projects a positive self-image, though she admits—highly unusual in secular autobiography of her time—to indiscretions and, on occasion, to poor judgment.[29] Her style—objective and without emotional embellishments—accurately mirrors her personality.

She is never at a loss to combine her highly sophisticated discretion, informed frankness, and confident self-possession to unravel dishonest intrigues or to settle touchy diplomatic niceties. Had she been a man during the turbulent times of the Civil War, she would have been a diplomat par excellence.

Even to her readers Halkett is diplomatic, explaining to us how she has selectively omitted tedious details or events that might be boring. The reported dialogue, the attention to detail, the stress on the emotional ramifications rather than on history or facts make her work more dramatic than any autobiography before her. She was "one of the most perceptive and skilful stylists among British autobiographers of her time,"[30] writes Delany. Filled with romance, excitement, and suspense, Halkett's *Autobiography* exhibits the skills of a psychological novelist.

• • •

Both Halkett's and Cavendish's autobiographies would be notable even if they had been written in the twentieth century, let alone more than three hundred years ago. Fanshawe's autobiography is less successful because its narrative reads almost like a diary, with few digressions from chronological order. However, it is a complete and shaped work with a unifying personal theme, her love for her husband. Rich's memoir, also basically chronological, is of a piece, and it advances women's autobiographical tradition by focusing on herself. Halkett and Cavendish are more selective than comprehensive in their content and more psychological than historical in their intention. Their variations from progressive narrative prompted their editors to comment in introductions on their impurities in factual continuity, and the editors take it upon themselves to summarize and fill in events in their correct order.

Both Halkett and Cavendish are also more subjective in their self-portraits than Fanshawe and Rich—Halkett in her novelistic treatment of others, Cavendish in braving censure by analyzing her personality, "eccentric" for her day, not for ours.[31] They continue and extend the personal and subjective element of autobiography found in such early works as Agrippina's family history and Kempe's and Teresa's confessionals. Donald Stauffer notes that these seventeenth-century autobiographies by women are as a class "far more interesting and important than the autobiographies of men—more personal, informal, and lifelike. Where the men tend to digress on questions of history, or grow prolix in controversial accounts, the women remain self-centered and confidential, engrossed in the more enthralling problems of their own lives."[32]

Women improved the genre of autobiography by freely adapting the conventional narrative forms practiced by men—the linear and progressive *res gestae*—and they advanced subjective over spiritual or political expression both in autobiography in general and in the female tradition specifically. They inaugurated psychological self-analysis and the fictional shaping of autobiographies, anticipating those by contemporary women.

· 3 ·

The Eighteenth Century:
Professional Beginnings

Eighteenth-century autobiographies by women further legitimized subjective narrative, not only for life studies but also for the developing genre of the novel. They also continued the female tradition by emphasizing the personal over the historical, family life over career, and disjunctive over progressive narratives—all in contrast to male autobiographies of the period.

The most important factor affecting the autobiographies of this century was economics. The Industrial Revolution had a profound impact on the status of women as well as on the rest of society. No longer could a single woman retain a comfortable niche in the rural family unit. With the mass movement to urban areas, the unmarried and usually uneducated woman became a financial liability to her family and was often forced into mercenary marriage arrangements, pressured to accept the charity of others, or compelled to live by her wits, and sometimes by her body. The result for the history of women's autobiography was a century dominated by confessionals—not religious ones, but secular pleas for acceptance by women forced by economic circumstances to adopt life-styles that violated the stringent moral standards of the day.

Many of the women who wrote autobiographies during this century of transition had once led "respectable" lives[1] but after widowhood or divorce found themselves without family connections. Desperate to find other means to support themselves and their children, some remarried out of necessity while others pursued careers in writing or acting, occupations even more insecure in their day than in ours.

Three such women were Laetitia Pilkington, Teresia Constantia Phillips, and Frances Vane, whose autobiographies share a common personal and subjective emphasis, similar disjunctive narratives, and the same effort to convince readers of their moral integrity. All three were talented literary women, independent in spirit, and determined to maintain their reputations even though living without marital sanctions. All three left unhappy marriages and wrote about them—in contrast to the happy marriages that Rich, Fanshawe, Cavendish, and Halkett described one hundred years earlier.

Perhaps it was the publication of *Pamela* in 1740 and *Clarissa* in 1747–48 that gave Pilkington, Phillips, and Vane the courage to publish their autobiographies—all within fifteen years of Richardson's novels. Their life studies are unhappy accounts of their frustrating efforts as women without wealth who must deal with would-be seducers or dishonest ex-husbands.

Unfortunately, their life studies were dismissed in their time as scandalous; in ours, they are discounted with a similar prejudice as mere *vies scandaleuses,* the honesty of their authors discredited, their writing considered mere hackwork.[2] Such pronouncements prevent an objective appreciation of their literary merit. When one looks at these autobiographies with an objective and contemporary eye, one can appreciate the significant contributions they made to the development of autobiography and the female tradition.

Laetitia Van Lewen Pilkington (1712–50) was a minor poet who published the three volumes of her *Memoirs* separately from 1748 to 1754.[3] The narrative is lively and with judicious editing could easily be read like a novel. But, of course, hers is a real life study of her own trials and courage.

Pilkington tells us little of her early years, concentrating on her adult life after her marriage at the age of fifteen to Parson Matthew Pilkington, an aspiring writer and dilettante. She astutely analyzes her husband's growing resentment of her superior poetic efforts and of her friendship with Jonathan Swift, who encouraged her literary endeavors. This patronage and her eventual separation from her ambitious and flamboyant husband earned her some notoriety during her lifetime. Pilkington describes her frequent literary visits with Swift—reporting their witty exchanges in often humorous dialogue—her husband's infidelities, his many schemes to make her appear unfaithful, their final separation (after he lived openly with a wealthy widow), her minor indiscretions (she is at first too trusting of scheming and lascivious suitors), and her financial destitution. She struggles to survive by writing poems for others and publishing her own, subsidized with a very small annuity gained only after she sadly agrees to give up her two children. All this may sound melodramatic, but contemporary women, especially single or widowed mothers, will have no trouble identifying with her problems.

Pilkington calls herself "a sad digressive writer"; indeed, although the three volumes are written in chronological order, they are constantly interrupted by long descriptions of events and people—often jumping ahead or back in time. But many are vivacious character sketches, often of her various patrons. She also interrupts the narrative with her poems (some of which are quite long); her purpose in inserting them, she tells her readers, is to illustrate her feelings. This reminds us of earlier women's similarly functional digressions.

Despite the hardships Pilkington endured, her memoirs reveal a confident self-image and a feminist consciousness. She often addresses her female readers directly, warning them that their reputations are "the immediate Jewel of their Souls." She advises them never to marry men with literary aspirations because such husbands will feel competitive and envious of their wives' talents. She sympathizes with women whom men seek to seduce and then condemn whether they succumb or not. A witty, confident, and spirited woman, Pilkington writes about personal matters women can identify with that are significant in the development of personal, secular autobiography: the nightmares she experiences, the deficient medical knowledge that attends her illnesses and those of her relatives and friends, and the difficulties of a woman alone seeking respectable lodgings.

Contemporary critics who call the *Memoirs* "scandalous" reveal their distrust of women.[4] Pilkington comes across as a sincere (if simple) woman who believed in her talent and was treated cruelly by her husband and by a snobbish society. Virginia Woolf admired Pilkington's personality, calling her an "extraordinary cross between . . . a rolling and rollicking woman of the town and a lady of breeding and refinement . . . [a woman] . . . in the great tradition of English women of letters."[5] Patricia Meyer Spacks misinterprets Pilkington's honest efforts to portray all her "faults, follies, and misfortunes" and underestimates her literary accomplishments by shortsightedly ascribing her diligent honesty to low self-esteem.[6] The reader may recall Delany's confessing that he found no seventeenth-century male autobiographers who admit to misdeeds or indiscretions;[7] the admissions by eighteenth-century female autobiographers are quite numerous. Pilkington's misfortunes took their toll, for she died in poverty when she was only thirty-eight.

The *Apology for the Conduct and Life of Teresia Constantia Phillips* (1748–49)[8] focuses on a specific period of Phillips's life when she was engaged in several lawsuits for financial support from her husband, Henry Muilman, who questioned the legality of their marriage. Thus, the descriptions of her family background, childhood, motherhood, and several unhappy liaisons with men who left her because of her indeterminate marriage/divorce status are subordinated to the central theme, the progress of this litigation.

As though to demonstrate her objectivity, Phillips (1709–65) casts her work in the third person and refers to herself as Mrs. Muilman. Moreover, to strengthen her case for honesty and clear thinking, she reproduces the legal briefs of both sides, excerpts of transcripts of court proceedings, and letters from Muilman to demonstrate his hypocrisy. All these factors militate against the reader's emotional involvement in Phillips's self-portrait, but they do attest to her tenacity and courage in the face of censure and social ostracism. They also contribute to the disjunctive narrative, as does the fact that the *Apology* was published in many installments over a two-year period. The only relief from the legal machinations are the digressions on the personal, more autobiographical aspects of her life.

Phillips's motive in writing her *Apology* is to convince her readers of Muilman's malice toward her and her family (she does not mention when she had children or whose they were) and of the righteousness of her legal claims. Another motive is her hope to earn money to pay for the lawsuits and to support herself. Lacking narrative continuity and containing little in the way of literary craft, the book can easily be viewed as hackwork. Nonetheless, it is a valuable document of the trials of a divorced woman in eighteenth-century England. It is also a remarkable portrait of a young woman of modest beginnings struggling for acceptance in respectable society.

Lady Frances Anne Vane (1713–88) was a more privileged woman than Phillips or Pilkington, yet her experiences with men—portrayed in her "Memoirs of a Lady of Quality" (1751)[9]—were equally trying, though she was staunchly befriended by many upper-class women and men who sympathized with her situation and admired her congenial personality.

Tobias Smollett was one of her many respected and respectful admirers, and he included her "Memoirs" as chapter 81 of his novel *Peregrine Pickle,* itself a chaotic, disjunctive narrative that allowed for easy insertion of the life study. He even included it in the title of the first edition of the novel, which reads: *The Adventures of Peregrine Pickle, in Which Are Included Memoirs of a Lady of Quality.*

Unlike Pilkington's and Phillips's nonchronological and digressive narratives, Vane tells her life story chronologically and with considerable literary merit, in a fluid style that far excels Smollett's. She describes her widowhood, which occurred early in a love marriage, after which her parents, believing that a respectable woman cannot survive without a mate, force her to marry again, this time to a husband who turns out to be paranoid and impotent. Vane details her futile efforts to compromise with her tyrannical husband and then describes what today we would call her "relationships." It was unusual even among secular confessionals to admit to such liaisons without apology and with pride. She tells us that she refused to involve herself with men of means solely for their wealth but chose two or three whom she truly loved. Women will recognize her pleas for acceptance, her claim that her unhappiness was "*because I loved, and was a woman.*"[10] "Memoirs of a Lady of Quality" may have been scandalous for her time, but contemporary women will see it not as the " 'true confession' story of a notorious woman," as one critic put it,[11] but as a sincere account by a strong and independent woman.

These three autobiographies, begun within three years of one another, continue the women's autobiographical tradition into the eighteenth century by focusing on the personal aspects of their lives, especially the harsh realities faced by women without mates or means. Pilkington and Phillips continue the tradition with their disjunctive, nonchronological narratives. In addition, these three autobiographies furthered the progress of the novel. Shumaker writes that the

> effect of these autobiographical romances . . . may have been important to the development of a subjective emphasis. . . . If autobiography was to conquer areas of more subtle meaning, the reading public had to be shown that writers could do with their own real lives what Richardson had done with his fictive ones.

But Shumaker errs when he says that "before the publication of these three amorous confessions secular lives regularly ignored the feelings, whereas afterward they often did not."[12] As we have seen, Margaret Cavendish and Anne Halkett in the seventeenth century expressed their feelings in their autobiographies with, if anything, even more sophistication and perception than these eighteenth-century women.

Another confessional and subjective autobiography of this period was written by the accomplished actress Charlotte Charke (d. 1760). However, hers is not considered "scandalous" because it focuses on her hardships and difficulties not with a wayward husband or unscrupulous suitors but with her unforgiving father, the infamous poet laureate Colley Cibber. *A Narrative of the Life of Mrs. Charlotte Charke, Youngest Daughter of Colley Cibber, Esq., Written by Herself* (1755)[13] was published in eight weekly installments in an effort to earn money, literally to keep from starving to death. Disowned by her father after her divorce, Charke pleads in vain for acceptance and financial help from the man she most loved and admired. Often in abject poverty when not performing at Drury Lane, Charke traveled throughout the provinces for nine years with small companies in order to support herself and her daughter. Talented and innovative, she became—when acting failed—a puppeteer, wrote plays and farces, managed small theater companies, established her own businesses in pastry and sausages, and even worked as a proofreader. Since she dressed most of her life in men's clothing, she was also able to get jobs as a waiter and a gentleman's valet, once for an Irish lord, who fired her five weeks later when he learned of her sex.

The tales of Charke's many escapades are full of wit and humor, which makes this picaresque life study a fast-paced, lively account. Were it not for the many spirited anecdotes, the narrative would be tedious, weighed down as it is by apostrophes to her father similar to Kempe's digressive weeping fits, such as: "What have I done so hateful! so very grievous to his Soul! so much beyond the Reach of Pardon! that nothing but MY LIFE COULD MAKE ATONEMENT?" The work is so episodic that it is hard to tell which are the digressions and which the narrative. There are interruptions with accounts of events occurring at the time of her writing, flashbacks, associative digressions on a variety of subjects, and some of her poetry. This haphazard narrative is often incoherent, attributable perhaps to the manner of her writing (in installments), the impulsiveness of her personality ("being universally known to be an odd Product of Nature"), and the conditions of desperate poverty and ill health under which she wrote.[14]

What gives the life study a modicum of unity is the central theme—as in the case of Rich—Charke's many futile attempts to gain the forgiveness and financial support of her father. Indeed, she was wasting her time trying to win approval for her flamboyant life-style from Colley Cibber, an extremely unpopular, social-climbing, and insolent man, who was ridiculed by critics and mocked by Pope in *The Dunciad.* Charke was too much her father's daughter, whose daring, independent life-style—for a woman—outmatched his. But also unifying the work is Charke's personality. Though lacking psychological depth, she reveals her astuteness and sophistication when describing childhood influences on her adult personality, the jealous nature of actors, the hypocrisy of theater life, and the difficulties of daily life in the provinces and in London—those "mundane" details so often found in women's autobiographies. These specifics, which give the feel and flavor of a time, a life-style, or a character, give autobiographies their personal immediacy. Thus, Charke's account, though hardly a literary achievement, reveals a little-known and fascinating side of the life of a struggling traveling actress during the eighteenth century.

Charke's chronicle was not scandalous, but the six-volume autobiography of another accomplished actress, George Anne Bellamy (1731?–88), *Apology for the Life of . . . , Late of Covent Garden Theatre, Written by*

Herself (1785), could easily be included among the *vies scandaleuses.* So could numerous other autobiographies by women, who, because of economic necessity, adopted occupations and life-styles contrary even to their own earlier standards. So many of these so-called scandalous life studies exist that one could write a book on them alone, and, indeed, it would be a long overdue rewriting of history to interpret these autobiographies in light of modern feminist consciousness. Some of these works include the anonymous *Memoirs of a Norfolk Lady* (1733), a life among gypsies and amours with the gentry; Catherine Yeo Jemmat's defense of her conduct for leaving her drunkard and bankrupt husband in *Memoirs* (1765); Elizabeth Steele's (pseud.?) *Memoirs of Mrs. Sophia Baddeley* (1787), which describes her own love affairs; Ann Sheldon's *Authentic and Interesting Memoirs* (1787–88), the life story of a fashionable courtesan; Elizabeth Sarah Gooch's (b. 1754?) *Life* (1792) of "sin," written in prison; Mary E. Bowes Strathmore's (1749–1800) *The Confessions of the Countess of Strathmore* (1793), taken from a deposition; Margaret Leeson's *Memoirs* (1797), about scandals in England and Ireland; Arabella Euston's *Lover's Looking Glass* (1800?), a milkmaid's affair with a tradesman's son; and the memoirs of Phebe Phillips, alias Maria Maitland, *The Woman of the Town* (1810?), the story of a "courtesan, family troubles, sexual urges, lovers, brothels, and street-walking."[15]

There were also autobiographies by women writing about experiences not usually associated with their sex. Some, in order to find work, disguised themselves as men,[16] such as Christian Cavenaugh (Mother Ross) Davies (1667–1739), whose *Life and Adventures* (1740) describes her experiences as a foot soldier under Marlborough, and Hannah Snell (1723–92) whose *The Female Soldier* (1750) tells of her adventures disguised as a sailor and soldier in her search for the husband who deserted her. The *Life, Voyages, and Surprising Adventures of Mary Jane Meadows* (1802) describes her business ventures, bankruptcy, shipwreck, and Crusoe-like existence on an island, and Eliza Bradley's (b. 1783) *An Authentic Narrative* (1820) details her shipwreck and capture by Arabs, whose customs and laws she also describes.

The century did not lack religious autobiographies, but their number decreased as economic conditions forced a greater concern with the here and now than with the hereafter. An example of a Quaker autobiography is *Sketches of Piety in the Life and Religious Experiences of Jane Pearson* (1735?–1816), published in 1817.

Finally, we must note the continuous outpouring of self-writing in the form of diaries and letters, such as the *Complete Letters* (1763) of Lady

Mary Wortley Montagu (1689–1762). One notable collection deserves mention before we leave the eighteenth century. *Letters Written During a Short Residence in Sweden, Norway, and Denmark* (1796) by the philosopher and feminist Mary Wollstonecraft (1759–97) is not really a collection of letters per se. Ostensibly a travelogue, it is actually a compendium of twenty-five essays that constitute a kind of subjective autobiography. Wollstonecraft imposes a continuity on this painful search for self-realization, which she explores with sophisticated awareness of female roles and problems.[17] Such philosophizing was rare in letters, autobiography, and, especially, the burgeoning genre of the travelogue. In combining elements from all three, Wollstonecraft also gave new sophistication to the travel genre, which, until then, had been written almost exclusively by men, who rarely philosophized about their lives and merely recounted actions.[18] It was not until the nineteenth century that women began to travel in greater numbers and to write about their experiences away from home, some with less philosophical or literary skill than Wollstonecraft but often, like her, with greater attention and sensitivity to people than to events (see chapter 4).

• • •

Economics played an important role in the development of British autobiographies during the eighteenth century. Subjective confessionals by assertive and independent women, usually those forced to support themselves after leaving unhappy marriages, were the dominant mode. With strong feminist consciousness and a sense of their differentness from other women, autobiographers such as Pilkington, Phillips, Vane, and Charke struggled to prove their honesty and respectability. Although none of their autobiographies achieves the stature of a classic, their emphasis on affairs of the heart furthered the subjective development of the genre; it may also account for the discontinuous and digressive narrative, which mirrors, if you will, their insecurity and efforts at acceptance and self-affirmation. We shall see this subjective element surfacing in an exotic strain in American autobiography a century later. Not until then do women on both sides of the Atlantic pursue accepted professions, legitimate careers for the "other" sex. Then, however, the subjective mode is smothered in respectability.

· 4 ·

The Nineteenth Century:
New Voices

The subjective autobiographies of the eighteenth century had little if any influence on the autobiographies by women or men during the nineteenth century. The confessionals of Pilkington, Phillips, and Vane may have contributed to the development of the novel, but they had little effect on later autobiography. (Such was also the case with that rare subjective autobiography by a man, Rousseau's *Confessions,* 1782.) Even before Victorianism took hold, the impulse to intimate revelation was silent. Women continued to treat personal matters, but at a distance. To protect their vulnerable private lives, they wrote objectively about themselves and others. It was not until the second half of the twentieth century that women began to come out of their emotional closets to write subjective life studies once again.

The century, however, ushered in a plethora of autobiographies, the result of the revolution in printing, increased economic stability, and, especially for women, advancements in education. There was a booming book industry, with many works from the previous centuries published for the first time, a proliferation of reprints, and hundreds of new autobiographies eagerly consumed by an increasingly literate populace. The public was eager to read about everyone—not just the famous. "Self-portraiture ceased to be considered an extraordinary activity . . . and came to be accepted as conventional."[1]

Two rare subjective autobiographies during the nineteenth century were by women whose fame gave them the courage to brave society's censure, for they wrote about romantic hardships similar to those of Pilkington, Phillips, and Vane. The first, like these eighteenth-century women's apologies, was Mary "Perdita" Darby Robinson's (1758–1800) *Memoirs* (1801).[2] Like them Robinson pleads her case as a devoted daughter and mother and a loyal wife despite an irresponsible and wayward husband; she also shared their reputations as accomplished women—she was a published poet and a renowned Shakespearean actress on the London stage. But Robinson only hints at the events that resulted in the loss of her reputation; a biographical sketch appended to her memoirs tells the reader of her seduction, brief affair, and betrayal by the prince of Wales (later George IV), all of which precipitated the loss of her reputation, prompting her to write a self-portrait to justify her moral character.

Thus, the *Memoirs* takes us through only a small portion of Robinson's life, ending abruptly when she is in her early twenties. It is a real loss to autobiography that she did not write her own account of the affair and her later life, for her work shares many of the characteristics of Halkett's life study. It is an eminently readable chronological narrative that is as gripping as a psychological novel[3] and includes considerable realistic dialogue. In occasional digressions she perceptively sketches the influences on her personality as a precocious, beautiful, and sophisticated child and adolescent, her own motives as a talented young adult, and the character traits of others. She creates suspense by teasing readers with hints of her impending seduction by the persistent prince and her final decision to capitulate—where the memoir ends.

Robinson struggles self-consciously to vindicate herself and pleads for readers' acceptance of her moral rectitude. She also takes pains to describe subjects of exclusively female interest. For the first time in autobiography, we find descriptions of the discomforts of pregnancy (though not of childbirth), the pleasure and inconvenience of breastfeeding, and the joy of a child's first words. She also details her efforts to reconcile her passive duties as a wife with her desire for a theatrical career—much encouraged by David Garrick. Even she felt that acting was not respectable work for a woman and chose it only out of economic necessity; as an established actress, she still had to ward off would-be seducers. Financial independence, she realizes, is her only hope for true freedom: "The consciousness of independence is the only true felicity in this world of humiliations."

Robinson also wrote a tract entitled "Thoughts on the Condition of Women and the Injustices of Mental Subordination," in addition to poems that were admired by Coleridge and Southey, and several novels, including *The Widow* and *Angelina.* Few actresses were as talented and sensitive as Robinson, and after her, few dared to brave Victorian censure by writing about their lives. It was not until late in the century that the actress Frances (Fanny) Anne Kemble (1809–93) published her trilogy *Record of a Girlhood* (1878), *Records of Later Life* (1882), and *Further Records* (1890). (Earlier Kemble had written about her unhappy experiences in America in *Journal of a Residence on a Georgian Plantation in 1838–1839*; see chapter 6.)

The second subjective autobiography was by Elizabeth Medora Leigh (1815–49), the alleged daughter of Lord Byron and his half sister Augusta.

Her brief *Autobiography* (1869)[4] elicited considerable attention when it was published twenty years after her untimely death, for it has all the "scandalous" elements that could easily qualify it as a *vie scandaleuse.* It begins with her rape at fifteen by her brother-in-law, Henry Trevanion, and then her forced life with him until she was able to escape ten years later after three pregnancies and only one surviving daughter. Alone, sick, and unable to obtain financial support from her family, including the alternately caring and vindictive Lady Byron, Leigh wrote the autobiography as a plea to her readers for understanding of her unhappy life and for financial aid from friends and relatives. Obviously, her pleas went unanswered, for her work was not published during her lifetime.

• • •

The absence of subjective autobiographies as a dominant mode during the nineteenth century appears all the more surprising because the period was so rich in other forms of subjective literary expression. The very people we would expect to write such autobiographies—women and men of poetic sensibility—and to continue the tradition initiated in the seventeenth and eighteenth centuries did not do so. Perhaps one explanation is that poets and novelists pour all their emotional energies into creative works, leaving little time for nonfictional renderings.

True, some of the Romantics lived short lives, but many others did not. Among the male literary giants of the Romantic and Victorian periods who did not write autobiographies are Shelley, Keats, Byron, Landor, Tennyson, Dickens, Robert Browning, Thackeray, D. G. Rossetti, Pater, Arnold, Swinburne, Morris, and Meredith. The exceptions are primarily by essayists: De Quincey's *Confessions of an English Opium-Eater* (1822) and *Autobiographic Sketches* (1853), Hazlitt's *Liber Amoris* (1823), and Hunt's *Autobiography* (1850). Coleridge includes only fragmentary personal notes in *Biographia Literaria* (1817), and Wordsworth's *Prelude* (written in 1804–5, revised in 1839, and published after his death in 1850) has autobiographical elements, but it is not a prose work, which is our sense of an autobiography.

The picture is similar for the female literary giants of the century. Virginia Woolf called the nineteenth century the "epic age of women's writing" in fiction, but though their letters have often been collected, none of these novelists wrote autobiographies: Jane Austen, the three Brontë sisters—Charlotte, Emily, and Anne—Elizabeth Gaskell, Frances Trollope, Caroline Bowles, and George Eliot, as well as the poet Christina Rossetti. Elizabeth Barrett Browning (1806–61) left only two brief and youthful essays: "My Own Character," composed when she was twelve, and "Glimpses into My Own Life and Literary Character," written when she was fourteen (the latter was published posthumously in *Hitherto Unpublished Poems* in 1914).[5] In girlish self-absorbed prose, Browning describes a happy and secure childhood, her devotion to poetry and the classics, her adoration of her brother, and her efforts to overcome her vanity. But these pieces do not qualify as complete or mature life studies.

It may surprise readers that most autobiographies are not written by literary people and that most male autobiographies that are considered classics were not written by novelists or poets. During the nineteenth century, the "full and luxuriant flowering" of autobiography that Shumaker posits[6] applies only to male autobiographies published in the last decades of the century, and they were, for the most part, written by men who were not creative writers; for example, Cardinal John Newman's *Apologia* (1864), philosopher John Stuart Mill's *Autobiography* (1873), novelist Anthony Trollope's *Autobiography* (written 1876; published 1883), art and social critic John Ruskin's *Praeterita* (1886–89), novelist George Moore's *Confessions of a Young Man* (1888), naturalist Charles Darwin's autobiography (1896), and the edited *Reminiscences* (1881) of essayist Thomas Carlyle.

Among female autobiographers, we do find a number by literary women, but they are totally unknown today—both for their life studies and their other works. Because more women were educated during the nineteenth century, more were able to earn a living by writing, whatever the subject matter or genre. However, a significant number of these women's autobiographical works center not on themselves but on others, often taking the view of Elizabeth Browning, who began "Glimpses" with that now famous line: "To be one's own chronicler is a task generally dictated by extreme vanity"; though written by a child, it is an accurate reflection of the attitude of most nineteenth-century female autobiographers. Accomplished women, even those who were successful if not famous, were usually apologetic or self-deprecating about their personal lives and careers. Many women whose lives crossed paths with famous male writers chose to concentrate on them rather than on themselves, believing, as Fanshawe and Rich did in the seventeenth century, that the public was more interested in the lives of these men than in their own.

Samuel Johnson was a particularly popular focus of such attentions. Just as Hester Lynch Thrale Piozzi (1741–1821) is known more for her *Anecdotes* (1786) about Johnson and her *Letters* (1788) to and from him than for her own *Autobiography, Letters, and Literary Remains* (1861), so too are

Laetitia Matilda Hawkins for her *Anecdotes* (1822) and *Memoirs* (1824) and Fanny Burney (1752–1840) for her *Diary and Letters* (1842–46)—all descriptions of their social life in Johnson's circle.

Especially popular objects of curiosity were the poets and writers of the Romantic era. Lady Marguerite Blessington (1789–1849), an accomplished novelist, penned a graphic journal, *Conversations with Lord Byron* (1834); Anne Richman Lefroy (b. 1808) described her literary friends the Burneys, the Lambs, and Hazlitt, among others, in *Good Company in Old Westminster and the Temple* (first published in 1925); and the novelist Elisabeth Lynn Linton (1822–98) portrayed her friendships with Landor, Dickens, Thackeray, and Eliot in *My Literary Life* (1899).

Dorothy Wordsworth's (1771–1855) *Alfoxden Journal* (1798) and *Grasmere Journals* (1800–1803)[7] contain personal reminiscences about people she and William encountered on their walks, as well as poetic descriptions of nature—notes her brother used in writing some of his famous poems. But strikingly absent from Wordsworth's journals are any of her own feelings, especially about her close relationship with William. The *Journals* of Mary Shelley (1797–1851) do reveal many of her intimate feelings, but most relate to her profound dependence on her husband.[8] The letters, diaries, and journals of other wives of famous authors are less personally revealing, though they did make the job of future biographers of their husbands easier.[9]

The focus of these autobiographies—whether by well-known or obscure women—on famous male writers indicates the low esteem in which these women—and society—held their own literary efforts. Lady Sydney Owenson Morgan (1783?–1859) wrote two life studies—*Passages from My Autobiography* (1859) and *Memoirs* (1862); though a successful novelist and historian, Lady Morgan, like many of her female contemporaries, is apologetic about her choice of a literary career over a strictly "feminine" life as a wife.

Mary Russell Mitford (1787–1855) was also a successful writer—a playwright (*Rienzi,* 1828), author of sketches (*Our Village,* 1824–32), and a novelist (*Belford Regis,* 1835, among others)—yet in her *Recollections of a Literary Life* (1852)[10] she writes very little about her career and even that is self-deprecating. Though this work is cataloged as an "autobiography," it is actually an anthology of selections of Mitford's favorite poets and prose writers. What we do learn about her writing and her personal life is scattered nonchronologically and fragmentedly in prefatory remarks and biographical sketches introducing the selections. In her preface Mitford honestly and accurately evaluates her *Recollections:*

> Perhaps it would be difficult to find a short phrase that would accurately describe a work so desultory and so wayward—a work where there is far too much of personal gossip and of local scene-painting for the grave pretension of critical essays, and far too much criticism and extract for anything approaching in the slightest degree to autobiography.[11]

The low self-esteem that writers such as Morgan and Mitford display by dismissing or downplaying their personal lives and careers is matched by their Victorian reticence. Charlotte Elizabeth Tonna (1790–1846) reveals a passionate nature in her novelistic social exposés of the sufferings of women factory workers in *The Wrongs of Woman* (1843–44) and of child labor in *Helen Fleetwood* (1839–40). Yet despite Tonna's concern for social and personal issues relevant to women, her *Personal Recollections* (1841)[12] omits any reference to subjects she considered indiscreet, such as her first unhappy marriage, all her living friends, even her writing career. Instead, 90 percent of this autobiography is devoted to moralizing about God and correct behavior—Tonna was a virulent anti-Catholic. Like Mitford, she gives only occasional glimpses of her personal feelings.

• • •

In addition to autobiographies by women connected to the literary world, there were the perennial religious narratives, especially by Quaker women. They were intended for moral instruction and to show the course of their spiritual progress. None of even passing interest survives. Upper-class women continued to write autobiographies about their happy marriages in the tradition established in previous centuries. For example, Lady Isabel Burton (1831–96) left a fragment on her happy marriage and travels, which was incorporated into her biography by W. H. Wilkins (*Romance*, 1897). Even Queen Victoria (1819–1901) contributed to this mode with two autobiographies, one in 1862, *Leaves from the Journal of Our Life in the Highlands*, and twenty years later, *More Leaves* (1883).

But new on the scene were autobiographies by women in occupations other than literature; these women were more independent in their activities and less apologetic in their life studies. A number of these autobiographies were by women in working-class occupations other than acting, such as Nelly Weeton Stock's (1776–1850) *Miss Weeton: Journal of a Governess* (first published 1936–39); missionary Sarah Nash Bland's *The Field and the Garner* (1854); domestic servant Elizabeth Cadwaladyr Davis's picaresque travels in the West Indies, Brazil, Australia, and South Africa as a nurse and housekeeper (*Autobiography,* 1857); Mary Ann Ashford's *Life of a Licensed Victualler's Daughter* (1844); and professional pickpocket Ellen O'Neill's *Extraordinary Confessions* (1850).

While some of these women wrote about travels to foreign lands from their vantage point as workers, there were other more routine travel autobiographies by wives accompanying their husbands to the colonies. Especially during the 1850s and 1860s, India was the place most of these women wrote about, and an amazing number of them seem to have been present at the siege of Lucknow. Women also wrote about their impressions of the American and French revolutions, of the war in the Crimea, and of visits to Russia and Africa.

New among travel autobiographies were those by women with the means to travel at their leisure, sometimes accompanied but often alone. They did not feel obliged to prove their marital contentment nor to focus on a popular event to appeal to their readers. Many of these works had real literary merit and, unlike writings by male counterparts, emphasized feelings over events.

One remarkable narrative about a three-month trip to America was *A Lady's Life in the Rocky Mountains* (1879)[13] by Isabella Lucy Bird (later Bishop) (1831–1904). Written in the form of seventeen letters, the work nonetheless maintains its continuity by the poetic sensibility that informs it. Like an early-day Annie Dillard, Bird describes her 1873 trip alone and on horseback, depicting in beautiful strokes the flora and fauna of the region, the rough terrain, the breathtaking beauty of the mountains, as well as the many primitive people she encountered in wilderness hovels. Though Bird tells us little about herself directly, her personality—independent, spunky, generous, and not at all snobbish—is conveyed, along with her self-confidence and sensitivity to people and nature alike.

Other examples of such travel autobiographies are Lady Lucie Duff-Gordon's (1821–69) *Letters from Egypt* (1865) and *Last Letters from Egypt* (1875), Baroness Annie Allnutt Brassey's (1839–87) *A Voyage in the Sunbeam* (1878), and Lady Anne Blunt's (1837–1917) *A Pilgrimage to Nejd, the Cradle of the Arab Race* (1881); Blunt's is an especially intense and personal narrative of her travels on horseback with her husband in Arabia. A charming journal by Victoria Wortley (1837–1912) written when she was fifteen—before she became the famous semanticist Lady Welby-Gregory[14]—is generously sprinkled with youthful slang as the sensitive and curious young woman reveals her fascination with the people and customs of America.

During the last two decades of the nineteenth century, a new element entered autobiographical writing, an interest in the development of the individual as both an intellectual and a psychological being. We saw the beginnings of this interest in the writings of Cavendish and Halkett; now we see it shaped by Darwinian notions of development and evolution as autobiographers write voluminously of the influences that affected their personalities and of their accomplishments. Some of the women who wrote such "developmental" autobiographies earned their living by writing—literary and otherwise—and they took their professional work and lives seriously, not apologizing for their lack of "femininity" in pursuing careers or for their "vanity" in writing a self-centered work. They are self-conscious about the practices of writing autobiography and tend to imitate the orderly progressive style of male "developmental" life studies while retaining the basic characteristics of the female tradition: emphasis on the personal and disjunctive narratives.

Harriet Martineau (1802–76) is probably the best known of these late nineteenth-century autobiographers. A prodigious writer on progressive politics for a quarter of a century, she was the author of *Illustrations of Political Economy* (1832–34), *Society in America* (1837), *Eastern Life* (1848), and *Household Education* (1849), among many others (her famous novel is *Deerbrook,* 1839). Like a nineteenth-century Upton Sinclair, Martineau transformed complex political and philosophical ideas into didactic fiction that was palatable to a mass audience eager for the new ideas of a century bursting with change. Her *Autobiography* (1877)[15] is in the spirit of her age and her temperament, both consumed by a scientific obsession with facts. It is a workhorse of a book, a long, meticulously detailed account of the career of a woman of phenomenal self-discipline, impeccable honesty, avant-garde egalitarianism, and, of course, Victorian discretion.

Martineau's *Autobiography* was written in 1855 at breakneck speed in three months when physicians told her that her death from heart disease was imminent. She had it printed, illustrated, and bound in 1855, but she lived another twenty years.[16] We cannot help but wonder why she never undertook a sequel to document those later years. At any rate, the haste with which she undertook her life study may help to explain its straightforward "scientific" objectivity, which was also the mode of her professional writings. Like them it is methodically organized, here around four basic subjects, with the most concentrated treatment given to her career. The first subject is her unhappy childhood and her early adult struggles to publish her writings. The second describes her twenty-some years of success as a working author asked to write on numerous subjects, which she researched thoroughly. The third emphasizes the many famous people she met and befriended—including Malthus, Macaulay, Wordsworth, Dickens, Thackeray, Carlyle, Godwin, and Wollstonecraft in England; and Margaret Fuller, Catharine Sedgwick, Fanny Kemble, Emerson, and Channing, among many others, in America, which she visited in 1834–36 and whose slavery she bravely spoke out against in her book. Finally, she describes her "declining" years of just a little less work, some travel, and stoic preparations for her death.

Though the autobiography is chronological within the four main subject divisions, it is often nonchronological from one to the next. The sketches of famous people, letters, articles, and stories—some by others as well as her own—often interrupt the narrative, as does her documentation of the sources of all her articles and books. This sometimes makes for tedious reading, but scattered throughout are hints of the private feelings of this very public person.

In the section on her childhood, a safe subject for revealing personal feelings, she describes herself as a bright, shy, but painfully sensitive child who was almost totally deaf and who suffered deeply from her mother's callousness ("I was more trouble than I was worth" was the sentiment her mother often conveyed to her). Martineau emphasizes how selfishly her mother behaved toward her self-deprecating daughter.

In the second section Martineau hints cautiously, indirectly, of her mother's jealousy and disapproval of her social position. Intensely afraid of her mother, she was unable to stand up to her domination, which resulted in a five-year illness, supposedly a tumor caused by "mental stress." Martineau was cured by mesmerism, which turned her to atheism, but her mother refused to see her again because atheism threatened her religious convictions. In the last chapters Martineau reveals some of her fears of impending death.

Martineau did not have the leisure to contemplate and reflect on her personal struggles when she wrote the *Autobiography* in 1855. Perhaps she did not write that sequel because she felt she had accomplished her objective, which was to demonstrate the overriding motive of her life: that with hard work and self-mastery anyone can accomplish anything. She is intolerant of individual weakness, including passion, and believes that with the proper education and self-discipline, women can accomplish anything that men can. Though she was very conscious of and sympathetic to women's oppression ("I want to be doing something with the pen," she writes, "since no other means of action in politics are in a woman's power") and though she supported many women's issues such as suffrage, she considered feminism itself as the cause of women with a gripe. Though she cared about people, it was her intellectual pursuits that drove her; and though she does not write in the psychological language familiar to twentieth-century readers, she is aware of how her mother influenced her need to prove her self-worth, to authenticate herself through her writing.[17] She is glad she never married; she says: "That life is not for those whose self-respect had been early broken, or had never grown. . . . I have ever been thankful to be alone. . . . I am probably the happiest single woman in England."

Less well known today than Martineau but equally prolific and famous during her lifetime was Annie Wood Besant (1847–1933), whose *An Autobiography* (1893)[18] divides itself naturally into two "lives." The first one, a third of the work, documents early developmental influences—her happy and secure childhood, her shock at the restrictions of married life, and then—abandoning her intense Christian upbringing—her divorce and turn to atheism. The second "life" leaves her personal struggles behind and focuses on her political and philosophical efforts in the public arena—her life as a frequently published writer and charismatic speaker on the causes first of atheism, then of socialism, and finally of the occult. The "two lives" are distinguished by different styles—the first introspective and subjective, the second discursive and polemical, less a narrative than a compendium of letters, articles, and speeches on various causes.

Of course, the first part of *An Autobiography* holds more interest to students of autobiography, exhibiting more of the personal, introspective reflections of Besant's inner feelings. The second part becomes a pedestrian, progressive history, a proselytizing tract by a woman caught up in public advocacy midway through life—when the autobiography was written.

Another woman well known during her time for her dedication to social reform was Frances Power Cobbe (1822–1904), a philanthropist, antivivisectionist, feminist, and religious writer—much criticized for her last views by the freethinker Besant. Cobbe wrote thirty books, including her *Life* (1894).[19] This autobiography has even less developmental history than Besant's and is weighed down intellectually by her thoughts on the many subjects that absorbed her social conscience. Crowded with selections from her writings on personal travels, social history, and feminist issues (especially divorce), Cobbe's *Life* lacks even the minimal personal reflection of Martineau's and Besant's autobiographies.

These three professional writers belonged to a growing class of women who earned their living by writing. Without husbands or children, they devoted their lives to their work. As a result their autobiographies focus on their professional lives and, therefore, like many men's, they are unidimensional, progressive, and less personal than autobiographies by earlier women, especially those who wrote about romantic complications in their personal lives. Thus, it is not surprising that a working writer who was also a destitute and widowed mother of three children produced a rare subjective autobiography at the end of the century.

Margaret Oliphant's (1828–97) work was as central to her life as it was to the more intellectually oriented Martineau, Besant, and Cobbe. In a period of fifty years she wrote one to four books a year, totaling over one hundred novels (her most famous is *Miss Marjoribanks,* 1866) and nearly thirty-five other books on history and biography. She also published over three hundred short stories and articles, primarily in *Blackwood's Magazine.* Yet her *Autobiography* (1899) concentrates almost entirely on her feelings, without being scandalous and with the usual Victorian discretion.

Oliphant merely mentions the dates when she completed her works, preferring to write about real people than about the "creatures of her [*sic*] imagination." After describing her happy childhood and marriage, she details without pity the loss of her beloved husband and then each child in succession. Too preoccupied with her family and her work to socialize with her literary peers, she writes self-consciously of her loneliness, her considerable financial difficulties, and also her "obstinate elasticity" in brief happy times. The life story ends on a mordant sense of futility at the death of her last child.

The autobiography was written in three installments, the first in 1860, the second in 1864, and the third twenty years later from 1885 to 1892. However, the installments shift back and forth in nonchronological order,[20] leaving huge gaps in her history. There are also many digressive but vivid character sketches of the friends and neighbors who helped her through her trials and of the very few who understood and encouraged her literary efforts. Thus, the work lacks the continuity of a progressive narrative, but it has a continuity of feeling and sensibility. It is an engaging portrait of a sensitive, shy, and reclusive woman whose greatest concern was her children and her friends. This fragmented autobiography is a moving and absorbing document of a struggling working writer who never lost touch with matters of the heart.

Oliphant's autobiography is atypical of women's life studies during the late nineteenth century, which are self-conscious about their careers and the new role of women. Increasingly, we find women speaking out against the oppression of women as a social class, but not until the first decades of the twentieth century do we find autobiographies by suffragists, such as

Emmeline Goulden Pankhurst's (1858–1928) *My Own Story* (1914). Their works are similar to Martineau's in their reticence to speak about personal matters, but there are forays into subjectivity and intimacy similar to Oliphant's in the autobiographies written by women during the second half of the twentieth century, especially in America after the great leap forward of the second women's movement.

• • •

This review of women's autobiographies from antiquity to the Renaissance and then to the end of the nineteenth century in England demonstrates a common emphasis on the personal. Until professionalism becomes their means of self-validation, women's approach is generally subjective. And they document not the events of male intellectual history but those of their own.

As early as Ahuri's "Tale" and Agrippina's *Memoirs,* the focus is on family matters. Kempe's *Book* is self-conscious and subjective, concentrating on people rather than events. Teresa's *Life* relentlessly examines her inner self while also paying attention to the practical details of establishing a holy order. In the seventeenth century, Hutchinson, Rich, and Fanshawe write about their happy marriages as well as themselves, and Cavendish and Halkett write about themselves and others with psychological subtlety. In the eighteenth century, Pilkington, Phillips, and Vane advance subjective autobiography with their intimate memoirs about their unhappy marriages and survival as single women. In the nineteenth century, women write about famous men in their lives or their professional achievements in light of the childhood influences on their lives.

Most of these women are self-conscious about their gender, aware that readers will accuse them of vanity for their autobiographical efforts. They are often apologetic and self-deprecating at the same time that they take pride in their accomplishments and assert their honesty and integrity. Kempe and Teresa battled the religious establishment for validation. Seventeenth-century autobiographers proved their authenticity by asserting that they were contented wives. In the eighteenth century women pleaded their innocence while pursuing independent lives. And in the nineteenth century they fought self-consciously as professionals for respect in a man's world.

Their struggles were not in vain but contributed much to autobiography and to women's history. Women added a major development to the genre: the analysis of self through subjective, personal treatment rather than abstract or philosophical analysis. It was women who dealt with the issues of heart and hearth, while men were touting their exploits in historical chronicles or *res gestae.*

In style, women's autobiographies follow a fairly consistent pattern. Unlike most men's progressive, unidirectional forms, most women's life studies tend to be disjunctive or discontinuous narratives—often interrupting the chronological order with flashbacks, anecdotes, and character sketches. Ahuri's "Tale" uses flashbacks to tell her story. Julian's *Revelations* alternates between the past and oncoming "shewings." Kempe constantly interrupts her narrative with apostrophes to God and long descriptions of her weeping fits. Teresa interrupts her story with a long digression on prayer and vivid descriptions of her raptures.

Other women digress from strict chronology by inserting anecdotes, poems, letters, articles, and the like. Fanshawe writes anecdotally, Cavendish writes according to subject categories, and Halkett edits for psychological suspense as a contemporary novelist would. In the eighteenth century a pastiche of anecdotes about Swift, episodic intrigues, and poetry interrupt the story of Pilkington's life. In the nineteenth century, besides anecdotal and fragmentary travel autobiographies and a profusion of journals, diaries, and letters, even the more career-oriented, unidirectional, basically chronological autobiographies by Martineau and Besant still rely on anecdote, flashback, and sketches. Theirs is an organization more unconscious than conscious, more "closely akin to free association,"[21] to the integral play of their personalities with forms suitable to their lives and their feelings.

Let us now turn to America to see how these patterns continue in the New World.

PART II:
American Autobiography to the Twentieth Century

· 5 ·

Seventeenth and Eighteenth Centuries:

Traditional Beginnings

By comparison with that in England, the autobiographical output by women in America before the twentieth century was small. During the seventeenth and eighteenth centuries, most American women not only lacked the leisure enjoyed by their aristocratic literary sisters in England but also were not even literate. By 1740 only about 40 percent of American women could read and write, and most of these were from British and middle- and upper-class backgrounds, usually tutored by their mothers or grandmothers in England or in their new homes.[1] By the late eighteenth century, there were a few female seminaries, but these were not much more than finishing schools. According to one report for the years between 1789 and 1822, Boston public schools established for boys allowed girls to attend primary grades from April to October, but only if there were vacancies by boys occupied with harvesting the fields.[2] The first female college, Mount Holyoke in Massachusetts, founded by Mary Lyon, did not open its doors until 1838.

It should come as no surprise, therefore, that the first autobiographical writings in America—diaries, journals, letters, spiritual autobiographies, and Indian captivity narratives—were mainly by men, even though increasing numbers were published during the nineteenth century. William Matthews's two bibliographies of American diaries cite many more by men than by women. The first, published in 1945, lists about 2,300 published diaries for the period of 1629 to 1861, with about 2,100 by men and 165 by women. The second, in 1974, lists unpublished diaries for the period 1580 to 1799, with about 1,119 by men and 26 by women.[3] The bibliography of American diaries compiled in 1983 by Laura Arksey, Nancy Pries, and Marcia Reed for the period 1492 to 1844 includes many more diaries than appeared in Matthews's 1945 bibliography, but their statistics do not significantly change the gender difference.[4]

For autobiographies, the situation is the same. Louis Kaplan cites 6,377 published autobiographies proper up to 1945 in his bibliography of American autobiography (1961), with a little over 1,000 by women. The fact that Kaplan excludes journals, letters, and narratives of Indian captivity, ex-slaves, and overland experiences may explain why he cites only three published autobiographies by women before 1800.

Recent feminist scholarship has uncovered many more autobiographical works by women before and even during the twentieth century; nonetheless, the difference in output by women and men is still considerable. The 1982 bibliography of American autobiographies compiled by Mary Louise Briscoe, Barbara Tobias, and Lynn Z. Bloom, which covers the period 1945–80, gives a total of 5,008, with only one-fourth by women[5]—a significant statistic in itself. Thus, they discovered over 5,000 autobiographies in a thirty-five-year period, whereas Kaplan found roughly 6,300 from the beginning of American history to 1945.

But quantity is not quality. Women wrote less than men, and we can guess that the quality of their works was inferior also because, among other factors, their education was poorer. However, excellent works have probably slipped through the critical cracks because women's personal expression has been given little notice until recent decades. During the late nineteenth century and into the early twentieth century, as literacy increased and the market for books expanded and as women benefited from social and political reforms, more women found the confidence to write about their personal lives and achievements. But until then, the status of women in American society did not encourage them to feel valued enough to write their autobiographies in the quantities that men did.

• • •

Though diaries, journals, and letters are episodic, repetitive, and often lacking in the structure that a retrospective account of one's life ideally takes, nonetheless, in America they were the forms from which a tradition of secular writing about the American experience began and through which it continues to the present day. In colonial America, the early settlers brought the diary tradition with them from England. One critic notes how striking it was that

> the colonists, engrossed in politics, toiling in the woods or fields, drilling with the train-bands, going to church, building schools and a college, opening roads and founding towns, keeping shops, and maintaining homes and raising families under what now seem unbearably difficult conditions, so often took precious minutes at the end of their arduous days to set down an account of them.[6]

This critic is speaking of men, of course. Colonial working women were too preoccupied with children, arduous domestic duties, and all the chores of survival to find time to write about their experiences. All the extant women's diaries from the seventeenth and eighteenth centuries were written by teenagers or well-to-do women, who describe their social and personal activities at home or on trips to coastal towns.

The two earliest extant diaries by women from the seventeenth century—published after their authors' deaths—are by the teenager Hety Shepard (b. 1660), who kept a private diary between 1675 and 1677 about the Puritan influence on her "feminine pleasures"; and Mehetabel Chandler Coit (1673–1758), whose diary covers a longer time period, 1688–1749(?), but is an undistinguished family history, primarily of "genealogical interest."[7]

Of the several dozen extant diaries and journals from the eighteenth century, a large number are by religious women, who kept records of their missionary travels or their own spiritual progress, such as those by the Quaker Esther Palmer (d. 1714) and Mary Weston (1712–66), and by the Puritan Esther Edwards Burr (1732–58). But secular diaries and journals of domestic and social affairs for personal amusement or distraction are also typical. Some focus on girlhood experiences, such as the flighty excerpts from Nancy White's diary published in her Brookline High School journal *The Sagmore;* or the more sedate reflections by Eliza Southgate (1783–1809), a bright, sociable, and lighthearted teenager, who displays uncommon shrewdness about her schoolgirl experiences and especially her feelings about men and women as her marriage day at seventeen approaches.

> I may be censured for declaring it as my opinion that not one woman in a hundred marries for love. A woman of taste and sentiment will surely see but a very few whom she could love, and it is altogether uncertain whether either of them will particularly distinguish her. . . . The female mind I believe is of a very pliable texture; if it were not we should be wretched indeed.
>
> Gratitude is undoubtedly the foundation of the esteem we commonly feel for a husband. . . . The inequality of privilege between the sexes is very sensibly felt by us females, and in no instance is it greater than the liberty of choosing a partner in marriage; true, we have the liberty of refusing those we don't like, but not of selecting those we do.[8]

Some diaries provided an outlet for unhappiness, sustenance in times of suffering. The unpublished diary of Lucy Park Byrd (d. 1716?) gives an entirely different view of her unhappy marriage from that in the slanderous diary of her husband, William Byrd, for the same period, 1709–11. A sickly, brooding, and passive wife, Byrd describes the burdens of caring for her many children and living with a temperamental and promiscuous husband, who was frequently away from their genteel Virginia home. The diary of Anne Home Livingston (1763–1841) (née Nancy Shippen) is a tragic self-portrait of a woman forced by her family to give up the man she loved for a marriage of convenience, which ended in divorce and the loss of her child. Mary Fish (1736–1818) writes in her letters and journals about the deaths of her three husbands and her struggles to support and educate her children.[9]

There were also a number of secular travel journals kept by sophisticated middle-class women, usually from New England, on trips to colonies further south. With America in a period of transition from a domestic to a market economy, it is not surprising that in their travels some of these educated women recorded such observations. Nowhere is this more evident than in the occasionally anthologized journal kept by Sarah Kemble Knight (1666–1727) (first published in New York in 1825).[10] This record is unusual among women's autobiographical writings for the self-confidence Knight displays (not unusual in travel journals), but it is also distinguished by its shrewd observations of practical differences among the colonies, seen almost as separate countries, and also by its very literate prose style.

Knight was a widowed shopkeeper and businesswoman who kept an almost daily account of her five-month trip on horseback in 1704 from her home in Boston to New York via New Haven, taken with only a guide and no chaperone. With a sharp eye and considerable wit, she describes the architecture, bridges, roads, and ferries she passes, the accommodations of inns—their food, hospitality, even the condition of their mattresses—and the weather when it makes fording rivers difficult. She also gives lively character sketches of the many people she met, revealing, by the way, her prejudice against blacks, Indians, and even women in more restricted situations than her own socially prominent one. The beauties of nature did not interest Knight, nor did religious or political matters. What she noted was what practical necessities each locale offered that made living there comfortable or owning a business profitable. Despite the fact that she recorded her observations after each day's journey, there is considerable continuity from one entry to the next, revealing a woman astute at observing and evaluating, whose prose had a decidedly literary touch.[11]

While I could find no autobiographies proper that were published by women who lived through the Revolutionary War, there are some letters, diaries, and journals from this period. The letters of Abigail Smith Adams (1744–1818), famous advocate of women's rights, to her husband, John, while he was in Philadelphia founding the United States and during his long years as ambassador to France, have been published in various editions.

Less well known are journals and diaries by well-to-do women who lived in the immediate vicinity of many of the battles fought near Philadelphia and in southern New Jersey. Some were written by Quakers whose faith made them ambivalent or even sympathetic to the British, but all deal more with personal matters than with the details of the battles or with the war's political significance. The journal of Elizabeth Sandwith Drinker (1734–1807) records her private and social life during the Revolution; Sarah Fisher Logan (1751?–96) describes the British occupation of Philadelphia (1776–78); Margaret Hill Morris (1737–1816) reflects seriously on the effects of the Revolution; and Lydia Minturn Post, an officer's wife, describes the hardships imposed on her Long Island domestic life during the period 1776–83.[12]

Sally Wister's (1761–1804) journal (1777–78), written from her family's summer estate, gives only a brief, peripheral description of the battle of Germantown, then a suburb of Philadelphia, concentrating instead on the many flirtations she enjoyed with the British soldiers who visited her home. At sixteen and writing to a school friend, Wister's interests were understandably less than political. Her editor notes the journal's "faithful and clever descriptions of personals and events, its quaint moralizings, its naive confessions of likes and dislikes, its roguishness and genial good humor, and . . . its dramatic spirit."[13]

Religion was usually an important element in the lives of the authors of these seventeenth- and eighteenth-century diaries and journals. Similarly, the first autobiographies in the New World were spiritual in nature. As in England, the women who wrote these religious life studies were educated and in fairly comfortable economic circumstances, with the leisure to write about their experiences. Quakers especially were encouraged to write about their lives, not only because of their strong faith in the value of the printed word,[14] but also as a means of documenting their belief that "all religious progress centered on the individual," that autobiographical records were part of an "absorbing personal quest for some assurance of salvation."[15]

Nonetheless, most of these early spiritual autobiographies centered on the conversion experience rather than on the personal lives of their authors. Unfortunately, few autobiographical works of this type are extant;

two from the seventeenth century are by Puritan women, who were not encouraged as much as Quakers to include personal details of their lives.

Elizabeth White's passionate and mystical autobiography, *The Experiences of God's Gracious Dealings with Mrs. Elizabeth White,* was written around 1660, the year of her death, but not published until 1741,[16] just about the time (1722–35) Jonathan Edwards (1703–58) was composing his journal of religious meditations and self-analysis, *Personal Narrative* (1765). White demonstrates a clear and logical mind as she methodically lists, first, the five improvements in her happiness since her conversion, which took place after her marriage in 1657; then, her three principles concerning God and the Scriptures; and finally, the three reasons for writing her life study. They were to praise God for helping her overcome her "unbelief," "to treasure up" her experiences of God's goodness, and to set forth her principles to test their validity.

White's self-doubt is evident earlier when she admits that her "first" conversion was more intellectual than emotional, an unusual revision here of testimony she originally gave for church membership. White's emotional honesty extends to the inclusion of descriptions of her many visions, such as Satan, three men representing the holy trinity, a ladder reaching up to heaven, and other dreams or hallucinations. Had White survived to the time of the publication of her work, she might have been closely cross-examined by church authorities, as Margery Kempe, Julian, and St. Teresa had been. Perhaps her methodical listing of principles and reasons was an effort to counterbalance the highly emotional character of these mystical experiences. For, as Daniel Shea notes, White was a "member of a generation that prided itself on its vigilance against enthusiasm."[17]

The other extant seventeenth-century spiritual autobiographical work was by another Puritan and America's first poet, Anne Dudley Bradstreet (1612–72). Her brief "To My Dear Children," written in 1660, is one of a small number of autobiographical narratives from colonial times, such as Massachusetts governor John Winthrop's impersonal *Journal* of public events (1630–49) and William Bradford's *History of Plimoth Plantation* (first published in full in 1856). Bradstreet's work was first published in 1867 as "Religious Experiences," a title supplied by the editor and by which it is still known.[18]

Bradstreet is remembered for her collection of poems, *Tenth Muse Lately Sprung Up in America* (1650), which was published in London without her consent or knowledge by her brother-in-law. Ten years later when she wrote "To My Dear Children," she had raised a large family, was in her late forties, and was ill and contemplating death. It is not unusual that she addressed her autobiographical narrative to her children, a common practice among Puritans, for whom deep family relationships and the parent-child tie entered into every aspect of living and thinking.[19]

Bradstreet immediately establishes an intimate tone,[20] dividing her words between her personal meditations on God and her private instructions to her children. But she does not dwell on sin, as Cotton Mather did when addressing his autobiographical work to his children. Instead, Bradstreet exudes motherly tenderness by assuring her children that God can always be trusted, that there is no reason ever to doubt him as she has.

Selective about what she considers essential to pass on to her children, Bradstreet, unfortunately, writes about neither her personal life nor her literary pursuits, as she had in the prologue to her poems, where she expresses her self-consciousness as a woman writer. Despite a fine education by tutors in England, where she was born, and the confidence of a secure marriage and pedigree—her husband, Simon Bradstreet, was a Puritan leader in the Massachusetts Bay Colony and her father, Thomas Dudley, was its governor—Bradstreet is still reticent and apologetic about her writing. No doubt, as the first American woman to devote herself to writing—at approximately the same time her British counterpart Aphra Behn (1640–89) was earning her living by writing—Bradstreet did not have the peer or social approval that is more typical of later centuries. However, her self-consciousness about writing is characteristic of the women's autobiographical tradition. Similar apologies as that at the end of "To My Dear Children"—a "very weakly and imperfectly done" work—or defensiveness or outright neglect of one's literary efforts occur repeatedly in the self-writings of Bradstreet's literary heirs.

The several extant spiritual autobiographies from the eighteenth century are about equally divided between Puritan and Quaker women, both of whom wrote rather conventionally and typically in this form. *An Account of Some Spiritual Experiences of Elizabeth Mixer* (1736) is a Puritan conversion autobiography. *The Life and Spiritual Sufferings of That Faithful Servant of Christ* (1771) by Jane Fenn Hoskens (b. 1694), a Quaker who emigrated from England in 1712, focuses both on her conversion and on secular themes. The *Account of the Convincement and Call to the Ministry of Margaret Lucas, Late of Leek in Straffordshire* (1797) is in the form of a letter to a relative in England, from which the Quaker Margaret Brindley Lucas (1701–69) emigrated. And *Memoirs of the Life of Catherine Phillips* (1797), a British Quaker missionary (1727–94), describes her work in isolated communities in New England.

There was one unusual spiritual autobiography from this time, that by the Quaker Elizabeth Sampson Ashbridge (1713–55). Unlike most such works, which skip the subject of their early lives to write about their religious experiences as adults, *Some Account of the Fore-Part of the Life of Elizabeth Ashbridge . . . Wrote by Herself* (1774)[21] includes her life before she became a missionary.

And what an extraordinary story she tells! First, she describes a "foolish passion" and elopement when she was fourteen, then her widowhood, her kidnapping, her discovery of a mutinous plot on board the ship taking her to America as an indentured servant, unusually cruel treatment from a master, and a second unhappy marriage. Though more subdued than the British confessionals by Pilkington, Phillips, and Vane, this first part of Ashbridge's autobiography does share some of their sensational characteristics.

However, what makes this a spiritual autobiography is Ashbridge's intention to document her resolute Quakerism, despite her second husband's resistance to her conversion and subsequent missionary work. The details of her early "desolute" life serve as an example to other women to overcome their past and embrace the Quaker faith. Thus, the major focus of the rest of the narrative is on her resistance to her husband, which she takes as a test of her own spiritual endurance. This theme unifies a basically anecdotal and episodic narrative, much as Ann Fanshawe one hundred years earlier had unified her work around the theme of her love for her husband. This technique was unique in early Quaker journals and an original conception. Shea notes: "Nothing in the tradition of the Quaker journal encouraged quite so vivid a portrait as [Ashbridge] provides of her moody, complex, and irresolute husband."[22] The fact that *Some Account* was composed at one sitting, whereas most spiritual autobiographies of the period were written over a period of time, also contributes to its continuity.

Like the spiritual autobiographies, the Indian captivity narratives written during the seventeenth and eighteenth centuries are essentially religious confessionals, composed with the intention of receiving absolution for the sins forced upon these women by their captors. Thus, they never discuss sexual abuse, which would have offended the sensibilities of their readers and, instead, discreetly recount only respectable subjects: their grief over the death of other family members during the invasion of their homestead, their separation from their captured children, their physical hardships, and, of course, their spiritual deprivation, which colors the entire narrative.

Most captivity narratives were published after the author's death, and they became so popular that they were frequently reprinted. In fact, by the eighteenth century these authentic accounts were in such demand that they were often bowdlerized, made more sensational by editors eager to capitalize on any evidence of Indian brutality, which was used to justify the extermination of the Indians and the confiscation of their lands. By the nineteenth century, it was hard to distinguish between authentic narratives and fictional pulp thrillers.[23]

However, there is no question about the authenticity of the very first Indian captivity narrative by a woman published during the seventeenth century, which was also the first to be published as a separate work.[24] Mary Rowlandson's (1635?–78) *A True History of the Captivity and Restoration of Mrs. Mary Rowlandson, a Minister's Wife in New England* (1682)[25] is typically discreet about very private matters, with most of the narrative focused on Rowlandson's efforts to see her children, who were separated from her during their capture. Often near starvation and forced to earn her keep by sewing and knitting for the Indians, Rowlandson nonetheless recounts no outright physical abuse. Thus, her title page is misleading: "Wherein is set forth, the cruel and inhumane usage she underwent amongst the heathens, for eleven weeks time; and her deliverance from them. Written by her own hand, for her private use: and made public at the earnest desire of some friends, for the benefit of the afflicted."

In fact, the tone of the whole account is quite unusual in that it appears self-aggrandizing when describing Rowlandson's social interaction with her captors. When one considers how assertively she chastized them, it is surprising that she was treated with so much tolerance. She records her expressions of indignation and anger toward the Indians at the servitude they force upon her and when they refuse her permission to visit her offspring at a neighboring camp. Of course, Rowlandson's intention is to absolve herself in the eyes of God; her resistance to these "heathens"—perhaps exaggerated—will earn her redemption.

To this end, Rowlandson frequently interrupts her narrative with quotations from the Bible to illustrate the sustenance it gave her during her trials. But despite its religious motive, the work also has some literary merit. Though comparatively uneducated, Rowlandson has a prose style that is graphic and dramatic. The work was not published during her lifetime, but she seems to be aware of the popular interest in her story. She is a skillful narrator, pacing her experiences to create dramatic tension. For example, as the negotiations for her release reach their conclusion, she builds suspense by interrupting the narrative five times to lecture the

English on specific mistakes they made when fighting the Indians. These sober interruptions also have the effect of assuring her readers of her reliability as a level-headed witness to the events she describes.

Of the Indian captivity narratives written during the eighteenth century, the publication of *A Journal of the Captivity of Jean Lowry* (1760)[26] during the author's lifetime was highly unusual; therefore it is not surprising that Lowry describes her three-year captivity—from 1756 to 1759—with a great deal of discretion about personal matters. However, her work *is* typical of many published in the eighteenth century in that it describes in great detail the brutality of the Indians, which was becoming a commonplace in anti-Indian literature. Lowry describes many harrowing experiences: beatings despite being pregnant when captured, the scalping and torture of fellow prisoners, and her torment as her five children are taken from her one by one. However, what saves Lowry's narrative from sensationalism is her sober and pedestrian prose style. Lacking Rowlandson's artistic pacing, Lowry's straightforward narrative, with the usual interruptions to declare her religious faith, makes her experiences seem more credible than would a more melodramatic rendering. Indirectly, the reader gains an appreciation of Lowry's courage in defying the Indians when she refuses to work on the Sabbath, and—when sold to the French—she resists their efforts to convert her to Catholicism. Lowry's stoicism suffuses a work aimed at informing her readers but also at protecting herself.

Other Indian captivity narratives exist from the seventeenth and eighteenth century, such as *A Narrative of Hannah Swarton,* appended to Cotton Mather's *Humiliations Follow'd with Deliverances . . .* (1697); *God's Mercy Surmounting Man's Cruelty, Exemplified in the Captivity and Redemption of Elizabeth Hanson* (1728); and *A Remarkable Narrative of the Captivity and Escape of Mrs. Frances Scott* (1786). None of these adds new insights to our review of this early form of autobiographical writing by women.

However, it should be noted that by the late eighteenth century and during most of the nineteenth, these stories had become so commonplace that their authors were frequently apologetic about writing yet another sensational—but true—captivity narrative; such was the case with Susannah Willard Johnson's 1796 account of her captivity. Others were defensive about the authenticity of their accounts because of the number of "hack writer[s] gone wild," as Roy Harvey Pearce described the many purely fictional stories written during the nineteenth century.[27]

Another element of doubt was cast upon narratives that professed any positive feelings about Indians. Such was the case with *A Narrative of the Life of Mrs. Mary Jemison, Who Was Taken by the Indians, in the Year 1755,*

When Only About Twelve Years of Age, and Has Continued to Reside Amongst Them to the Present Time (1841), dictated when Jemison (1743–1833) was eighty years old to James Everett Seaver, who plays down Jemison's respect for the Indians.[28] And Fanny Wiggins Kelly (1845–1904) attached affidavits by military personnel to substantiate the authenticity of *My Captivity Among the Sioux* (1872),[29] in which Kelly expresses her ambivalence toward the Indians, noting their savagery but also their humaneness and their mistreatment by whites.

• • •

As limited as the sources are for an evaluation of the autobiographical writings of women during the first two centuries of America's history, we can still draw some insights from these basically traditional beginnings.

The forms in which women were writing were not different from men's—diaries, journals, letters, spiritual autobiographies, and Indian captivity narratives. Most of these are episodic and anecdotal by the very nature of their form. Even where there is a basic chronological narrative, as in the spiritual autobiographies and the captivity accounts, it is usually interrupted by biblical quotations, apostrophes to God, or even mini-lectures.

Although the subject matter of these works is similar to that in men's autobiographical writings of this time, it is altered by a female perspective. While the Puritan Cotton Mather (1663–1728) was writing obsessively about sin and the Quaker John Woolman (1720–72) was writing about divine experiences—both shifting the focus off themselves—spiritual women such as Bradstreet and Ashbridge were focusing on personal matters, especially their children's happiness. Secular women emphasized practical and concrete realities, such as Knight's detailed descriptions of the domestic efficiency of towns, and considered military battles peripheral to their own personal concerns, such as Sally Wister's flirtations with British soldiers during the long encounter in Germantown. We saw the same pattern in England—a tendency among female writers to relate the personal rather than the abstract, excluding even the political or military in the midst of such male-dominated events.

In addition, we see an exotic strain emerging in women's self-writing, as early as the spiritual autobiographies by White and Ashbridge and also in the Indian captivity narratives. This element did appear in Teresa's *Life* and a few eighteenth-century British autobiographies, but in America it becomes a major strain in women's autobiography in every century.

Finally, there exists in the writings of most of these seventeenth- and eighteenth-century women a dual or paradoxical self-image. Since it was considered indiscreet for women to reveal anything truly personal about themselves and since most were not writing with the idea of publication, their works share a common defensive or apologetic tone; even Bradstreet, a published poet, apologizes for her writing. Or they need to prove that they can write—"Written by Herself" appears more frequently in their titles than in men's. Or, like those who wrote about their captivity, they struggle to prove their respectability and the authenticity of their accounts, just as Kempe and Teresa did years earlier.

At the same time, however, these apologetic women display a pride and self-confidence in their conduct under unusual circumstances. Unusual circumstances—Southgate at seventeen contemplating the behavior of men and women on the eve of her marriage, Knight coolly estimating the worth of people and locales, Ashbridge resisting her husband's objections to her Quakerism, women captured by Indians confronting their captors. These women feel their uniqueness and their difference, and they speak out.

They speak out because it is the singularity or the novelty of their experiences that was the justification for their writing at all. Rather than covering their entire lives, their "life" stories focus on a specific experience that has special meaning. These autobiographers do not feel yet that their lives as a whole are of interest to readers, but to satisfy their urge to write, they capitalize on their unusual experiences.

Lacking a nobility, early America produced no "polite" life studies of happily married "ladies," as England did. Instead, the "remarkable" experiences of these American women come out of the harsh circumstances of their lives. Our modern estimate of their life as a "success"—though they may not have defined it that way—may be inherent in the nature of self-writing. And the combination of this positive image with the authors' defensiveness may help to explain the fragmented nature of their writing. We shall see these same themes, the paradoxical self-image, and similar stylistic patterns in the autobiographical writings of the nineteenth century.

· 6 ·

Early Nineteenth Century:

Stirrings of Adventure and Defiance

Throughout the nineteenth century, female autobiographers continued to write in the same disjunctive forms as during the two previous centuries, maintaining the same emphasis on the personal and concrete over the intellectual and abstract. But in addition to traditional forms and modes of expressions, the century produced a variety of new types of autobiographies. Rather than adhere to a strictly chronological order in discussing these works, I will discuss each new type of autobiography when it first appeared. The early, middle, and late periods each produced more autobiographies of a particular type than the others, but, of course, there was overlapping between periods.

The reader should keep in mind, however, that all through the century, there was an abundance of the usual diaries, letters, journals, captivity narratives, and spiritual autobiographies. As in the past, most of the religious confessionals were written by Quakers, and they were usually published after the author's death. A few examples are *A Short Account of the Life and Remarkable Views of Mrs. Chloe Willey* [b. 1760], *of Goshen, N. H., Written by Herself* (1807); Rachel Hinman Lucas's (b. 1774) *Remarkable Account* (1806), about a miraculous healing; Mary Mitchell's (1731–1810) *A Short Account of the Early Part of the Life of Mary Mitchell, Late of Nantucket, Deceased, Written by Herself* (1812), the life of a gospel preacher with the Society of Friends in New York, New Jersey, and Rhode Island; the *Narrative of Religious Experience* (1826) by Harriet Livermore (1788–1868), a traveling preacher; the *Memoirs* (1833) of Elizabeth Collins (1755–1831), a Quaker minister in New Jersey; *A Narrative of Some of the Exercises and Christian Experiences in the Early Part of Her Life* (1838) by another Quaker, Jane Reynolds; and later, Margaret Cummins's *Leaves from My Port Folio, Original and Selected Together with a Religious Narrative* (1860). Cummins collected her poems and a miscellany of personal reflections on such topics as dress, prayers, friendship, enjoyment, and women's power; to this she appended her spiritual autobiography, which reads more like a missal encouraging young women to trust in God than it does a life study.

More appealing than these spiritual autobiographies, however remarkable or miraculous their accounts, was a new expression of the domestic autobiography, one less sanguine than those earlier polite diaries of women of leisure such as that by Eliza Southgate. Now, women in Puritan America were daring to write about unhappy marriages and experiences, sometimes for their sensational content, more often out of a need for self-vindication. These memoirs appealed to the more prurient appetities of readers, just as the fictionalized and distorted Indian captivity narratives of the century did. They provided an outlet for the developing exotic, even erotic, impulse in American literature. In his discussion of several nineteenth-century male autobiographies, Thomas Cooley notes:

> Such narratives satisfied the reader's appetite for high adventure in a culture where out-and-out fiction was held morally suspect. In a climate officially hostile to "frivolous" literature, autobiographies (or domestic romances disguised as autobiographies) could enjoy a place even on sparse bookshelves because they professed to record not what writers imagined or dreamed but what had actually happened to living witnesses.[1]

They served a similar function as our contemporary mystery thrillers, and some of them no doubt incorporated elements of fiction within authentic accounts.

Abigail Abbot Bailey's (1746–1815) *Memoirs* (1815) is a "lengthy account of her sufferings at the hands of a 'depraved and deceitful' " husband.[2] Another sensational life study was Elizabeth Monro Fisher's (b. 1759) *Memoirs of Mrs. Elizabeth Fisher* (1810),[3] written after Fisher had served six years in prison for allegedly forging papers to land in New York state inherited from her father—at the instigation of her half brother, who also claimed the land. By our standards, this is not thrilling fare, but her shame at the scandal must have made it so in her day: "My children, just stepping on the stage of life, to have such a slur of character on them, as to be told—'Your mother had been in the state's prison for FORGERY!' My readers, you who have become parents, how does this impress your minds?"

Only forty-four pages long, Fisher's memoirs barely sketch the events of her life, at first chronologically: her unhappy childhood with a cruel stepmother; a strained marriage to a husband, who is, nonetheless, acquiescent to her needs (at least at first); and her decision to leave this increasingly brutal man and to support herself and the youngest of her five children. At this point Fisher asks her readers' forgiveness:

> Without observing the order of time, I must go back and relate some circumstances which may not be uninteresting to the public. I at first thought it best to omit them; but as they tend to fill some chasms in the foregoing narrative, and as it is my object to give a correct outline of my history, I will here relate them.

Fisher now relates three exciting incidents, though not in the order of their occurrence: her disguising herself as a man in order to rescue a devoted slave girl sold by her husband, the "mischiefs" she practiced to avenge her stepmother's cruelty, and her vindication when her husband interrogates a male traveling companion about her virtue.

Fisher's imprisonment occupies a very small portion of her narrative, as does her life with her husband in a British camp in upper New York state during the Revolutionary War. Instead, like others who were imprisoned, Fisher emphasizes her life before her imprisonment, especially her relationships with her family, first with a stepmother and father and then with her husband. The portrait that emerges is that of a plucky, industrious, and clever woman. Her imprisonment was a punishment typical in her day for outspoken and assertive women.

Many other "thrilling" domestic autobiographies were written by women incarcerated for real or imagined crimes, not only in prisons, but also in mental institutions and convents. Among those who were imprisoned and wrote their life stories to vindicate themselves was Josephine Amelia Perkins (b. 1818), who wrote two intriguing life studies: *The Female Prisoner: A Narrative of the Life and Singular Adventures of . . .* (1839)[4] and *A Demon in Female Apparel: Narrative of the Notorious Female Horse Thief, Again in Prison—and for Life* (1842). More serious than horse theft was the crime of murder leveled at Mary Jane How (1816–47) and Bridget Dergan (1843–67), whose short lives were both chronicled in works called *Life and Confession,* each published the year of its author's death.

Hannah Hanson (Witham Freeman) Kinney was imprisoned for allegedly poisoning her husband. *A Review of the Principal Events of the Last Ten Years in the Life of* Mrs. *Hannah Kinney: Together with Some Comments upon the Late Trial, Written by Herself* (1841) is a sad commentary on the scandal divorced women were subject to early in the nineteenth century.[5] Omitting her childhood because "nothing of interest occurred until I was married," Kinney tells of her divorce from her first husband, Witham, because of his adultery, and her resuming her single name of Hanson for herself and her three children. Deeply religious and struggling to support herself as a seamstress, she eventually had two more husbands, both of whom died within a year of their marriage, causing rumors that she had murdered the last one, Mr. Kinney—and possibly the other as well! After four months in prison awaiting trial, she was acquitted, all the evidence indicating that her husband had committed suicide. Kinney's *Review* is written in the form of letters with occasional narrative transitions to provide continuity. The letters show her desperation and perseverance despite social condemnation, and her successful effort to prove her honesty and integrity.

Even less fortunate than Kinney were women who became the victims of a new source of captivity, the mental institution. A number of their life studies were published in the nineteenth century, especially during the second half. Examples are Ada Metcalf's *Lunatic Asylums: And How I Became an Inmate of One: Doctors, Incidents, Humbugging* (1876); Anna Agnew's *From Under the Cloud; or, Personal Reminiscences of Insanity* (1886); and Clarissa Caldwell Lathrop's (1847–92) *A Secret Institution* (1890).[6] Lathrop was imprisoned in an insane asylum merely for voicing her suspicions that her husband was attempting to poison her. Written novelistically, her autobiography clearly documents the sordid and cruel conditions under which female inmates lived and her own lengthy efforts to get a fair hearing before she was finally released. *A Secret Institution,* like the others of this type, was an exposé of these institutions, which were often used to confine outspoken women.

Kinney's and Lathrop's trials were matched by even more sensational accounts by ex-nuns whose life in convents during the nineteenth century were, in some cases, exceptionally harsh, even criminal. Such life stories appealed to the popular interest in thrilling adventures, especially after the publication in 1836 of the sensational, ghostwritten autobiography by a black nun, Maria Monk (1816–50?);[7] they also contributed to a growing anti-Catholic movement in America.[8]

Such was the case with Josephine M. Bunkley's *Testimony of an Escaped Novice* (1855)[9] and Edith O'Gorman's (b. 1842) *Convent Life Unveiled* (1871).[10] Both Bunkley, a convert to Catholicism at sixteen, and O'Gorman, born of devout Irish Catholic parents, entered the nationally powerful order of the Sisters of Charity; both were outraged by the cruelty and hypocrisy they found among the older nuns; and both escaped and soon after wrote of their experiences not only to warn innocent girls against entering the convent but also to attack "Romanism." Both interrupt their narratives for the purposes of edifying Protestant readers with a history of their particular convent and of the order; with an explanation of the vows of poverty, chastity, and obedience; with letters and/or articles that attack their accounts, and with their rebuttals.

Otherwise, the narratives themselves differ substantially. Bunkley's is rather novelistic, with an objective, relaxed style; her convent life seems to have been less harsh, although both women were beaten arbitrarily and were frequently ill from the spartan regimen. But, in addition, O'Gorman suffered from the persistent attempts of a priest to rape her (she awakened from a drug just in time, she avers—à la Clarissa—to prevent her rape) and could get no one to believe her or to transfer her to another convent. Thus, O'Gorman endured six years of gross mistreatment whereas Bunkley, after two years, made her escape, which is narrated with much suspense. Once free, Bunkley was fortunate in finding friends and her relieved Episcopalian parents almost immediately.

O'Gorman's harder lot affects her prose style; almost breathlessly, sensuously, she describes both her attraction to and repulsion of the priest's advances. When she finally does escape, her prose is highly emotional, desperate and despairing because she is afraid to contact her family and unwilling to expose the church or the priest—it is the system, not the man, that is accountable, she argues. O'Gorman suffers many humiliations, rejections, and near starvation (even attempting suicide) until she is befriended and finds work as a secretary. Then, gaining confidence and overcoming her former reticence, she becomes a "fearless" public speaker—braving censure, catcalls, and even an attempted assassination by outraged Catholics—lecturing on such topics as "Cruelty to Orphans," "Convent Life," "The Roman Catholic Priesthood," and "The Confessional." The second half of her life story, after her escape, has none of the drama of the first half and consists mostly of letters and articles (and her rebuttals) pertaining to the lawsuit brought by her sister against the priest (who eventually was suspended).

Both Bunkley and O'Gorman wrote their accounts very soon after their defection and while they were still being harassed, Bunkley (in 1855, the year she escaped) under the protection of her family, and O'Gorman (in 1871, three years after her escape) when safely married.

Safety—under the protection of family or friends—was a prerequisite for publication of these "domestic" thrillers. This was also true of the women who disguised themselves as men, became sailors and soldiers, especially during the War of 1812, and lived to write about their extraordinary adventures. These women changed into men's clothing for various personal and economic reasons—usually to search for or accompany a husband or lover or to escape poverty or the lure of prostitution as a living; some fought in military battles while others robbed banks or engaged in less dangerous occupations. The many accounts we have probably represent only a fraction of the women who dared but did not write about their disguise experiences.[11]

Deborah Sampson (later Gannett) (1760–1827) is the first American woman we know of who disguised herself as a soldier, using the name Robert Shurtleff; we know that she fought in the Revolutionary War and was wounded in combat, not from an autobiography but from Herman Mann's biography of her, *The Female Review,* first published in America in 1797. Perhaps the first American disguise autobiography was *The Adventures of Lucy Brewer (alias Louisa Baker) . . .* (1815) by Lucy Brewer (later West) (b. 1793?). It went through several printings and aliases[12] before it was published as *The Female Marine* a year later. There appear to be at least two versions, with the second one more vivid and concrete in its details and more angry about the indignities she suffered, but the tale is basically the same: her rape by a suitor, her shame, running away from home, her futile search for respectable work, her three years in a brothel, her three years disguised as a sailor in combat during the War of 1812, and then her reconciliation with her family.

Brewer concentrates most of her life story on the sins and evils of brothel life and of prostitutes in general, warning unwary girls and boys alike of the deceptions practiced by her former colleagues. In a shorter section of this already brief life study, she describes her escape from the brothel, and then her military exploits, with as much pride as a man. The second version adds a portion of her life between her return to her parents and her eventual marriage. It describes a trip she took to Boston and New York disguised again as a man, during which she comes to the rescue of an unescorted woman and avoids a duel by outwitting her opponent. Brewer also inserts socially conscious criticism of the decadent conditions of American prisons and almshouses, which she is able to tour in her disguise. Both versions of *The Female Marine* are episodic, written with the wit and zest of an eighteenth-century picaresque novel.

A modern editor of Brewer's life study, Alexander Medlicott, argues in his introduction that the autobiography is a "literary hoax." Citing both external and internal evidence, he avers that its author, Lucy Brewer, never existed, that a woman could not have succeeded in disguising herself as a sailor and gotten away with it—a frequent response to these disguise autobiographies—and that inaccuracies about naval battles abound, among other minor points. Nonetheless, too many authenticated disguise autobiographies exist to credit such a defensive reaction.[13]

Concurrent with the publication of Brewer's disguise autobiography was the life study by Almira Paul (b. 1790). The *Surprising Adventures of Almira Paul, a Young Woman, Who, Garbed as a Male, Has . . . Actually Served as a Common Sailor, on Board of English and American Armed Vessels Without a Discovery of Her Sex Being Made* was first published in 1816, then republished in 1840 appended to another disguise autobiography, *The Cabin Boy Wife* by Ellen Stephens (discussed below). The publisher of Stephens's work, C. E. Daniels of New York, took it upon himself to attest to the authenticity of Stephens's account by including Paul's story and by commenting on his strong belief that women could disguise themselves without being discovered; he cites several other cases as proof.[14]

Paul's original motive for disguising herself was to avenge her husband's death, which occurred in an American attack on his British ship during the War of 1812. Born in Halifax, Nova Scotia, of "reputable parents," Paul, as a widow, had no means of support, so she left her two children with her mother, donned her husband's clothes, and enlisted as a cook's mate on a British cutter. Her story is unusual for being less a summary of events than an account of her feelings, for example, her pride—like Brewer's—in her behavior during battles ("the bullets whistled about my ears, but I think I was much less terrified than what many women would have been in my situation"); her fear of exposure if her tight-fitting garment is ever removed; and a particularly amusing account of her anger at a persecuting cook whom she tries to trip overboard.

Paul's emotional growth is evidenced by her gradual development of respect for the Americans because they comport themselves well in battle; eventually she realizes that her husband's death was "the fate of war," and she gives up her revenge motive. She must now look out for herself. She also shows feminist feelings familiar to contemporary women. When she is relieved of her duties as a cook for the more rigorous life of an ordinary seaman, she wants to "convince the world that the capacities of women were equal to that of the men." Paul as a man indulges in less moral behavior than her proper female upbringing would have sanctioned. She admits to testing her disguise by proposing marriage to a widow, then skipping out on her "fiancée"; she squanders her savings, reenlists because she is ashamed to return home empty-handed, deserts, then decides to return to female dress and her family to avoid capture as a deserter. Episodic and thrilling, Paul's narrative bears the stamp of credibility both because she describes the details of ship life very realistically and because she admits to blatantly unethical behavior.

Brewer disguised herself to escape brothel life, Paul because her husband died and left her poor, and Ellen Stephens because she was seeking her child, whom her adulterous husband had kidnapped. Published in 1840, *The Cabin Boy Wife*[15] lacks the excitement or lucid prose of both Brewer's and Paul's accounts. In summary form with long awkward sentences, Stephens describes her duties as a cabin boy, serving meals and waiting on passengers of a Mississippi steamboat as she makes four passages up and down the river in eight months hoping to find her child. Half the brief and frequently interrupted narrative is occupied with Stephens's admonitions to "the *young* and *unmarried* of my sex" against marrying a man solely for his money; better to choose a poor but honest, industrious, and moral man, she advises, than a rich and dissolute one.

In contrast to these three credible disguise narratives is *The Female Warrior* (1843)[16] by Leonora Siddons (b. 1822). Written when she was only twenty-one, this life study is so filled with melodramatic language and improbable events (besides inaccurate history) that it reads more like a fairy tale than a nonfictional account. It does, however, show an inventive imagination at work, if not a credible one.

Orphaned as a teenager, Siddons decides, with patriotic ardor, to help her country by disguising herself as a soldier and joining the Texan army under General Sam Houston. Seemingly the sole survivor of the battle of San Antonio, Texas, in 1836, she is unaccountably imprisoned instead of killed and taken by ship to Mexico. A Yankee disguised as a doctor in the Mexican service helps her in an attempted escape. Recaptured, she is tied behind a cart and made to walk 250 miles to Vera Cruz "barefoot over burning sand beneath the tropical sun." When her sex is revealed just before she is to be whipped to death by Santa Anna, she refuses to become his mistress. She is able to escape when she finds a file concealed in her cell along with a note from a previous prisoner indicating which bars have already been cut! Making her way back to Vera Cruz, Siddons embarks on a three-year voyage as a sailor until she is able to return to her home in Mobile, Alabama, in 1843. Perhaps part truth and part fiction, perhaps entirely fictional, this account is different from the other disguise autobiographies; Siddons may have been indulging a schoolgirl joke as she romanticizes her life in heroics more typical of male adventure stories.

Another, more credible, disguise autobiography was *Life and Sufferings* (1844)[17] by Emma Cole (later Hanson) (1775?–1829). This is a sentimental account that focuses only on the sensational aspects of her first twenty-two years of life, omitting entirely the subsequent thirty-three happily married years. Orphaned at the age of seven and a servant until the age of fourteen, Cole resisted the economic temptations to work in a brothel by disguising herself as a sailor. She describes in summary form her frightening adventures when captured by pirates and her near death sentence by an English court. But her sufferings come to an end when she (as a man) saves a child from drowning, becomes a ward of the child's parents (after revealing her sex), is given an education, and eventually marries. Cole's motive is clearly a moral one, as she states, to prove that virtue is rewarded.

Later in the century there were other disguise autobiographies by women in military situations, such as Madeline Moore's *The Female Officer, or, The Wonderful, Startling, and Thrilling Adventures of Madeline Moore* (1851; adapted in 1862 into a sensational Civil War novel called *The Lady Lieutenant*); *A Sketch of the Life of Elisabeth Emmons* [1817–41], *or The Female Sailor* (1841); and Loreta Janeta Velazquez's (b. 1842) *The Woman in Battle* (1876), whose exploits as a Confederate spy under the alias Lieutenant Harry T. Buford were followed after the war by adventures as a secret agent, broker, and miner.

Nonmilitary but still unusual experiences are described in the autobiographies by Amanda Bently Bannorris (1817–46)—*The Female Land Pirate; or Awful, Mysterious, and Horrible Disclosures of Amanda Bannorris, Wife and Accomplice of Richard Bannorris, a Leader in That Terrible Band of Robbers and Murderers, Known Far and Wide as the Murrell Men* (1847); Eliza Allen Billings (b. 1826)—*The Female Volunteer; or, the Life and Wonderful Adventure of Miss Eliza Allen, a Young Lady of Eastport, Maine* (1851); Jemima (Thompson) Luke (1813–1906)—*The Female Jesuit; or, The Spy in the Family* (1851); Zilla Fitz James (b. 1827)—*The Female Bandit of the South-West; or The Horrible, Mysterious, and Awful Disclosures in the Life of the Creole Murderess . . .* (1852); and Lucy Ann Lobdell (b. 1829)—*The Female Hunter of Delaware and Sullivan Counties, N. Y.* (1855)—who presents a convincing argument for equal pay for comparable work. From the number of such accounts, of which the above are only a sampling, we can see that the public had an insatiable curiosity for these titillating life stories by women engaged in activities unusual for their sex.

• • •

In nineteenth-century America, in every type of female autobiography—whether about unhappy marriages; Indian captivity; incarceration in prisons, mental institutions, and convents; or women disguised as men—this sensational-exotic strain continues. These autobiographies also exhibit the same personal perspective that we have seen before, as well as the same need by authors to prove their honesty to win the acceptance and respect of their families and friends. At the same time, these women also affirm a pride in their successes, despite a self-consciousness about their inferior place in society. Episodic, often fragmented, these early life studies of adventure and defiance have the distinction of being among the first expressions of feminism in American literature.

· 7 ·

Mid–Nineteenth Century:
Breaking the Bonds

Rivaling disguise and domestic autobiographies during the mid–nineteenth century in providing vicarious thrills to an increasingly literate readership was a new type of autobiography, the ex-slave narrative. It dominated not only the nineteenth but also the early twentieth century.

The abolition movement, which mushroomed during the early 1830s when William Lloyd Garrison began publication of the *Liberator* (1831) and when the American Anti-Slavery Society was organized (1833), gave impetus to the flight of slaves to the North. During the three decades before and during the Civil War, the abolitionists published many ex-slave autobiographies for the purpose of propaganda. Most of these were by men, who were physically more fit for the arduous journey North than the women were. According to Sidonie Smith, these accounts "offered northern readers, many of them descendants of Puritans and Quakers, a very literal description of the flight of the soul from bondage in the hell of slavery."[1] They were also the beginnings of black literature in general, black protest literature in particular, and, even more enduring, black literature of personal affirmation. Black autobiographies today share with these first efforts a common theme—they are "success" stories in the most literal sense.

Only 12 percent of these antebellum publications were by women who escaped to the North and had their life stories published during their lifetime by sympathetic Northerners. And a good number of these were written by others. Abolitionist editors, in their zeal to get their message across, often shaped these "as-told-to" narratives with such long dramatic dialogues, long digressions on the evils of slavery, and long romantic descriptions of the slave's escape—as thrilling as any Indian captivity narrative—that there is little doubt that someone other than the ex-slave wrote the account. Some of these include the *Memoirs of Margaret Jane Blake* (1834); the *Memoirs of Elleanor Eldridge* (1785–1865), published in 1838 as an "object lesson to colored people as an example of the worth of industry and perseverance," and *Elleanor's Second Book* (1839), both written by a white woman, Frances Whipple Greene; and *Aunt Sally* [Williams]; *or, the Cross the Way to Freedom* (1858).[2]

The Narrative of Sojourner Truth (1850) also presents no problem of authenticity because it is a biography by the New England abolitionist Olive Gilbert;[3] *Running a Thousand Miles for Freedom; or, the Escape of William and Ellen Craft from Slavery* (1860) was written by William Craft alone; and after the Civil War, *The Story of Mattie J. Jackson . . . a True Story* (1866) was "written and arranged by Dr. L. S. Thompson [Jackson's stepmother] as given by Mattie."

Although it is highly questionable that the *Autobiography of a Female Slave* (1857) was written by Mattie Griffiths (also Browne) (d. 1906),[4] its frequent mention in studies of black literature warrants some analysis of it here, especially as an example of the characteristics of such "edited" narratives.

Griffiths[5] was typical of slave women who escaped to the North before the war who had similar backgrounds. She had learned to read and write at an early age; she lived in or near an urban environment; she was light-skinned and beautiful; and as she was a house slave, her lot was a little less wretched than that of a field laborer. There can be little doubt about the factual accuracy of this life story in its descriptions of the brutality and degradation experienced by Griffiths and other slaves in the house where she worked. However, what casts doubt upon her autobiography, even to the most sympathetic contemporary reader, is the improbability inherent in her presentation. First are the untold number of coincidences, the melodramatic and sentimental treatment of events, and, especially, the profusion of alleged dialogue—so much so that the work might easily be converted to the stage.

Written when Griffiths was an old woman teaching recently freed black children in a small Massachusetts town, the book is clearly intended as a lesson on the immorality of slavery for student readers. The pedagogic intention is also apparent in the extremely long conversations that contrast the dialect of the uneducated slaves with Griffiths's own sophisticated language, often Homeric in its rhapsodic details. The reproduction of the other slaves' speech may be highly accurate, but it is unlikely that they could have understood Griffiths's philosophical, college-level vocabulary—even as a child! In addition, the narrative is burdened with many digressive apostrophes and exhortations on her fervent faith in Christ.

Clearly, whoever was the author of the *Autobiography of a Female Slave* was not sensitive to nuances in style and was probably trying to duplicate the sensation caused by the publication of *Uncle Tom's Cabin* five years earlier. Although *Female Slave* was written for the usual audience of ex-slave narratives, white Northerners, to enlist them in the abolitionist cause, one must wonder how successful it was because the portrait of Griffiths—her self-righteousness, superior attitude, and lack of any anger—must certainly have diluted its credibility and literary impact even in her own day.

This is not the case with the ex-slave narrative *Incidents in the Life of a Slave Girl, Written by Herself* (1861), by Harriet Jacobs (ca. 1815–97) under the pseudonym Linda Brent.[6] The book is a realistic treatment of the seven years Jacobs spent hiding in a small shed to escape from her slave owner. It is a rare picture of a slave-master power struggle. In her preface, Jacobs reveals her motive for writing her life story: to alert women of the North to the plight of virtuous black women who are sexually harassed by their white owners—a subject known to Southern white women but rarely discussed and bound to enlist Northern women in the abolitionist cause.

Jacobs skips over her unusually happy childhood, spent surrounded by parents, siblings, and other relatives, including a devoted grandmother. She was six before she learned that she was a slave when she went to work in the house of her owner, "Dr. Flint." It is on Flint's persistent attempts to rape her and her success in eluding him that Jacobs focuses the bulk of her autobiography; it has all the suspense of a Richardson novel of seduction.

Unique among ex-slave narratives, Jacobs's not only describes the sexual harassment of slave women but also the jealousy of the wives and daughters of the masters. Cleverly, she skirts the accusations of Flint's wife and unattractive daughters and avoids Flint's constant subterfuges. The doctor appears to have been obsessed by Jacobs's beauty and piqued by her fearless resistance to his advances. Fortunately, the fine reputation of Jacobs's family and Flint's position as the town's doctor restrained him from raping her.

Jacobs also depicts herself as a cunning adversary, choosing—however reluctantly, she says, because of her Christian upbringing—to frustrate Flint's passion by giving herself to another respectable, but respectful, white man, by whom she has two children. Finally, to elude Flint, Jacobs "escapes" by hiding for seven years in a tiny—$9' \times 7' \times 3'$—shed on her grandmother's property.

Despite this summary of events, most of *Incidents* centers on Jacobs's static life in the shed. Although it is chronological for the most part, the editor, Lydia Maria Child, notes that she had made a few changes "for the purposes of condensation and orderly arrangement," so we do not know how much to credit Jacobs for the dramatic pacing or whether the original account approximated the disjunctive style of women's life-writings.[7]

Jacobs does preface the story of her seven-year confinement with historical summaries of the kind of treatment slaves received on various plantations. She seems to have been well informed about her context, unlike the Griffiths author, who depicts her as isolated and aware only of her immediate surroundings. Jacobs writes with sensitivity as well as anger about the humilation and dehumanization of slavery, yet she analyzes with a historian's eye the moral degeneration of both races caused by the "peculiar institution," the significance of slave rebellion, and the implications of submission.

Jacobs's title, *Incidents in the Life of a Slave Girl,* seems too pedestrian for this well-crafted autobiography. Without self-consciously analyzing herself or the other "characters," she conveys, like a good novelist, her own and others' personalities through their actions, incorporating dialogue selectively and in a language midway between dialect and educated speech. Her autobiography deserves reading for much more than its historical content; the slave dimension adds to a story filled with all the suspense and drama of an eighteenth-century novel in the tradition of *Clarissa.*

These "thrilling" ex-slave autobiographies written before the war are replaced soon after the war by more sedate and expository life studies. These were written to prove that blacks can succeed in the white world. As such, they rarely express anger toward whites or the institution of slavery; the authors focus instead on themselves as women with pride in their race and their accomplishments.

Elizabeth Hobbs Keckley (1824–1907) suffered a reasonably benign servitude through her work as a competent seamstress, until she earned her freedom, at the age of thirty-six, in 1860, but she devotes only about one-sixth of her autobiography, *Behind the Scenes; or, Thirty Years a Slave and Four Years in the White House* (1868),[8] to her slave life. Instead she concentrates on her independent and free life in Washington, D.C., where she became the dressmaker of many of the prominent women of the capital and eventually also the confidante of Mary Todd Lincoln.

Keckley's life study is lively, articulate, and always positive in outlook, giving us an insider's view of the fashions of the day and homey but discreet anecdotes about the personalities of cabinet officers, President Lincoln, and his family. We see her charming and confident, a woman of intelligence and with moderate or liberal principles. She is tactful and amiable but also forthright in expressing opinions to her employers, and she proves a devoted friend to Mrs. Lincoln during the presidency and after, especially during her bereavement and the poverty that resulted when Congress refused her an annuity. Keckley also founded fund-raising organizations to feed and clothe the hundreds of blacks who poured into Washington during the war, free but unused to a life of independence.

Keckley is selective in her narrative, emphasizing her public life rather than her personal one. Perhaps because she expects her readers to be whites exclusively, she displays more grief at the deaths of Abraham Lincoln and, earlier, his son, than she does at the death of her own son as a soldier in the war. Her anecdotal account of the people she knew is occasionally interrupted by flashbacks and natural dialogue; it is also sprinkled with letters documenting her freedom, demonstrating her continued friendships with Southern whites after the war, and discussing Mrs. Lincoln's futile efforts to sell her luxurious wardrobe and jewels. Indeed, Keckley wrote *Behind the Scenes* to earn money after she gave up her sewing business in order to work full-time to help Mrs. Lincoln.

Keckley's stated intention in writing her life story was to explain the "stirring" influences that affected her life—both in slave days and in her free life as a respected person in white and black circles. She reveals a great deal of psychological insight about individuals, but displays no anger toward whites, even judiciously appraising the positive aspects of slavery—it taught her self-reliance! Despite her apparent condescension, which this summary may imply, Keckley never demeans her race and always expresses her pride as a black woman with a sense of self-worth.

After years of freedom and as the war and slavery receded in people's memories, blacks felt much freer in their autobiographies to criticize whites, slavery, and the prejudice that still existed decades after the war. An example is Susie King Taylor's (b. 1848) *Reminiscences of My Life in Camp* (1902),[9] a brief, straightforward, and mostly historical account by a woman who served without pay for four years (1861–65) as a cook, laundress, and nurse to the first black regiment in the South during the Civil War.

Like Jacobs and Keckley, Taylor first writes—all too briefly—of her happy childhood: She can trace her family back to her great-great-grandmother, she learned to read and write at an early age albeit clandestinely (she later helped slaves escape by writing passes for them), and she never "served" on the slave farm where she was born near Savannah, Georgia. As the narrative progresses, these personal experiences are set aside for the more methodical descriptions that make up the bulk of the text: the operations of the black regiment, especially details of military tactics and battles. Taylor's intention is less to write about herself than to extol these black fighters.

Taylor does not have the novelistic skill or intent of Jacobs. Her study, like Keckley's, is more historical than dramatic. She constantly reminds readers that she is an author looking back to the 1860s from the perspective of twenty to thirty years later. This disjunctive narrative, alternating between past and present, allows Taylor to voice her anger at the younger black generation who take their liberation for granted, failing to appreciate the contribution of the "colored boys" who helped free the slaves. She also expresses anger at white prejudice that still exists in the North and especially in the South: On a trip in 1898 she witnessed or heard about daily lynchings, murders, and other incidents of continued Southern hatred toward blacks.

Neither Keckley nor Taylor experienced slavery the way Jacobs did, and both had a more privileged upbringing than even house slaves. But like most black autobiographies after the war, theirs show an ambivalence of loyalties: pride in their black contribution but also—by current standards—too much respect for their white employers and readers. (Taylor's book is chauvinistically filled with high praise—and pictures—of the white officers, especially the regiment commander, whom she sees as having given her and other blacks the opportunity to serve their country in the cause of emancipation.) As a group, the ex-slave autobiographers (especially those writing before the war) protest slavery's evils and proclaim their own self-worth, all the while aware that their readership is white. But the further away they are from their slave experiences when writing, the less time they spend on those experiences and the more likely they are to express anger. However, like white autobiographers, all focus on experiences that set them apart from the ordinary person. They see their lives as success stories, and they are proud of their accomplishments.

• • •

Autobiographies by black women who were born free in the North usually lack the thriller element of the pre–Civil War, ex-slave narratives. Some were predominantly spiritual, such as the unusual early printing of excerpts from the journal of the missionary Betsy Stockton in the *Christian Advocate* in 1824–25; the autobiography of the unordained preacher Jarena Lee (b. ca. 1783), *The Life and Religious Experiences of Jarena Lee, a Coloured Lady, Giving an Account of Her Call to Preach the Gospel . . . Written by Herself* (1836); Zilpha Elaw's *Memoirs of the Life, Religious Experiences, Ministerial Travels, and Labours of . . .* (1846), the life of a Methodist minister in both Northern and Southern states; and Amanda Berry Smith's (1837–1915) *An Autobiography: The Story of the Lord's Dealings with Mrs. Amanda Smith, the Colored Evangelist; Containing an Account of Her Life Work of Faith, and Her Travels in America, England, Ireland, Scotland, India, and Africa, as an Independent Missionary* (1893). But Nancy Gardner Prince's (b. 1799) *A Narrative of the Life and Travels of Mrs. Nancy Prince, Written by Herself* (1850) is an exciting account, first, of this free black woman's early life and that of her sister—who was "deluded away" to prostitution—and then her twelve years in Russia as the wife of a black man in the service of the czar; Prince had a thriving business in St. Petersburg before she returned to America and became an active feminist and abolitionist.

Like Taylor's *Reminiscences,* many ex-slave autobiographies were not published until late in the nineteenth century or early in the twentieth. Before Taylor's, there was *The Narrative of Bethany Veney* (1889), Lucy A. Berry Delaney's *From the Darkness Cometh the Light; or, Struggles for Freedom* (1891), and Lucy N. Coleman's *Reminiscences* (1891). After, there was Annie Louise Burton's (b. ca. 1859) *Memories of Childhood's Slavery Days* (1909). Some were not published until the Harlem Renaissance or during the 1930s, when a new interest in sociological authenticity and the Federal Writers' Project spurred collections of surviving ex-slave narratives.[10] Indeed, *The Journal of Charlotte L. Forten: A Free Negro in the Slave Era* was not published until 1953. Forten (later Grimké) (1838–1914), a wealthy Philadelphian whose family had never been slaves, became an abolitionist when she moved to New England. In her *Journal* she describes her frustration at her isolation from less fortunate blacks, and then her experiences as a teacher in the Port Royal project on the Sea Islands off Georgia in 1862–63, a successful experiment, which proved that recently freed black children and adults left by fleeing plantation owners could learn to read and write.

Among the autobiographies from the period before, during, and after the Civil War, few exist by white Southern women critical of slavery. The British actress Frances Anne Kemble (1809–93) created a sensation when she published a scathing account of the institution in the midst of the war, in 1862. *Journal of a Residence on a Georgian Plantation in 1838–1839*[11] was published in the form of letters to a close female friend. Aware of the irony of her position as the wife of a plantation owner, nonetheless, Kemble bravely denounces the horrors she witnessed and exposes her own feelings of helplessness. Eventually she divorced her husband, who was granted custody of their children by the Southern courts, returned to her native England, where she resumed her acting career, and wrote three additional autobiographies near the end of her long life (see chapter 4).

Though not critical of slavery, there were many accounts of the Civil War by white Southern women who told about their dramatic experiences from the Confederate perspective—many more, in fact, than autobiographies by Union women.[12] These women focused their attention on other matters than the war itself and rarely even mentioned its political implications. Instead, most concentrated on the difficulties of maintaining a semblance of domestic life while under siege. Two works by young women are Eliza Frances Andrews's (1840–1931) *The War-Time Journal of a Georgia Girl, 1864–1865* (1908) and Sarah Morgan Dawson's (1842–1909) *A Confederate Girl's Diary* (1913). Fannie A. Beers, a nurse, wrote *Memories: A Record of Personal Experience and Adventure During Four Years of War* (1888).

A well-known autobiography by a white Southerner is *My Cave Life in Vicksburg* (1864) by Mary Ann Webster Loughborough (1836–87).[13] Loughborough, the wife of a Confederate officer, gives a civilian and female perspective on the three-month Northern siege on and defeat of Vicksburg, Mississippi (April to July 1863). The narrative is filled with poetic descriptions of nature, to which Loughborough always remained responsive despite harsh wartime conditions ("Admidst the constant falling rifle balls, the birds sang as sweetly, and flew as gayly from tree to tree, as if there were peace and plenty in the land"). While shrapnel spewed all about her from daily bombardments, she paints a vivid picture of the "ladies" watching from a safe hilltop the shellings that resembled fireworks. Living in a cave to be near her husband, she describes the day-to-day hardships—obtaining scarce food, keeping dry and clean in her underground home—although as the wife of an officer she was more privileged than the common soldiers or her black servants, who continued to serve her loyally despite the war.

Loughborough is not chauvinistic about the South, but her love of the land is apparent. As a "lady," she does not tend the wounded, and although she never comments on the institution of slavery, she attacks war in general: "Verily, war is a species of passionate insanity." She is a sensitive woman, her compassion extending to starving animals, even when their death provides her family with food; to dying Northern soldiers; and especially to the black women whose children are wounded or killed in battle:

> The screams of the women of Vicksburg were the saddest I have ever heard. The wailings over the dead seemed full of a heart-sick agony. I cannot attempt to describe the thrill of pity, mingled with fear, that pierced my soul, as suddenly vibrating through the air would come these sorrowful shrieks—these pitiful moans!—sometimes almost silmultaneously with the explosion of a shell.

Though it contains little dialogue or narrative variety, *My Cave Life* is literary and articulate, offering striking contrasts between the beauty of nature and the terrors of war.

A well-known account of the Civil War and slavery was written by Mary Boykin Miller Chesnut (1823–86), a novelist, who kept an extensive diary from 1861 to 1865 and expanded and synthesized her sensitive and astute reflections twenty years later in a remarkable historical and human document.[14] *Mary Chesnut's Civil War* is a deviation from the usual apolitical accounts by women. As the wife of an aide to Jefferson Davis, Chesnut was in a position to see at close hand the sufferings of both the soldiers and the civilians, especially the abandoned and starving ex-slaves. She was also "an interesting individual herself: intelligent, outspoken, articulate, widely read. She was . . . candid about the faults of others and of herself [and] . . . she understood both intellectually and emotionally the sexual connotations of slavery and its relationship to the marriage institution as a misuse of power."[15] Chesnut's compelling personal observations are common in the women's tradition, though her *Civil War* is more a portrait of an era than a self-study.

The fewer autobiographies by Northern white women were written from the sidelines of the war, usually by nurses in hospitals around Washington, D.C., and Virginia. They were not published until the closing decades of the century or during the twentieth century. One is by the wife of a Northern general, Setima Maria Levy Collis (1842–1917), *A Woman's War Record, 1861–1865* (1889). Another is Mary Ames's (1831–1903) *From a New England Woman's Diary in Dixie in 1865* (1906). *The Personal Memoirs of Julia Dent Grant* (1826–1902) were begun in 1886, a year after the death of her husband, Ulysses, when her narrative ends, although she survived him by almost twenty years. Not published until 1975, the memoirs cover Grant's life as the child of a slaveholder and give personal insights about the Civil War and its personalities; but she concentrates primarily on her private life with her husband, with whom she shared a happy marriage.

• • •

Although the Civil War dominated America's political and social life during the mid–nineteenth century, ex-slaves such as Jacobs focus on their personal experiences of slavery rather than on the political institution per se. These women project a sense of achievement—even of victory—in their escape from extraordinary adversity, but their life studies are directed at the evils of the system only in order to justify their own personal rebellion. The autobiographies of black women born free or freed at a young age, such as Keckley and Taylor, are documented proof of their successful adaptations to a new life, of making it in the white world. A similar sense of achievement also informs the memoirs of white women from the South who survived the hardships of the war from the sidelines, coping with imminent death, domestic duties, and harried husbands and children.

Thus, for both black and white women during this period, the personal is inextricably bound with the political, in fact even if not in theory. Except for Taylor, who touts the black regiment's achievements, there is little focus on the military aspects of the war or the moral issues of slavery. When narrating their stories of suffering and achievement, these women incorporate dialogue, anecdotes, flashbacks, and letters, which give a poignant reality to their ordeals and their successes. Though most center on a particular time of their life—that with the most public interest—their positive self-image is a step in women's progress toward self-assertion, which was manifested in new areas of women's endeavor later in the century.

· 8 ·

Late Nineteenth Century:

Pioneering in Literature, the Land, and Social Reform

The autobiographies of the last decades of the nineteenth century mirror the continuing progress of women's emancipation. As political, social, and economic forces resulted in greater freedom and opportunities, women plied their literary craft, settled the western frontiers, and forged the reform movements that transformed the lives of the oppressed in America. In these three areas especially, autobiographies poured forth from women proud of their achievements and increasingly bold in their expression.

During the early decades, while women were breaking their bonds by disguising themselves as men, escaping from institutions, and winning their freedom from slavery, literary women flourished in the first renaissance in American letters. From 1820 to the 1850s, twelve novelists—all unread today—achieved best-seller status, yet, as in England, few of these or the other female writers of the time wrote autobiographies. Society was not ready to accept their success, even denounced it as unnatural, and perhaps the writers themselves suspected their talents and accomplishments.[1] However, some of them did leave letters, which have been invaluable to biographers. A few such writers, well known today but who did not write life studies, include Louisa May Alcott, Sarah Orne Jewett, Catharine Beecher, Harriet Beecher Stowe, Julia Ward Howe, Emily Dickinson, and Constance Fenimore Woolson.[2] However, this is also the case with most of the literary men of this period, such as Hawthorne, Melville, Poe, Simms, Lanier, Emerson, Longfellow, Whittier, and Irving.

The historian Hannah Adams (1755–1831), the first American woman to support herself by writing, published *A Memoir of Miss Hannah Adams, Written by Herself* in 1832; unfortunately, it is a dryly written and impersonal history of the publication of her many religious tracts, such as *History of the Jews* (1812) and *Letters on the Gospel* (1824).

Of greater interest is the brief autobiographical work by Margaret Fuller Ossoli (1810–50). Fuller was one of the most influential personalities of her day in American literary circles, a leader of the Transcendentalist movement, and an ardent feminist; her unfinished *Memoirs* (1852) are, however, unsatisfactory as a complete life study. Written when she was thirty but published two years after her tragic death at sea, the memoirs cover only her childhood. They describe Fuller's lonely existence as an only child forced, like John Stuart Mill, into intensive study by her father before she had enjoyed the toys and games of childhood: "With me," she writes, "much of life was devoured in the bud."[3] Even when her father realized his mistake and sent Fuller to boarding school, she was incapable of socializing with her peers. The memoirs are unusual for her time because of their psychological analysis of the ill effects such a utilitarian and unloving upbringing has on children. But when speaking of the most unpleasant incident of her own childhood, Fuller distances herself from her material by quoting her fictionalized version, the short story "Mariana," which, unfortunately, ends this unfinished memoir.

During the second half of the century, many women took on the "respectable" profession of writing, most often to earn a living. More like the working writers of the same period in England than their American forerunners, who were usually from the leisure class, these women were very prolific and popular in their day but are all but unknown in ours. Their novels, poetry, and plays now lie in obscurity, and their autobiographies are rarely noteworthy. Economic necessity is not often the mother of greatness. In fact, a consistent pattern that appears in these life studies is the authors' ambivalence or reticence about their writing careers. Circumstances were not ripe for a women's renaissance in writing; neither self-affirmation nor social acceptance of aesthetic pursuits by women existed, as they would a century later.

Thus, these literary women, consciously or not, employed various means of skirting their careers in their autobiographies. One way was by concentrating exclusively on their girlhood. Fuller's early death explains her not writing about her adult achievement, but Catharine Maria Sedgwick (1789–1867) wrote her "Recollections of Childhood" (published after her death in *Life and Letters,* 1871)[4] when she was in her sixties and already a well-known novelist—*A New England Tale* (1822) and *Hope Leslie* (1827) are her most famous works. But like many writers of this period, she felt the justification for writing her autobiography was to educate and entertain a young person, a devoted niece. "Justification" for writing about oneself seems to have been a necessity for these women—even successful writers.

Sedgwick's "Recollections" covers only the period of her life up to the age of fourteen and includes no mention of literary activities or ambitions. Instead, she writes about her ancestors, her beloved parents, and anecdotes about her two sisters and four brothers; and she makes perceptive and cheerful historical comparisons between the customs and amenities of her childhood, when the country was in its infancy, and those of her niece's time. Written in three installments over a period of seven years (from 1853 to 1860), "Recollections" lacks continuity, regularly jumping out of chronology and interrupting one anecdote to free-associate it with another. The result, however, is a charming and informative work, exuding a sense of "continuity in discontinuity," as Hart aptly put it.

Another autobiographer who describes only her early life is Lucy Larcom (1824–93), whose *A New England Girlhood* (1889)[5] has gained an enthusiastic twentieth-century audience. Larcom skips almost forty years of her professional career as a teacher and writer and instead describes, nostalgically, her life up to 1852, when she was twenty-eight. The audience for Larcom's autobiography is, like Sedgwick's, young girls, whom she urges to learn about life not just from formal schooling, to be proud of being girls and not to wish to be boys, and to accept the "divine dowry . . . of receiving and giving inspiration."

A New England Girlhood was written over fifty years after Larcom began work at the age of eleven at the Lowell textile mill. She describes both her work life and her love of learning, studying German and botany and writing poems after a thirteen-hour day. Despite this working-class background, she expresses no interest in labor reform, and though she displays strong feminist feelings and was writing during the heyday of the first women's movement, she reveals no interest in women's suffrage.

Larcom's nature is a conservative and unrebellious one. The autobiography is simple, unpretentious, and uncomplicated in thought, but rich in lyrical and sensuous descriptions. And despite years of teaching, three years at college, and the attention of many of New England's male literati, Larcom writes timidly of her achievements, claiming no ambition, merely a longing to fulfill her spiritual and literary callings. But the autobiography does display Larcom's intense pride in the self-reliance she learned at the mill and in the camaraderie of the mill girls. She is especially proud of the newspaper they printed. There she published her teenage poems, many of which interrupt her otherwise strictly chronological narrative. Larcom concludes her autobiography with the modest words: "Let us all try together to be good and faithful women, and not care too much for what the world may think of us or our abilities! My little story is not a remarkable one, for I have never attempted remarkable things. . . . I never had a career."

Other literary figures whose autobiographies concentrate on their childhood include Grace Greenwood (pseudonym for Sara Jane Clarke Lippincott) (1823–1904)—*Recollections of My Childhood and Other Stories* (1883); Frances Eliza Hodgson Burnett (1849–1924)—*The One I Knew the Best of All: A Memory of the Mind of a Child* (1893); Laura Elizabeth Howe Richards (1850–1943)—*When I Was Your Age* (1894); Mary Antin (1881–1949)—*From Plotzk to Boston* (1899); and Mary MacLane (1881–1929)—*The Story of Mary MacLane* (1902).

Some autobiographers at the turn of the century avoided writing about their literary careers by focusing almost entirely on personal anecdotes about their times and the people they knew.[6] Examples are Mary Elizabeth Wilson Sherwood (1826–1903)—*An Epistle to Posterity: Being Rambling Recollections of Many Years of My Life* (1897); Ednah Dow Littlehale Cheney (1824–1904)—*Reminiscences* (1902); Rebecca Blaine Harding Davis (1831–1910)—*Bits of Gossip* (1904); *Marion Harland's Autobiography: The Story of a Long Life* (1910) by the novelist Mary Virginia Hawes Terhune (1830–1922); Constance Cary Harrison (1843–1920)—*Recollections Grave and Gay* (1911); and Adele Sarpy Morrison (b. 1842)—*Memoirs* (1911).

Some writers took a defensive stance toward their careers, such as the poet Lydia Howard Sigourney (1791–1865)—*Letters of Life* (1866)—and Caroline Nichols Churchill (1833–1926)—*Active Footsteps* (1909). Others distinguished between their career and noncareer personas, such as Emma Bullet (1842–1914)—*Autobiography* (1906); Margaret Elizabeth Munson Sangster (1838–1912)—*An Autobiography: From My Youth Up: Personal Reminiscences* (1909); and Amelia Edith Huddleston Barr (1831–1919)—*All the Days of My Life: An Autobiography: The Red Leaves of a Human Heart* (1913). And, finally, there were those who were less reticent about their careers or literary development, such as Elizabeth Stuart Phelps (also Ward) (1844–1911)—*Chapters from a Life* (1896); Elizabeth L. Banks (1870–1938)—*The Autobiography of a "Newspaper Girl"* (1902); and Ella Wheeler Wilcox (1850–1919)—*The Story of a Literary Career* (1905).

Two versatile women who were successful writers chose to concentrate their autobiographies on their careers as actresses because their intention was to defend themselves against the common accusation that the theater was an immoral profession for a woman. Neither *The Autobiography of an Actress* (1854) by Anna Cora (Ogden) Mowatt (later Richie) (1819–70) nor *Before the Footlights and Behind the Scenes* (1870)[7] by Olive Logan (1839–1909) is a commendable literary work, but both are entertaining documents that attempt to prove the respectability of their authors, of acting as a profession for women, and of the theater in general as a place where respectable people perform and attend.

Mowatt's life study was written at the dying request of her devoted husband. She apologizes for undertaking a public career but justifies it by citing her husband's financial ruin and illness as explanation. First she was a successful novelist (*The Fortune Hunter,* 1844; *Evelyn,* 1845; *Fairy Fingers,* 1865; and *Mute Singer,* 1866), then a popular reader of poetry, and, finally, reluctantly, an actress. Mowatt achieved instant fame when she first performed in her own plays—*Fashion* (1845) and *Armand* (1849), both popular hits—and then other domestic comedies and a significant Shakespearean repertoire. She discusses extensive tours in America and in England, during which she was—strangely—alternately bedridden from recurring tuberculosis and in excellent health.

Mowatt's narrative is unassuming and lively but burdened by excessive details that proceed in strictly chronological order. When she is on tour, the *Autobiography* reads like a travelogue of events; when she acts, it describes every role and includes innumerable anecdotes about the plays and performers. She also inserts poems, articles, letters, and reviews, some by her, some by other people. Entertaining and earnest, the work argues for the respectability of its author and of the difficult but rewarding life of an actress.

Before the Footlights, unlike Mowatt's life study, reveals almost nothing about Olive Logan's personal life. Logan was not a successful actress, but she was a successful lecturer, and her twelve-year lecture career took her into active participation in the women's suffrage movement. She wrote several plays and novels, was a sought-after translator from the French, and she penned two other collections of personal commentary on social problems and the theater: *Apropos of Women and Theatres* (1869) and *Get Thee Behind Me, Satan!* (1872). Yet Logan chooses to ignore these aspects of her professional life in this quasi-autobiography, including only a smattering of personal information. A compilation of her lectures on the history of "the show business," it covers the many topics amusingly listed in her complete subtitle: *A Book About "The Show Business" in All Its Branches: From Puppet Shows to Grand Opera; from Mountebanks to Menageries; from Learned Pigs to Lecturers; from Burlesque Blonds to Actors and Actresses; with Some Observations and Reflections (Original and Reflected) on Morality and Immorality in Amusements: Thus Exhibiting the "Show World" as Seen from Within, Through the Eyes of the Former Actress, as Well as from Without, Through the Eyes of the Present Lecturer and Author.* Logan's free-swinging style is distinguished by an earthy sense of humor, which was applied unfortunately only to her efforts to legitimize her acting career.

Although most of the writers noted above are unfamiliar to us today, the fact that they took their lives seriously and wrote about them—even if reticent about their accomplishments—indicates a significant change from the literary figures of the earlier part of the century who did not write autobiographies at all. Also, however conscious they are of their being "female" writers, most of them did not challenge the "woman question" or the "cult of true womanhood" in their autobiographies. Rose Norman points out that "there is a direct relation between avowals of devotion to domesticity and the professional success of the writer." It is perhaps because of this unconscious repression that, as Norman notes, most of these autobiographies by literary women manifest discontinuous structural patterns rather than straightforward chronological narratives.[8] We will see a similarity in the attitudes and structural patterns in the autobiographies of literary women in the twentieth century (see chapters 10 and 11).

• • •

The second type of autobiography that figured prominently during the nineteenth century, but especially during the latter half, was written by women who made the journey west to the new territories. While all these works are invaluable as historical and social documents of women's contribution to the settlement of the West, few of exceptional literary merit survive.[9] However, they complete the picture of westward migration omitted in traditional histories of the nineteenth century.[10] In contrast to pioneer autobiographies by men, which concentrate on migration routes, technological successes, or male entrepreneurship, these female autobiographers emphasize the personal, specifically the people they met and the day-to-day hardships of domestic survival.

The pioneer autobiography in America was similar to the many travel autobiographies in England except that the latter were usually written by missionaries or by wealthy women touring rather than establishing colonies. While some American missionaries wrote autobiographies from far-off places such as China and Africa, more wrote from the interior of their own country, especially from the South, where they worked among Indians and migrant workers. Fortunately, most of these accounts were more secular than religious in content, but few focused entirely on their authors. Some wrote about the new lands they settled while others centered on the people they were converting. For example, Harriet E. Bishop (1817–83), who left her pious and proper New England home for missionary work, concentrated her *Floral Home; or, First Years of Minnesota* (1857) more on the history of that state than on her own personal reminiscences. And accompanying her missionary husband, Narcissa Prentiss Whitman (1808–47), one of the first of six white women[11] to cross the plains and Rocky Mountains, describes in her letters and journals—collected in *The Coming of the White Women, 1836* (1937)[12]—the surprise of hunters and trappers in seeing white women for the first time in years. Later, when settled at the mission in Oregon, Whitman reveals her initial enthusiasm for missionary work, then her gradual disdain for the Indians and discontent with her life, which came to an abrupt end when the entire mission population was massacred. Indeed, the pioneering by missionaries was just as grueling and dangerous as that by the many secular women who joined the westward expansion for other reasons.

Most of these women were poor and were accompanying husbands seeking economic improvement and self-fulfillment. Few of these women wrote autobiographies proper, but hundreds found the time—amazingly—to keep diaries and journals that focus, unfortunately, on only a brief period in their lives—usually the time of their journey and/or settlement struggles, concentrating on their efforts to establish new communities and schools, build homes, and farm the land.[13] They tell of the hazards of bearing children en route over rugged terrain, of living with their children in isolated settlements with few or no other women for companionship, of husbands away from home hunting and trading for months at a time.

Even those accounts that are written retrospectively, autobiographies as opposed to diaries and journals, are episodic, for the most part chronological, and rarely literary. Most of these autobiographical works were not published until the twentieth century,[14] but the earliest ones to be published often provided a "thrilling" appeal similar to that of the disguise and ex-slave narratives.

A good number of the pioneer autobiographies proper were written by women from the genteel class, usually from New England, who had more leisure than poor women. The autobiography of Christiana Holmes Tillson (1796–1872) is a typical example of the accounts of these more privileged women. From a comfortable Massachusetts family, Tillson joined her wealthy husband on their honeymoon trip to the "Far West." *A Woman's*

Story of Pioneer Illinois (1873),[15] her account of her first four and a half years in that state (1822–26), describes many hardships, but a life still less difficult than that of poor pioneer women.

Tillson's story is personal and unusually concrete. She first describes in detail the route the couple took on their grueling eight-week trip and their many troubles with horses and fording rivers. She also sketches both the dignified and "vulgar" people they met along the way. Tillson's inordinate concern with propriety and cleanliness runs throughout. In the second half she describes the difficulties of maintaining domestic comforts—furnishing their increasingly larger log cabins and then brick homes, feeding the many workmen and transients, and the arduous task of candle making. Educated and cultured, Tillson felt isolated and superior to the "white folks," a derisive name given to the first emigrants to the western states by the "gentry" or "Yankees" of her class (writing in 1872, she is apologetic about having kept slaves, but claims they would otherwise have been sold down the river). Tillson's intention is clearly to omit anything not pertaining to her brave pioneer experience. She tells us nothing about her childhood or early family life, nothing about her courtship and marriage, and, as a discreet "lady," nothing about the birth of two sons in an outpost that lacked a resident physician. The autobiography is written with some dialogue but with little narrative variety.

Other examples of pioneer autobiographies are more typical of the working-class life of their authors. The unpublished manuscript by Arvazine Angeline Cooper (1845–1929), "Journey Across the Plains,"[16] describes the long trek from Missouri to Oregon in 1863 at the age of eighteen, accompanied by her sixteen-month-old child and pregnant with her second, who was born during the arduous trip. Cooper's account is a modest one; at one point she explains to her readers that she is shifting to the third person because she is self-conscious about the personal nature of her narrative; yet she merely tells of her terror at the difficulties she and her family endured as the oxen pulled them precariously up and down rough mountainsides. In *The Story of a Pioneer* (1915), Anna Howard Shaw (1847–1919) describes her life in the wilderness of Michigan, where her father sent her, four brothers and sisters, and her mother to build a house and prepare the land for his arrival. By the time she was fifteen, she was teaching school and eventually earned enough money for college. She became a minister at twenty-three, then a lecturer for women's suffrage, and eventually president of the National American Woman Suffrage Association.

Shaw's success story is not atypical. She and other pioneer women display a pride in their achievement akin to that of the women who gained their freedom from slavery. Not surprisingly, many of these pioneers became avowed feminists and contributed greatly to the reform and suffrage movements of the late nineteenth and early twentieth centuries. Their experiences convinced them that they were the equals of any man. Maria Mitchell (1818–89), who later became a professor of astronomy at Vassar, records in her pioneer diary on 15 February 1853:

> It seems to me that the needle is the chain of woman, and has fettered her more than the laws of the country. . . . No woman should say "I am but a woman!" But a woman! What more can you ask to be? . . . The eye that directs a needle in the delicate meshes of embroidery will equally well bisect a star with the spider-web of the micrometer.[17]

• • •

In fact, the third type of autobiography written and published in great numbers during the last two decades of the nineteenth century—and also into the first two of the twentieth century—came from these reform-minded and feminist women, whose many life studies constitute a veritable renaissance in women's autobiographical history. This was the most movement-conscious era in American women's history, extending beyond World War I, when, as never before, numbers of women were graduating from universities and becoming professionals engaged in social and political activities. They were now writing very long and detailed autobiographies, attesting to the seriousness with which they took not only their careers but also their entire lives—not just specific experiences of popular or "thrilling" interest. The fact that their life studies went through many editions and, in a few instances, earned their authors enough financial security to continue their work indicates their popularity with the reading public.

Among the most active reformers were the suffragists. Efforts for women's rights had been growing steadily throughout the century. Early works calling for the equality of women included, for example, Lydia Maria Child's *The History and Condition of Women* (1835), Margaret Fuller's *Woman in the Nineteenth Century* (1845), and innumerable articles in magazines such as *Una* and *Godey's Lady's Book.* But the suffrage movement, after its 1848 Seneca Falls beginnings, was responsible for ushering in an unprecedented era in women's history. Women predominantly from the privileged white middle class, who had the time or financial security, responded in large numbers to the cause.

And they wrote autobiographies in large numbers also. Ironically, however, though these women were confident and relentless fighters, on the whole their autobiographies manifest varying degrees of insecurity about their acceptance, especially as women. Suffragists, it seems, more than other female reformers, were under the often unspoken but nonetheless present charge of proving their "femininity." In order to counter the public's image of them as "mavericks" or as "unladylike," they devote more of their autobiographies to their early years than to their later careers. Some spend a disproportionate amount of their life studies demonstrating what a normal, happy, and religious upbringing they had. As adults, they depict themselves as people with whom other white, middle-class, conservative, and religious women can identify without feeling threatened.

This reaction is similar to that seen in works by literary women. However, these reformers do not omit their careers or minimize the importance of their suffrage work; instead, they devise various means of putting their careers in the background or somehow camouflage them. Since most of them wrote their autobiographies before their cause had succeeded—the Nineteenth Amendment in 1920—it is not surprising that the emphasis in their autobiographies indicates doubts about being accepted as professionals by the public.

In a way, this is a blessing in disguise, because the emphasis on the earlier and personal aspects of their life relieves the often wordy and ponderous prose of their autobiographies. It is as though they used their style to prove their seriousness and professional capability, and their content to prove their humaneness and interest in female pursuits, reflecting a fear that they will be denounced for their eccentricities or simply ignored. I doubt that this dichotomy was so much planned as unconsciously executed.

Such was the case with Frances Elizabeth Willard (1839–98). When she published *Glimpses of Fifty Years: The Autobiography of an American Woman* (1889)[18] at the age of fifty, she had been president of the National Woman's Christian Temperance Union (WCTU) for ten years and had seen the organization grow, as she writes, from a group of "conservative women of the churches" who held "aloof from the 'suffragists' by fears as to their orthodoxy" to a group "eager to clasp hands for a more aggressive work than such women had ever before dreamed of undertaking." It was due to Willard's untiring drive, superb organizational abilities, and charismatic personality that the WCTU expanded its activities into the political arena and eventually joined with the women's suffrage movement.

However, two-thirds of Willard's autobiography documents in profuse detail her childhood environment of love, intellectual encouragement, independent thinking, and religious devotion, as well as her earlier professional career as a teacher and worker for expanding and improving women's educational opportunities. The work for which she is most famous, in the WCTU movement, occupies only the last third of *Glimpses of Fifty Years.* This long narrative—written in grand and undulating prose with reasonably spaced dialogue providing some relief—reads like a history, relentlessly chronological and ponderous like that of her English contemporary Harriet Martineau. Incorporating a great deal of political and philosophical discussion into her life study, Willard constantly interrupts the narrative with letters, articles, speeches, selections from her voluminous journals, and even contributions by siblings, parents, and friends.

It is not until we reach her appendix, "Silhouettes," that we find a lighter prose style and more personal descriptions of her family, her early writing efforts, her many friends and colleagues, even a "silhouette" on why she never married. Had Willard been able to integrate this material into her autobiography, we might today have a fine literary work.

Mary A. Rice Livermore (1820–1905), Civil War worker, temperance and suffrage leader, and lecturer, published her autobiography, *The Story of My Life; or the Sunshine and Shadow of Seventy Years,* in 1897.[19] Like Willard, Livermore devotes considerably more of her life study to her formative years than to her twenty-three-year professional career as a feminist lyceum lecturer. In lively anecdotes, she tells of her happy childhood in a financially comfortable family; of her education; of her experiences on a visit to a Southern plantation (almost a third of the book, attesting to the importance the visit played in formulating her values and ideas), where she experienced the injustices of slavery and from which she returned an avowed abolitionist; of her marriage to and domestic life with the Universalist minister Livermore, who was a devoted husband and a staunch supporter of women's rights; and of her work as a nurse during the Civil War, which made her more confident of her own and all women's abilities. All these experiences are narrated with more detail than that devoted to her active participation in the women's suffrage movement in Illinois or her long and brilliant lecture career, during which she gave over one hundred lectures annually on every conceivable topic—all from a feminist perspective: history, politics, religion, reform, suffrage, temperance, ethics, city life, marriage and divorce, and the afterlife.

Livermore's style is more novelistic than Willard's because, like many others, her intention is to inform her grandchildren about life in days gone by. To "entertain" them, she includes 120 engraved illustrations replete with captions in the style of a nineteenth-century novel in order to captivate her young readers. Thus, she admits in her preface her intention to omit anything unpleasant about herself, her life, or the people she knew:

> Every human soul has its secret chamber, which no one is allowed to invade. Our uncomforted sorrows, our tenderest and most exquisite loves, our remediless disappointments, our highest aspirations, our constantly baffled efforts for higher attainments, are known only to ourselves and God.

Even without such intimate disclosures, Livermore's account is lively, though overburdened with details; apparently she was not able to condense the many volumes of her journals and letters and the accounts by others that she used as sources for her autobiography. But, unlike Willard, she rarely interrupts her narrative with inserted letters, lectures, or other material, leaving to an appendix six of her most popular lectures.[20] Strictly chronological, the narrative incorporates much dialogue, even black patois from Livermore's Southern experience. The lively anecdotes guaranteed the dissemination of the weightier subjects treated in the life study of this contented and successful professional woman.

Other suffragists who pay less attention in their autobiographies to their careers than to their private lives include Jane Grey Cannon Swisshelm (1815–84), whose autobiography, *Half a Century* (1880), is defensive about her work as a newspaper editor fighting for abolition and women's rights in Pennsylvania; and Elizabeth Cady Stanton (1815–1902), who underplays her successful career as the cofounder of the women's suffrage movement in *Eighty Years and More: Reminiscences, 1815–1897* (1898), which will be discussed in detail in chapter 9.

Besides life studies by suffragists, there were many at the turn of the century by reformers in other areas. Many were written by women whose temperance work overlapped with or was a prelude to suffrage advocacy. The temperance movement itself produced many autobiographies, such as Eliza Daniel Stewart's (1816–1908) *Memories of the Crusade: A Thrilling Account of the Great Uprising of the Women of Ohio in 1873, Against the Liquor Crime* (1888). Elizabeth Blackwell (1821–1910), the first woman to graduate from an American medical school, wrote *Pioneer Work in Opening the Medical Profession to Women* (1895), also known as *Autobio-*

graphical Sketches. Union organizing was the passion of Mary Harris "Mother" Jones (1830–1930), who at the age of fifty changed her profession from teacher and dressmaker to full-time union organizer, on which she focuses *The Autobiography of Mother Jones* (1925). Others wrote autobiographies about their work in court reform, in health reform and disease prevention, and many other fields of social activism.

As a group, these reformist autobiographers reveal less concern with their image as women than did the suffragists, but this may be because their life studies include very little about their personal lives, even about their childhood. This lack of a personal dimension or any ambivalence makes their autobiographies less interesting and less noteworthy than a work like Stanton's, which, in attempting to "hide" her career, nonetheless gives us a more balanced view of her life. The work-centered life studies are less efforts at self-portraiture than progressive histories of their authors' work lives, more like the autobiographies by men, who tend to write predominantly about their professional achievements.

The fact that the autobiographies by both the suffragists and other reformers reveal an inability to integrate the professional and personal lives of their authors indicates how shaky nineteenth-century women were about society's acceptance of both aspects of their lives. But time and the major social and political changes of women's liberation during the twentieth century gave reformist women a securer footing and more confidence in their identity as women *and* professionals.

• • •

We have seen how during the nineteenth century, American women's autobiographical writings followed the course of women's history, especially their efforts to defy or combat established institutions. Disguise autobiographies, ex-slave narratives, and confessionals about experiences in mental asylums, prisons, and convents during the first half of the century; and autobiographies by literary women, pioneers, and social reformers during the second half—all reflect the progress of women in attempting to control and shape their lives despite admonitions and restrictions.

Whatever the events or subjects of their life studies, the perspective is personal and distinctly female—whether the autobiographies focus on extraordinary adventures or domestic realities, whether they were published for popular appeal or for posterity, whether the author is black or white, poor or financially secure. A military battle, the abuses of slavery, the difficulties of wilderness homesteading, even social and political activism—all the autobiographers' experiences are cast within the purview of their personal and female identities.

This female identity is not a heroic one. For the most part, women do not see themselves as legends or representatives of their times, as critics interpret the self-image in men's autobiographies. Most traditional critics concur with Emerson's estimate of *Walden* as a "symbolic autobiography of the self"—"the only true America"[21]—and equate the private with the national. But this archetypal view of the American identity is almost exclusively male.

On the contrary, what we glean from women's autobiographies of this century is a sense of the female identity as a "local" one—personal and "different." These women feel that they are unusual, even eccentric—that exotic strain—compared not only with men, but also with other women. Like the British autobiographers, nineteenth-century American women, especially those who lived early in the century, feel the need to authenticate themselves, to prove their worth, even to apologize for their apparent eccentricity. Those writing in the early and middle decades of the century feel that only their unusual experiences or adventures, not their lives as a whole, are worthy of autobiography. Even when later in the century women began to take their work and their entire lives seriously, they were not yet able to accept their careers as normal or as equal to their personal lives.

However, the personal emphasis or ambivalence that informs most of these autobiographies gives them a more interesting and human dimension than autobiographies that project a heroic self-image and focus almost exclusively on professional achievements. And even with a sense of difference, there emerges in these female life studies a strong sense of success. Without heroics, women project a pride in themselves different from that usually expressed by men. It is a pride in having accomplished what was not expected of them, either by their families or by society, of having surmounted obstacles only women have to overcome, whether disguised as men to escape family difficulties or throwing off the bonds of slavery or mental institutions. Successful professional women in new occupations, often ones they created themselves—settlement house work, the birth control movement, women's suffrage—or women in traditionally male occupations—writing, acting, and pioneering—all express a pride in their hard-won accomplishments.

Thus, many of these nineteenth-century autobiographers convey a feminist awareness even before the suffrage movement began raising women's consciousness about their oppression and exploitation. Mothers, wives, incarcerated women, women engaged in unusual occupations—all reveal various degrees of discontent with their second-class status in society, even if unable to express their anger or dissatisfaction directly.

Since these women write from a self-consciously female perspective, it is not surprising that their autobiographies document *women's* social, political, and cultural history, not traditional male history. If one looks in these women's works for evidence of the usual political and military events found in men's life studies of this century, one finds huge gaps, because they are writing from a perspective adjacent or peripheral to men's experiences—disguised as men, watching battles from the sidelines, or participating in women's politics. Theirs is a different history from the traditional American experience, just as in England women were outside mainstream (male) society.

Critics who argue or assume that the history of America and the history of autobiography have developed together and that the periods of greatest productivity in autobiography correspond to the most important events in American history are short-sighted.[22] If they included women in their documentation, they would find a different history, one that would mandate a revision of their theories or at least an acknowledgment that their theories are limited to men's autobiographies.

For example, we find that the periods of increased diaries by men, during the Revolutionary War and the Gold Rush, are periods of decreased productivity for women. During the Civil War period, there was an increase in men's autobiographies, especially by military men, but an increase in women's autobiographies did not occur until the last decades of the century, after the war. The number of autobiographical works by women increased only after their educational opportunities improved. The peak periods of autobiographical productivity for women occurred during the Progressive Era—1890 to World War I—an era of unprecedented public service by women; during the thirties, when the younger generations reaped the benefits of the Progressive Era; and, more recently, during the decades of the second women's movement. Gerda Lerner notes:

> The periods in which basic changes occur in society and which historians commonly regard as turning points are not necessarily the same for men and women. This is not surprising when we consider that the traditional time frame in history has been derived from political history. For example, neither during nor after the

American Revolution, nor in the age of Jackson did women share in the broadening of opportunities and in the political democratization experienced by men. On the contrary, women in both periods experienced status loss and a restriction of their choices as to education or vocation, and had new restraints imposed upon their sexuality, at least by prescription. Thus, the traditional political and military chronology is largely irrelevant to the history of women.[23]

With women writing their autobiographies within the contours of their own experience and history, a history not powered by a heroic self-image but driven by a need for self-affirmation, it is not surprising that the style and forms of their autobiographies reflect a different mode of expression from men's. Rather than the progressive, linear, unidimensional works that men wrote—chronicles, *res gestae,* intellectual histories—most women's self-portraits are cast in discontinuous forms and disjunctive narratives. Diaries, letters, and journals, which flourished throughout the century, are accessible forms for women whose emotional, intellectual, and practical lives are fragmented by domestic responsibilities that leave them little leisure time to contemplate or integrate their experiences. Even in more shaped narratives and autobiographies proper, a disjunctiveness persists. Although the women attempt to maintain some chronology, to show some progression in their lives, they interrupt their narratives with anecdotes, character sketches, lectures, letters, and flashbacks—no matter what the subject matter, from Indian captivity to reform movements.

Thus, American women's autobiographies during the nineteenth century, and even before, mirror not so much their era as their own personal and practical realities. And paradoxically they project a tentative yet proud self-image, which may also help explain the disjunctive nature of their narratives. Their life studies document not the events of their times but the emotional conscience of America. The American female autobiographical tradition follows the progress of a "subversive" American history, subversive to the "traditional" (male) one. We shall see this tradition continued in the autobiographies from the modern era, which are discussed in Part III. These women write more about the process of their lives than its products, more personal history than American history, from the angle of vision of outsiders to the dominant society, sometimes even to their own sex.

PART III:
American Autobiography in the Modern Era

· 9 ·

Traditional Autobiography Liberated:

The Ordinary and Superwoman Elizabeth Cady Stanton

Elizabeth Cady Stanton (1815–1902) was the major intellectual figure of the women's reform movement during the late nineteenth century. She was also a transitional figure, very much a woman of the nineteenth century with her reticences and discretions, but also a twentieth-century woman with her independence, outspokenness, and pride in herself and her work. Her autobiography is representative of those written by women who devoted themselves to reformist careers. Not only were these women forging a new politics outside the mainstream (male) sphere, but they were also bucking male and female establishment expectations of them as women. They did not feel accepted solely as "career" women and acquiesced to the public's need for assurances that they were first of all ordinary and feminine, only secondarily "eccentric," that is, professionals. When writing their autobiographies, their overriding objective was to present their lives in such a way that their reputations and, concomitantly, their cause were protected. Because they wanted to convince readers of the rightness of their mission, they painted a rosy picture of themselves and their work, excluding anything negative or controversial. They also placed their public and professional lives discreetly in the background or within the context of their personal lives, the "personal," however, never being intimate or very subjective, but instead including descriptions of respectable families, friends, and travels, often supported with letters, articles, speeches, poems, and other artifacts. These insertions, along with anecdotes and flashbacks, interrupt the basically chronological and progressive order of their success stories, either enlivening long-winded accounts or contributing to already tedious reading.

For none of these works is very literary, even though most are well written, informative, and sometimes entertaining. Divided as they were between two selves, the public and personal, unaccepted as both, these autobiographers were unable to integrate their lives in public autobiographies. Such integration had to wait several decades, for Margaret Sanger's

Autobiography (1938) and especially Kate Millett's *Flying* (1974). The turn-of-the-century autobiographies are, therefore, discursive and historical life studies, the fate, it seems, of works that aim at demonstrating the progress and success of a public career. In spite of this similarity to autobiographies by men in public careers, these reformers' works demonstrate the characteristics we have found typical of past women's autobiographies.

• • •

In 1895, when Stanton began *Eighty Years and More: Reminiscences, 1815–1897* (1898) at the age of eighty, she was still a vigorous and active person, still writing and publishing. The autobiography followed close on the heels of two of her major publications, *History of Woman Suffrage* (1881–86) and *The Woman's Bible* (1895, 1898). Stanton had also been a prolific writer of speeches and articles during the fifty years of service to the cause that occupied her life—and shaped her autobiography—the women's suffrage movement.

Her intention, Stanton states in her preface to *Eighty Years,* is to write about her "private life" as opposed to her "public career":

> The story of my private life as wife of an earnest reformer, as an enthusiastic housekeeper, proud of my skill in every department of domestic economy, and as the mother of seven children, may amuse and benefit the reader.
>
> The incidents of my public career as a leader in the most momentous reform yet launched upon the world—the emancipation of women—will be found in "The History of Woman Suffrage."[1]

This is not, however, an accurate description of the book's contents. In *Eighty Years* Stanton spends little space on her private life as wife-housekeeper-mother. Though her marriage to Henry Stanton lasted for forty-seven years, until his death in 1887, she hardly mentions her role as his wife. Except for a brief sketch of their meeting and marriage journey, Henry himself is hardly present in the book; from 1848, when Stanton's political work started in earnest, until 1885—a period of thirty-seven years—he is never mentioned, and thereafter only three times, very briefly and insignificantly.

On the subject of housekeeping, Stanton offers many helpful suggestions, such as the value of efficient stoves, of circulating heat through a house, of adequate ventilation, and of the joys of creative cooking. But the anecdotes on these matters are scattered throughout the book and hardly constitute a major theme. She barely touches on her role as a mother and then only, after mentioning the birth of the first of seven children, to suggest that other new mothers trust their own judgment rather than the dictates of rigid and ignorant doctors. Though Stanton did not undertake her out-of-state lecturing until 1869, when her youngest child was eleven, we hear little about these children until the 1880s when they are all grown, married, and pleasant to visit in her less active years.

Stanton's actual intention in writing *Eighty Years* was twofold. First, she wanted to present herself as an ordinary human being, but *not* because she was a wife, housekeeper, and mother. She considers herself ordinary because she mixes easily with ordinary people, has a cheerful disposition, is self-reliant and healthy, and has varied domestic interests in addition to her political ones. This ordinary person plays an important role in the anecdotes that relieve the narrative of its second, more weighty goal (though it is never directly stated): to educate her readers about the women's suffrage movement in order to convert them to her cause. Everything she includes or excludes in *Eighty Years,* even the way she portrays her self-image, is determined by this overriding educational aim. Her "public career" is indeed the major objective of the autobiography, but she tries to make it as inoffensive as possible by means of humorous, human interest anecdotes designed to persuade her readers to accept her reformist ideas.

When Stanton wrote her life study she was a celebrity among reformists, a person who had figured prominently in the news for fifty years. By casting her views within the framework of an "ordinary" life, she was attempting to counter her unidimensional public image as a brilliant, argumentative, sharp-witted, unrelenting reformer from a prestigious upper-class family. How was she to integrate this overdetermined image of herself as an exceptional human being, certainly one worthy of full and equal citizenship with men, with a multidimensional image of an ordinary human being in a way that her readers would remain receptive to the "most momentous reform yet launched upon the world"?

Reconciling this paradoxical self-image was the struggle of her entire life as a feminist, and it remains a dilemma for today's feminists. For Stanton, and for us, there is the dialectic between the ordinary woman, product of the conditions that produce women in this society, and at the same time, the *not* ordinary but exceptional woman who is not trapped in those conditions but can see her way out of them.

It is evident from reading *Eighty Years* that Stanton intended to present both her personal life and her public work as successful.[2] However, in the effort to submerge the superior person, to present herself as an ordinary woman whom her readers can trust, she produces a narrative that is rife with paradox, contradictions, and ambivalence. While she writes an apparently linear and chronological narrative that emphasizes the stability of her personality and her faith in the order and progress of the world, the narrative is constantly interrupted by a variety of discontinuous forms—anecdotes, for the most part, but also letters and excerpts from speeches and published articles by herself and others. Though she writes about weighty and controversial issues, she often uses light and humorous anecdotes to make her points. While she wants to convince us that her childhood was a happy and normal one, she also shows the unusual emotional and intellectual sources of her dedication to the cause of women's rights. Though she treats her father with the greatest respect, it is apparent that even in her eighties she still thinks of him with fear and a great deal of unrecognized anger. While she regales us with her exploits aboard trains, bathing crying babies or airing stuffy parlor cars, she also depicts herself valiantly turning out speeches, lectures, petitions, and pamphlets, traveling day and night under superhuman conditions. In her travels on the lyceum lecture circuit, she feels comfortable and sisterly with ordinary women whose hospitality she accepts despite often unhealthful food and unsanitary sleeping conditions. Nevertheless, she has easy access to the homes of famous people in and out of the reform movement in her own country and abroad because of her family's social position. While she is completely reticent about her own intimate life, she is outspoken on such controversial issues as hypocrisy in the Bible, incompatibility as grounds for divorce, and the enfranchisement of former male slaves only on condition of enfranchisement of all women—positions that produced a barrage of attacks upon her not only from the mass public but even from within her own movement.

The final paradox is that at the time Stanton wrote her autobiography, she had not achieved the goal to which she had dedicated her entire life—the enfranchisement of women. Yet campaigns, attacks on bills, struggles for propositions and amendments, petitions, speeches—all the various efforts she describes—appear as victories. We complete this autobiography with the impression that Stanton's public career was a success.

The primary way she conveys this image of her work as successful, despite the suffrage failure, is to omit anything that might cast a negative light on her achievements, always emphasizing the positive. She excludes anything about her personal or public life that is irrelevant to the movement or that might give detractors ammunition against the cause. Stanton's unflinching self-confidence and her positive vision of her work—

qualities that produce leaders and heroes—made a success of her effort to educate her readers, convincing them of the justness of her cause and leading them to accept her dual self-image. How she resolved the dialectic between being ordinary and one with all women and at the same time special in her extraordinary talents has contemporary overtones; Kate Millett's efforts in her autobiography, *Flying,* to reconcile her individual needs with the collective goals of her cause reflect a similar concern.

Let us look at how Stanton develops her two unstated intentions—presenting herself as an ordinary human being and furthering the cause of women's suffrage. In the first third of the book, she deals with the influences that shaped her personality and character during her childhood, girlhood, marriage, and early motherhood, to 1848, when she was thirty-three. Here we see the most ambivalent or paradoxical aspect of her life study, for she is dealing with her personality more than the movement. In the second and longest section, the emphasis shifts to her efforts for the cause, from 1848 to 1881; here we see less ambivalence and more direct omission of information. In the final section, which continues the theme of her work for women's suffrage, she spends more time describing her travels and visits with her grown children; here, too, there is both omission and paradox, but to a lesser degree than in either of the two earlier sections.

First, let us consider the ambivalence evident in Stanton's description of her early years. She pictures herself, on the one hand, as a healthy, romping girl full of enthusiasm and energy, enjoying her schoolwork, her games with her two younger sisters, and all kinds of outdoor activities at her central New York state home of Johnstown. Her upper-class family supported a number of servants, nurses, and tutors, and the three girls played joyfully in the attic or the cellar, where the many barrels of produce from their father's tenants served as playthings. She presents no terrifying experiences and no sense of emotional or physical deprivation in these descriptions.

So intent is she on demonstrating that she had a happy childhood that whenever she does introduce a "sorrow" from her childhood, it is immediately followed by a joy. Some complaints are common to children, like the starched collars that tore at her neck, but she was rebuked for complaining about them. She and her younger sisters also had to wear red outfits throughout their childhood, leaving Stanton with a permanent hatred of that color.

Her more sorrowful memories are of the worms that dangled from the poplar trees of the town, the sight of which made her tremble, and the bells that tolled on numerous occasions and seemed to her like "so many warnings of an eternal future"(2). Years later, in her sixties, she experienced the same frightened reaction to the mournful sound of church bells. Of the many festivities that early nineteenth-century Americans celebrated with enthusiasm like the Fourth of July, it is the terrifying sounds of the cannon she most remembers.

Stanton evidences ambivalence not only toward the "joys and sorrows" of her childhood but also toward authority. In one instance, she is incapable of defying her nurses until her younger sister convinces her that they will be punished anyway, so they might as well have fun. "Having less imagination than I, she took a common-sense view of life and suffered nothing from the anticipation of troubles, while my sorrows were intensified fourfold by innumerable apprehensions of possible exigencies" (11). On the other hand, she rails against the nurses, who "were the only shadows on the gayety of these winter evenings. . . . I have no doubt we were in constant rebellion against their petty tyranny" (6). Her upbringing must have been strict and rigid, though she gives us little information about the rules that suffocated her enthusiasm and energy.

> I have a confused memory of being often under punishment for what, in those days, were called "tantrums." I suppose they were really justifiable acts of rebellion against the tyranny of those in authority. I have often listened since, with real satisfaction, to what some of our friends had to say of the high-handed manner in which sister Margaret and I defied all the transient orders and strict rules laid down for our guidance. If we had observed them we might as well have been embalmed as mummies, for all the pleasure and freedom we should have had in our childhood. As very little was then done for the amusement of children, happy were those who *conscientiously* took the liberty of amusing themselves. (12)

But perhaps the source of her fear of authority came as much from a severe religious code of behavior as from the nurses in her home. At the time Stanton was writing her autobiography, she was also writing *The Woman's Bible,* an exegesis and attack on the Bible and the clergy who preached women's inferiority. Writing the *Bible* must have reawakened her anger against the tyranny of the church, one childhood authority about which she evidences no ambivalence: "I can truly say, after an experience of seventy years, that all the cares and anxieties, the trials and disappointments of my whole life, are light, when balanced with my suffering in childhood and youth from the theological dogmas which I sincerely believed" (24).

When in her teens she attended Emma Willard's Troy Seminary for girls, she was so overcome by the hellfire sermons of the Reverend Charles G. Finney, that "terrifier of human souls," that because of "my gloomy Calvinistic training in the old Scotch Presbyterian church, and my vivid imagination," she became one of the first of his "victims" (41). She roused her father so often at night to pray for her soul that he, her sister, and her brother-in-law took her on a six-week summer trip where the subject of religion was taboo and they talked about nothing but "rational ideas and scientific facts." She then concludes this unpleasant subject with a rapid reassurance, lest her readers be too saddened by her account, that after this trip, "my mind was restored to its normal condition" (44).

Stanton's mention of waking her father at night to help her and of his taking her on a trip to cure her would seem to indicate a warm relationship; however, she exhibits much ambivalence toward him. He was, she writes, "a man of firm character and unimpeachable integrity," "sensitive and modest to a painful degree," and though "gentle and tender, he had such a dignified repose and reserve of manner that, as children, we regarded him with fear rather than affection" (3). Stanton had probably the most traumatic experience of her childhood with her father. When she was eleven, her only brother, who had recently graduated from college, died. "He was the pride of my father's heart. We early felt that this son filled a larger place in our father's affections and future plans than the five daughters together" (20). Stanton yearns so much for her father's affection that she accompanies him on his almost daily visits to the boy's gravesite. When she tries to comfort him, he says:

> "Oh, my daughter, I wish you were a boy!"[3] Throwing my arms around his neck, I replied: "I will try to be all my brother was."
>
> Then and there I resolved that I would not give so much time as heretofore to play, but would study and strive to be at the head of all my classes and thus delight my father's heart. All that day and far into the night I pondered the problem of boyhood. I thought that the chief thing to be done in order to equal boys was to be learned and courageous. So I decided to study Greek and learn to manage a horse. . . . They were resolutions never to be forgotten—destined to mold my character anew. (20–21)

Her efforts are futile, however, though she accomplishes her two goals:

> I surprised even my teacher, who thought me capable of doing anything. I learned to drive, and to leap a fence and ditch on horseback. I taxed every power hoping

some day to hear my father say: "Well, a girl is as good as a boy, after all." But he never said it. (22)

In 1854, when Stanton was thirty-nine, her father asked to hear her first speech, which she was to deliver before the New York legislature. It was on divorce.

On no occasion, before or since was I ever more embarrassed—an audience of one, and that the one of all others whose approbation I most desired, whose disapproval I most feared. I knew he condemned the whole movement, and was deeply grieved at the active part I had taken. (188)

When she finished her rehearsal, Judge Cady offered no opinion for or against her political work (then or ever after) but "gladly gave me any help I needed, from time to time, in looking up the laws, and was very desirous that whatever I gave to the public should be carefully prepared" (189).

More important to this study is the fact that Stanton evidences no bitterness toward her father's disapproval of her as a female. She simply treats him as one more influence on her life. At the above meeting, Judge Cady's response to her speech is primarily surprise at her emotional complaints:

Surely you have had a happy, comfortable life, with all your wants and needs supplied; and yet that speech fills me with self-reproach; for one might naturally ask, how can a young woman, tenderly brought up, who has had no bitter personal experience, feel so keenly the wrongs of her sex? Where did you learn this lesson? (188–89)

And Stanton's response is, "I learned it here, in your office, when a child, listening to the complaints women made to you" (189). Stanton does not remind her readers of her emotional crisis at eleven lest they attribute her devotion to her cause to a neurotic source.

Even her father's objection to her marriage to Henry Brewster Stanton did not seem to change her affection for him. Her cousin Gerrit Smith, the abolitionist, at whose Peterboro, New York, home she met Henry, also objected to the marriage and for similar reasons—that an abolitionist reformer and orator like Henry would not be a good provider. After their wedding trip to Europe, however, Judge Cady took Henry into his law office to train him for the bar, and for three years the couple and their growing family lived in the Cady household. Apparently Daniel Cady was both a stern father and a reasonable man. Though Stanton does not include it in her autobiography, it is known that at one time he disinherited his suffragist daughter but changed his mind before his death in 1859.[4]

Of her mother, Mary Livingston, from a prestigious colonial family, Stanton writes hardly anything at all. We know that her mother took the deepest interest in her father's political campaign for Congress. (He was elected the year of Stanton's birth.) To her mother's side of the family, she attributes her self-reliance, derived no doubt from General Livingston, whose Revolutionary War fame came from the fact that he took it upon himself to attack a British man-of-war. Stanton describes her mother as a "tall, queenly looking women, . . . courageous, self-reliant, and at her ease under all circumstances and in all places" (3). One wonders how she evidenced her courage and what control was mustered to be at "ease under all circumstances and in all places." It is clear that Stanton, who was short and progressively stouter as she grew older, must have envied her mother's queenliness, because she attributes this characteristic to women she most admires. Stanton never mentions her mother after the first few pages, a curious omission, for which she gives no explanation.[5]

Stanton's relationship with her husband seems to have been a satisfactory one, although she tells us very little about him in the autobiography. When she met him, he was considered

> the most eloquent and impassioned orator on the anti-slavery platform. . . . Mr. Stanton was then in his prime, a fine-looking, affable young man, with remarkable conversational talent, and was ten years my senior, with the advantage that that number of years necessarily gives. (58)

On their first outing together alone (on horseback), they seem to have fallen immediately in love, though they had been together previously but in the presence of others.

> When walking slowly through a beautiful grove, he laid his hand on the horn of the saddle and, to my surprise, made one of those charming revelations of human feeling which brave knights have always found eloquent words to utter, and to which fair ladies have always listened with mingled emotions of pleasure and astonishment.
>
> One outcome of those glorious days of October, 1839, was a marriage, in Johnstown . . . and a voyage to the Old World. (69–70)

That is the extent of Stanton's description of her courtship and marriage to Henry Stanton. We can only guess whether or not he objected to her taking out the word *obey* from their marriage ceremony, but she does tell us, quite objectively, that at the World's Anti-Slavery Convention in London in 1840, which they attended as part of their honeymoon trip, when the issue of women's participation in the proceedings came up for a vote, Henry voted against it. She expresses no feelings on this early event of her marriage, but she does recount enthusiastically the position of abolitionist William Lloyd Garrison, who sat in the observation gallery with the women and refused to take part in the segregated proceedings.

She briefly mentions that Henry, because of frequent travels to courts and abolitionist meetings, delegated to her the complete management of their homes, first in Boston and Chelsea, later in Seneca Falls. After 1848, when Stanton's political work began, Henry is not mentioned until thirty-seven years later at his eightieth birthday celebration in 1885.

There must have been a policy of live-and-let-live during their forty-seven years together (Henry's death in 1887 also is not mentioned). We know from sources other than the autobiography that though reformist in every other political cause, he, like her father, always objected to her work for women's rights. We know that he threatened to leave town if the first women's rights convention was held in their town of Seneca Falls, and he did.[6] We also know that Stanton's father frequently helped the couple financially and that she undertook the lyceum tours in part to earn money for their children's education. But Elizabeth Stanton does not include this information in her life study; it might discredit her husband, herself, and the movement. Writing in 1897, in *Eighty Years,* of their minister's superstitious objection to their marrying on a Friday, she sums up her relationship with her husband:

> As we lived together, without more than the usual matrimonial friction, for nearly a half a century, had seven children, all but one of whom are still living, and have been well sheltered, clothed, and fed, enjoying sound minds in sound bodies, no one need be afraid of going through the marriage ceremony on Friday for fear of bad luck. (71–72)

Though Stanton also leaves out any personal references to sexuality, her awareness of it is evident. For one thing, she frequently notices the good looks or fine physiques of the men she meets in her travels, but even earlier, she writes of her experiences as a child when she studied with boys at the Johnstown Academy, then moved to Emma Willard's Troy Seminary for girls only. She was flabbergasted by the intrigue stirred up by the girls there without boys present and argues strongly for coeducation, which most adults of her time opposed. Stanton describes the period between her graduation from Willard's seminary to her marriage as "the most pleasant years of my girlhood" primarily because she "rejoiced in the dawn of a new day of freedom in thought and action" (45). Her description of this time of her life is filled with echoes of sexual awakening:

> Then comes that dream of bliss that for weeks and months throws a halo of glory round the most ordinary characters in everyday life, holding the strongest and most common-sense young men and women in a thraldom from which few mortals escape. The period when love, in soft silver tones, whispers his first words of adoration, painting our graces and virtues day by day in living colors in poetry and prose, stealthily punctuated ever and anon with a kiss or fond embrace. What dignity it adds to a young girl's estimate of herself when some strong man makes her feel that in her hands rest his future peace and happiness! Though these seasons of intoxication may come once to all, yet they are seldom repeated. How often in after life we long for one more season of supreme human love and passion! (45)

Closely following this passage is Stanton's effusive description of her brother-in-law Edward Bayard, "ten years my senior . . . an inestimable blessing to me at this time" (45). We know that Stanton was infatuated with Bayard, but she judiciously rejected his advances beyond a platonic attachment[7] and soon after fell in love with Henry Stanton, like Bayard ten years her senior. She excluded any hint of an attachment to Bayard, a member of her own family, which might have been construed as an unrequited love affair "explaining" her "discontent" with the male way of running the world.

Of the intellectual influences on her life, we have already learned how, as a youngster, Stanton frequented her father's law office and heard the complaints of abandoned wives and mothers who had no legal recourse. Nonetheless, from these experiences and her frequent visits to the county jail, she writes, "I gleaned some idea of the danger of violating the law" (14). Her respect for the law explains why Stanton was conservative when it came to tactics and deferred in that department to her complement Susan B. Anthony; it also explains why she was such a logical and thorough debater. But her respect never seems to have intimidated her or deterred her from fighting laws she felt were unjust or that discriminated against women.

Stanton's political and reform spirit was nurtured in the home of Gerrit Smith, where as a late teenager she met her first runaway slave. But Stanton never felt the force of the tyranny of slavery as much as she did that tyranny of her own childhood and womanhood. When push came to shove, she opposed enfranchisement for male blacks when it was still denied to women after the Civil War, though she had put aside her suffrage efforts for five years in order to help the cause of the North.

It is not surprising that the tyranny exercised over Stanton as a child was the foundation for her later rebellion against the tyranny over all her sex. And it is not surprising that she should use the very same phrase to describe those two areas of tyranny over her life: "the constant cribbing and crippling of a child's life" (11) and "the most cribbed and crippled of Eve's unhappy daughters" (204).

The crucial experience that ignited her already aroused sympathies for the lot of women came at that antislavery convention in London on her honeymoon trip. It was not until eight years later, when longing for more intellectual challenges than those provided by the management of a large house, servants, and many children, that she and Lucretia Mott placed a brief notice in the local newspaper. Four days later, fifty women met at the Methodist church in Seneca Falls, New York, and started the first feminist movement in North America.

At this point in her life story, female readers probably have no trouble in identifying with Stanton's frustrations after eight years of dedicating herself exclusively to domestic duties. She has convincingly proved herself an ordinary human being and justified her gradual involvement in a "public career." Perhaps now her audience will be receptive to her as a person and treat her ideas seriously.

We now turn to the bulk of *Eighty Years and More,* where Stanton concentrates on her public career, the unstated purpose of her book. While the first part was informed by ambivalence and paradox because of the need to convey the self-image of both an ordinary and a superior person, with some omission to protect the women's movement, the second section is characterized more by omission than by paradox because her political work is the central focus. Her aim is to educate her audience about women's rights, and she does so by creating a positive image of the cause by leaving out anything that might discredit it in any way. There is still some paradoxical treatment or ambivalence in her presentation of herself, but it is less evident here than in the first section. Here everything is positively shaped for the cause.

All the chapters in the middle section have titles that refer to issues or events in the women's rights movement. Nonetheless, the subjects of these chapters are usually minimally treated. As in the first section, Stanton continues to use amusing and pleasant anecdotes, here to educate her audience painlessly about serious issues. The transition chapter, "The First Woman's Rights Convention," deals less with that event than with Stanton's preconvention boredom at tedious duties, with her postconvention relief in talking to women about their rights, and with her door-to-door efforts for signatures to petition the state legislature for more liberal property and divorce laws. No doubt her female readers could more readily identify with her concrete domestic experiences than with the convention itself, though she manages to convey its significance as the first organized protest against women's inferior legal position. True to her determination to be positive, Stanton tells us nothing about her husband's negative reaction to that meeting in Seneca Falls.

The next two chapters, which constitute a portrait of Susan B. Anthony, break the chronology, for it extends from 1851, when the two women met—three years after the Seneca Falls convention—to the 1890s. By including this portrait of Anthony (a revision of one she wrote for *Eminent Women of the Age,* 1868), Stanton reveals how far from her stated intention this autobiography is. For Anthony was the lifelong friend of her public career, and her portrait emphasizes how closely the two worked together.

> In thought and sympathy we were one, and in the division of labor we exactly complemented each other. In writing we did better work than either could alone. While she is slow and analytical in composition, I am rapid and synthetic. I am the better writer, she the better critic. She supplied the facts and statistics, I the philosophy and rhetoric, and, together, we have made arguments that have stood unshaken through the storms of long years; arguments that no one has answered. Our speeches may be considered the united product of our two brains. (166)

Stanton omits any mention of tension or problems with her friend. Their partnership was, indeed, predominantly a harmonious one, but they did disagree at times. Though Stanton was more revolutionary in respect to the movement's ideas, Anthony was more militant when it came to tactics. Nonetheless, Stanton exposes no disagreements or tensions in the upper echelons of the movement, nothing that might give cause for dissension in the ranks or for gossip among their detractors.

In this chapter Stanton also reminds her readers that she is not neglecting her children while she and Anthony work. She describes the mischievous games her children play around them that often require quick rescues and adult participation. She also directly faces the issue of Anthony's single life, which she knows her readers are curious about. She uses the portrait as an occasion to praise all single women who dedicate their lives to important causes: "All honor to the noble women who have devoted earnest lives to the intellectual and moral needs of mankind!" (157). She quotes Anthony's stand on the question of marriage, thus educating her audience in the process:

> She could not consent that the man she loved, described in the Constitution as a white male, native born, American citizen, possessed of the right of self-government, eligible to the office of President of the Great Republic, should unite his destinies in marriage with a political slave and pariah. "No, no; when I am crowned with all the rights, privileges, and immunities of a citizen, I may give some consideration to this social institution; but until then I must concentrate all my energies on the enfranchisement of my own sex" (172).

One may also infer Stanton's awareness and pride in having accomplished what few women before, during, or since her lifetime have managed, and that is the total dedication to a political cause *and* the achievement of a career as wife and mother.

It is in the next chapter, "My First Speech Before a Legislature" (in 1854 on behalf of the civil rights of married women), that Stanton explains to her father the intellectual source of her sense of the "keenly felt wrongs" against women, which was hearing the complaints of women in his law office, as opposed to the "negative" personal explanation of her traumatic emotional experience at eleven. Certainly, it was a common experience in her day for female children to be treated as inferior to boys, but Stanton's explanation reflects that she prefers to emphasize the law as the basis for her struggle.

In chapter after chapter, Stanton treats her material from a positive point of view. In "Views on Marriage and Divorce" she manages to convey the impression of success in 1860 as she traveled around New York state trying to get a liberal divorce bill passed. We hear amusing anecdotes about generous people and her pleasant experiences while traveling from one city to another, but nothing of the results of the bill. In "Westward Ho!" she describes her trip in the early 1870s to lecture throughout the state of Nebraska for a proposition to strike the word *male* from the state constitution. She gives a favorable description of the results of her efforts, but we really do not know if the proposition passed or not. For the 1876 centennial celebration, she attempted to get enough tickets so that every state was represented by a woman, but received only six tickets in response to her polite but firm letters, which she quotes in their entirety. But what she concentrates on is Anthony's daring rush to the platform to shove the Women's Declaration of Rights into the presiding officer's hand, thus succeeding in making it a part of the day's proceedings. Of the Women's Pavilion at the centennial, though she praises the woman engineer who ran its turbine to the surprise of the male organizers, she was obviously not satisfied with its contents. Rather than criticize them, however, she lists all the things that should have hung on its walls: "the yearly protest of Harriet K. Hunt against taxation without representation," "all the laws bearing unjustly upon women," "the legal papers in the case of Susan B. Anthony, who was tried and fined for claiming her right to vote under the Fourteenth Amendment," and "decisions in favor of State rights which imperil the liberties not only of all women, but of every white man in the nation" (316–17).

It is only in the case of the proposition to extend suffrage to women in Kansas in 1867 that Stanton evidences any anger at the failure of their efforts. She blames the failure on those in the East who "feared the discussion of the woman question would jeopardize the enfranchisement of the black man" (247). But women also learned another "important lesson—namely that it is impossible for the best of men to understand women's feelings or the humiliation of their position. When they asked us to be silent on our question during the War, and labor for the emancipation of the slave, we did so, and gave five years to his emancipation and enfranchisement. . . . I am now . . . sure that it was a blunder" (254).

The issue of black enfranchisement without women's suffrage split the women's movement into two factions, those who were willing to wait and take a back seat to black (male) suffrage and those who were not willing to support one without the other. Stanton led the latter camp, but nothing is mentioned in *Eighty Years and More* of this split in the movement nor of the establishment of two rival women's organizations in 1869. The union of the two groups eleven years later is easily missed in a quoted letter in which she mentions her election to the presidency of the new national organization.

Though Stanton expresses some anger about the Kansas failure early in the chapter "Pioneer Life in Kansas," the dispute over black men's and women's suffrage is largely ignored thereafter as she concentrates on her harrowing experiences in the backwoods, sleeping in soiled and flea-ridden beds and eating starchy and sometimes inedible foods, but always admiring the frontier women whose sacrifices in settling the West go unrecognized. Many of the anecdotes in these chapters, where Stanton is touting her seemingly successful efforts, focus on her encounters with people, usually women, whom she praises with obvious pride in their accomplishments—a soprano, a superintendent of schools, an understanding mother, young women traveling alone showing their independent spirits, and others.

Some anecdotes, however, have to do with her own experiences traveling around states as a lyceum lecturer from 1869 to 1881, from the age of fifty-four to sixty-six, from October through June, enduring an extremely physically demanding regimen with crowded schedules, often twelve- to eighteen-hour train rides with no time to rest or eat before appearances, even frequent blizzards that kept the hardiest snowbound. But not Stanton: "As I learned that all the roads in Northern Iowa were blocked, I made the entire circuit, from point to point in a sleigh, traveling forty and fifty miles a day" (261–62).

Stanton never complains about the many difficulties she encounters in her travels but describes her experiences with enthusiasm and cheerful good humor. For example, in Dubuque she arrives by train at a desolate station in the early hours of the morning but manages to attract attention by shouting, "John! James! Patrick!" When her feminist friends rib her for not hollering for "Jane, Ann, and Bridget," she retorts, "as my sex had not yet been exalted to the dignity of presiding in depots and baggage rooms, there would have been no propriety in calling Jane or Ann" (281). In Kansas, where her experiences seem to have been the most trying physically, she writes, "In spite of the discomforts we suffered in the Kansas campaign, I was glad of the experience. It gave me added self-respect to know that I could endure such hardships and fatigue with a great degree of cheerfulness" (252).

The amazon image that Stanton conveys throughout this second section of her autobiography is juxtaposed with her image as an ordinary person. On trains, she continues to dole out advice to mothers of crying infants and to open ventilators in smoky and stuffy parlor cars. Though many of the situations she describes make her seem ordinary, they also require a very hardy constitution. She sleeps on a lounge in the woman's salon of a ship during a two-week voyage because she can open a window there and avoid the stuffy staterooms. While all others are suffering with seasickness below, she enjoys the ocean breezes on deck, strolling or reading. For four hours, she precariously descends a mountain in Yosemite National Park, grabbing for roots and branches to steady herself, an undignified but impressive picture for a heavy woman in her sixties. Stanton never mentions a single illness in her life study; she rarely, and then discreetly, refers to her weight, which grew considerably each year; and only parenthetically does she refer to her lameness from a "severe fall" in her seventies.

Not only do we get this paradoxical self-image of Stanton as both an ordinary person and one of almost superhuman physical stamina, but in her descriptions of the people she meets and stays with, we also get a double message. On one hand, she stays with poor pioneer women in cabins in the Midwest and West; on the other, she is hosted by famous people in the United States and abroad. Her egalitarian attitude came from her genuine political commitment, whereas her pleasure in meeting the famous came from her upper-class family background, which opened doors to her not accessible to the average suffragist. It is also clear from the many names listed, most of which are unknown to readers today, that she is using this autobiography to thank people for their generous support of the women's movement in hosting her and financing her efforts. There is no question, finally, that her name-dropping is meant to indicate her superior status not just in intelligence but also in social position, implying that in a just society she would be entitled to full citizenship with the right to vote and hold office.

In her travels Stanton emphasizes the women she meets rather than their usually more famous husbands. And on only one occasion does she deviate from her usual tolerance for women who are unable to support the movement:

> The history of the world shows that the vast majority, in every generation, passively accept the conditions into which they are born, while those who demand larger liberties are ever a small, ostracized minority, whose claims are ridiculed and ignored. . . . That only a few, under any circumstances, protest against the injustice of long-established laws and customs, does not disprove the fact of the oppression, while the satisfaction of the many, if real, only proves their apathy and deeper degradation. That a majority of the women of the United States accept, without protest, the disabilities which grow out of their disenfranchisement is simply an evidence of their ignorance and cowardice, while the minority who demand a higher political status clearly prove their superior intelligence and wisdom. (317–18)

Such an outburst, which might antagonize those she most wants to win to her cause, is a rare exception rather than the rule in *Eighty Years.* Generally, the presentation and tone of the autobiography are mild and low-keyed. Stanton explains how she and the other women, often writing as a group, would argue, discuss, and plan their strategy in order to prepare speeches with acceptable arguments that would not reap the abuse so often leveled at them:

> So long as woman labors to second man's endeavors and exalt his sex above her own, her virtues pass unquestioned; but when she dares to demand rights and privileges for herself, her motives, manners, dress, personal appearance, and character are subjects for ridicule and detraction. (241)

Anyone reading Stanton's *History of Woman Suffrage* or *The Woman's Bible* will be startled by the comparison with *Eighty Years.* The effort not to antagonize readers of her autobiography made her soften the presentation of her ideas here with anecdotes. Her other writings are complex and brilliantly argued expositions; this life study appears simple and straightforward, almost childlike, by comparison. Where her public writings express the full force of her anger and rage at the injustice of the laws against women, here there is no anger, no rage, no bitterness.

Although men have sometimes felt uncomfortable reading the autobiography, it is not because she ever affronts them personally but because of the force of her very logical attacks on the laws that discriminate against women. She is no man-hater and often expresses her appreciation of men who supported the movement and her understanding of those who could not. Though she wore the bloomer outfit for years, she desisted when it was apparent that it caused her male companions too much embarrassment. When she reflects on how much abuse and ridicule men have suffered in supporting the women's movement, she understands, even in her eighties, why so few have been its supporters.

The third section of Stanton's autobiography, after 1881, when she was sixty-six and had retired from her lyceum lecturing chores, relies on the diary she began keeping at the suggestion of friends. The result is a more precisely documented narrative with notations of day, month, and year scrupulously recorded. The narrative thus becomes choppy and less integrated, with fewer extended anecdotes and much less humor. Though it describes her continuing public activities—writing, delivering speeches, and attending the annual meetings of the National American Woman Suffrage Association—the emphasis in this last section is once again on her private life. In the ten years between 1881 and 1891, she made six trips to Europe, primarily to visit her two children most active in women's work, Harriot Stanton Blatch and Theodore Stanton, who together edited her letters and other writings in 1922.

The emphasis here returns to the two-faceted image of ordinary woman and exceptional person. Though in 1881 her youngest child was twenty-two, she describes her joy at spending time with her "seven boys and girls dancing around the fireside, buoyant with all life's joys opening before them" (322). Invited to give an address at the sixtieth anniversary of her graduation from the Troy seminary, she regales her audience with the memory of the time when she and a friend woke the entire school by ringing bells in the middle of the night without being caught. Her observations on the differences in domestic accommodations between England and France continue the image of a woman concerned with ordinary matters. But she clearly also wants to keep alive her image as exceptional person. Even in her seventies, she boasts of hiding her fatigue after a long trip when she arrives at a friend's house. And wherever she goes all over the world, she is treated as a celebrity with receptions in her honor and invitations to give keynote addresses at women's convocations.

Stanton ends her autobiography with a chapter on her eightieth birthday celebration in 1895, when she was honored for her fifty years of service to womankind with a gala reception at the Metropolitan Opera House. She leaves her readers here with the final paradox of the autobiography, the impression that her efforts were a huge success. She achieves this effect here by quoting several pages of an effusive article that reviewed the occasion, and then by quoting her own address, in which she summed up her life's work. Now it no longer required courage "to demand the right of suffrage, temperance legislation, liberal divorce laws, or for women to fill church offices—these battles have been fought and won and the principle governing these demands conceded" (467).

As to the most important effort of her life, women's suffrage, rather than conclude with what still needed to be accomplished, she summarizes the victories: "Municipal suffrage has been granted to women in England and some of her colonies; school suffrage has been granted to women in half our states, municipal suffrage in Kansas, and full suffrage in four States of the Union" (465). Though it was not until 1920, seventy-two years after her first call for suffrage in 1848 and eighteen years after her death in 1902, that the Nineteenth Amendment was finally passed, the reader closes this autobiography with the distinct impression that Stanton's life was a success.

For after all, it was, and *Eighty Years* is indeed a success story. Without

Elizabeth Cady Stanton, ordinary *and* exceptional woman that she was, the present women's liberation movement would be in its infancy. Her leadership and work provided the foundation and the tradition for contemporary feminists, who are closer—because of her—to an amalgam of the sexual with the political, the private with the public.

In terms of the women's tradition in autobiography, we have seen, first, how Stanton concentrates on the personal and domestic perspective when dealing even with political and intellectual issues. Her efforts to demonstrate her oneness with all women lead her to relate every political issue to a domestic or personal experience with which her female readers can identify. And she demonstrates her consciousness of her womanhood not only domestically but also politically as a member of a caste that is deprived of full citizenship.

Second, while she felt very keenly her difference from her contemporaries, her genteel nineteenth-century background forces her to write objectively and historically about her life. Thus, she is never sensational about her differences, as many of her predecessors were, but she does reveal her exceptional qualities as a woman of extraordinary physical stamina and one who succeeded at two careers. A third feature that is typical of women's autobiographies is the concentration on areas outside the mainstream of society. Though the women's suffrage movement, as well as the many reform movements of the nineteenth century in which women were involved, occupies a very important place in American history, it has until recently been considered of minimal importance in most history books. Protest against laws that discriminate against women was then, and still is, considered only an annoyance to the predominant male culture, but we have seen how Stanton viewed all her experiences in the context of furthering the cause of the women's movement.

Fourth, *Eighty Years* proceeds fairly consistently in chronological order, more typical of her century than of the twentieth. But like her predecessors, she depends to a great extent on anecdotes—usually amusing ones—to tell her life story. She also inserts letters and speeches, sometimes hers, sometimes others', which occasionally interrupt the narrative, and she does not hesitate to interrupt chronology to complete a portrait of an important figure or to give the reader follow-up information, usually about a state's progress in granting women equal rights.

Fifth, the many anecdotes serve indirectly to provide information about Stanton herself. The anecdotes about others inform the reader about the "external" Stanton but do not tell us about her inner feelings. Their humor distracts readers from the fact that while they are being entertained, they are not learning much that is intimate about the author. Not only does she exclude intimate information about her life, but she also excludes adult fears, doubts, inhibitions, conflicts, or problems, whether with her family, her friends, or her work. In order to protect herself and to achieve her autobiographical intention, Stanton's primary tool was deliberate and calculated omission. Her method is direct and straightforward, nothing complicated like understatement, ellipses, or other subtle camouflaging tools that we will see in the twentieth century. She was a nineteenth-century woman using the autobiographical mode for a public cause, and while a positive self-image dominates her autobiography, it was achieved at the price of compromise in her struggle to placate her readers, indicating how much she was a product of her times and the extent of her liberation.

· 10 ·

Exotic Autobiography Intellectualized:

The Legitimation of Gertrude Stein

When Gertrude Stein's autobiography appeared in 1933, a huge, second insurge of women's self-writing was under way. Considering that the depression dominated the decade, one must wonder that so many women's autobiographies (as well as all types of books) were published. This second wave was made up of women born during the second half of the nineteenth century, the beneficiaries of those women of the last decades of the century who ushered in the first women's liberation movement. For these autobiographers, a good education was a given, they now had the right to vote, they were an accepted and normal part of the work force (even if many were unemployed because of the depression), and they were less constricted by society's mores than their nineteenth-century sisters. Particularly for women writing in the late twenties and thirties, an independent and career-oriented life was a palatable choice. Unlike the suffragists, they write about actual successes, without ambivalence, in a voice that is unmistakably confident. And they are more selective about their material, less obsessed with presenting detailed, scientific records of their lives. We find as the century progresses, the more they are able to integrate their personal and professional lives, the more crafted are their autobiographies.

This progression is especially evident in the many autobiographies by reformers and political activists, who continue to dominate autobiographical activity. For example, Jane Addams's (1860–1935) *Twenty Years at Hull-House* (1910), about her role in establishing the first settlement house in America—in Chicago in 1889—is a holdover from the late nineteenth century, when reformers tended to concentrate only on their work. But even this autobiography has considerable literary merit as a result of its topical rather than chronological organization, its concrete human interest anecdotes, and its simple, direct, and lucid prose style. Addams tells us very little about her personal life, because she claims her own history is indistinguishable from that of Hull House. She seems unconcerned with proving her "normality" or her "femininity," or perhaps as a single woman she did not feel as confident or comfortable about writing about her personal life as she did about her career.

By the late twenties and thirties, however, autobiographers were less inhibited in writing about their personal lives as an integral part of their political activities. In *Crusade for Justice* (1928), a black political autobiography—rare at this time—Ida B. Wells-Barnett (1862–1931) chronicles her longtime efforts on behalf of black civil rights, especially her thirty-five years as an antilynching activist, but she devotes equal space to delineating the trials and joys of raising a large family. In her two-volume *Living My Life* (1931), Emma Goldman (1869–1940) balances her political activities and those of her anarchist colleagues with personal details of her own life and portraits of theirs. Gilman's (1860–1935) *The Living of Charlotte Perkins Gilman* (1935) documents both her career as a feminist and labor reformer and also her long struggle with personal illness. In *A Footnote to Folly* (1935), Mary Heaton Vorse (1874–1966) first describes her happy middle-class childhood, her widowhood and parenting, and her many travels; then she tells of being inspired by the Lawrence strike in 1912, which resulted in her ten-year journalistic efforts on behalf of labor organizing, especially the Industrial Workers of the World (IWW)—all told, however, from the point of view of the movement's impact on children.

Perhaps the socialist Vida Dutton Scudder (1861–1954) needed to protect her long tenure as a literature professor at Wellesley College when she wrote *On Journey* (1937), a more than usually discreet and digressive autobiography that tells us much more about her travels, friendships, and religious views than about the settlement work and union activities for which she is remembered. Margaret Sanger (1883–1966) skillfully shapes *An Autobiography* (1938) to include the history of her revolutionary work in legalizing birth control and her personal, compassionate involvement with the poor women she wanted to help. And muckraker and feminist Ida Minerva Tarbell (1857–1944) integrates the process of her prolific journalistic career with her personal growth in a fine autobiography, *All in the Day's Work* (1939).

Though these authors are less afraid to be introspective in public, none of their works is more intimate than the reformist autobiographies of the previous century. For example, Goldman excludes her ten-year relationship with Ben Reitman out of fear that her public image will be even more tainted or devalued by intimate disclosures.[1] And Sanger does not describe her two marriages, her divorce, or her intimate friendship with Havelock Ellis.

Neither do these reformers and political activists reveal any conflict or ambivalence toward their work. Their omissions and other means of self-protection not only safeguard their cause, as Stanton did, but they reflect the still-prevalent moral restrictions of their day, especially the double standard of acceptance with which, as women, they all had to contend. Undeniably, however, their self-image is strong and positive.

In Patricia Meyer Spacks's reading of several twentieth-century political autobiographies—Emma Goldman's *Living My Life* (1931), Eleanor Roosevelt's *This Is My Story* (1937), Dorothy Day's *The Long Loneliness* (1952), Golda Meir's *My Life* (1975), and English suffragist Emmeline Pankhurst's *My Own Story* (1914)—she finds that "though writing in a genre which implies self-assertion and self-display . . . [these writers] find indirect means of declaring personal power and effectiveness, . . . [doing] so, as it were, in disguise." Spacks's interest in probing the psychological sources of ambivalence in women writers may have colored her emphasis on isolated passages she found in the several autobiographies she cites. In my reading, the autobiographies project, on the contrary, a positive self-image and a definite sense of "personal power and effectiveness."[2] While some of their authors admit personal doubts, this honesty gives their life studies a more human quality than works—by men and women—that hide behind masks of superhuman and unbelievable self-confidence.

In addition to the autobiographies by political activists the second and third decades of the century saw the publication of many autobiographies by women writing about exciting experiences in areas where women had rarely, if ever, been before, and, thus, which had fewer expectations of or restrictions on women. These autobiographers could write assertively of their adventures, with confidence in the public's perennial interest in "thrilling" stories by so-called eccentric women.

Paralleling pioneer autobiographies in their accounts of hardships were life studies by working-class women. Examples are Adelheid Dwořak Popp's (1869–1939) *The Autobiography of a Working Woman* (1912) and Anne Ellis's (1875–1938) three novelistic autobiographies—*The Life of an Ordinary Woman* (1929), *"Plain Anne Ellis": More about the Life of an Ordinary Woman* (1931), and *Sunshine Preferred* (1934). Ellis worked at many occupations, including mining camp cook and seamstress; she was one of the few Western pioneers who lived in poverty most of her life. Yet her autobiographies portray a simple working-class woman with a great deal of spunk and self-confidence.

Other autobiographies by women in new areas were Esther Bengis's impersonal account of her dutiful, husband-centered life, *I Am a Rabbi's Wife* (1935); Rosalie Morton's (1876–?) *A Woman Surgeon: The Life and Work of Rosalie Slaughter Morton* (1937); and Amelia Earhart's (1898–1937) *20 Hrs., 40 Min.; Our Flight in the Friendship* (1928), *The Fun of It: Random Records of My Own Flying and of Women in Aviation* (1932), and *Last Flight* (1937).

A few women focused on personal traumas or physical disabilities for an ever more receptive reading audience. Joanna Field (Marion Milner) (1900–) kept a reflective journal in which she analyzed the process by which she found her true identity, published as *A Life of One's Own* (1934). Helen Keller (1880–1968) wrote several works about her life as a deaf and blind child, author, and activist in various social causes. Her most popular was *The Story of My Life* (1903), which recounts her childhood ordeal and success with the help of her teacher, Anne Sullivan, but there were also *The World I Live In* (1908), *The Song of the Stone Wall* (1910), *Midstream: My Later Life* (1929), and *Helen Keller's Journals, 1936–1937* (1938). And Opal Stanley Whiteley (1899–), extraordinarily sensitive to the natural world, was encouraged to piece together her torn-up six-year-old's diary and publish it, which she did in 1920 as *The Story of Opal: The Journal of an Understanding Heart.*

Other "thrilling" autobiographies were as-told-to narratives by Native Americans, such as *An Indian Girl's Story* (1921), *The Autobiography of a Fox Indian Woman* (1925), *Red Mother: A Crow Indian* (1932), and *Autobiography of a Papago Woman* (1936); today these early accounts appear self-conscious, revealing the many pressures on these women to acculturate. And prostitutes—silent about their role in the Western migration[3]—began, finally, to tell their story. Published anonymously in 1919, when most cities had laws criminalizing prostitution, *Madeleine: An Autobiography* was prefaced by a judge, who viewed its author as a victim of society's evils. By 1928 Mary Churchill Sharpe (1877–1929) was quite forthright about her "exotic" occupation in *Chicago May: Her Story.*

Autobiographies by women in the fine arts were sparse during this period, perhaps because independence in this area was still a new phenomenon for women. Two from the twenties are interesting contrasts. Though both focus on the progress of their work and both reveal women confident in their talent, they differ strikingly in voice and style. Janet Scudder's

(1869–1940) *Modeling My Life* (1925) is a sober but engaging account of economic and professional hardships encountered in the process of becoming a successful and nationally known sculptor of distinctly American garden fountains, whereas Isadora Duncan's (1877–1927) *My Life* (1927) is a hyperbolic and poorly written glorification of her very legitimate achievements as a dancer and revolutionary choreographer.

Literary women did not write with the degree of confidence evident in the works by Scudder and Duncan. Though members of the most respected and long-lived profession for women and though they published autobiographies as prolifically during the thirties as the political activists, they rarely focus on their careers, usually omitting them entirely or dealing with them in indirect ways—Anne Bradstreet's heirs in the twentieth century. There are no autobiographies on the process of becoming a creative writer and few that even record the accomplishments of their authors. Perhaps, as one writer put it, her novels themselves would have to speak for her imaginative efforts and achievements.[4]

Especially during the first two decades, writers tended to focus their autobiographies entirely on their early years or their personal growth. This is not to say that they lacked confidence or that their work was not meaningful to them. But until the late twenties and thirties many women still felt apologetic about their careers and successes, not yet secure in their own or the public's acceptance of their professional commitment or the value of their work.[5] By the thirties, however, women were attending universities in greater numbers, feeling the immediate effects of their voice in electoral politics, and entering professions in greater numbers and with a greater degree of self-confidence and social acceptance. It is not surprising, therefore, that with each succeeding decade, even literary women, like the political activists, began to incorporate their work life much more into still predominantly personal life studies.

For some literary women, especially those who wrote during the early decades of the twentieth century, as in the past, their autobiographies are the literary endeavor for which they are now known. Following the example of many predecessors, they skirted—most often, intentionally—the issue of their careers, successful or not, by concentrating on their girlhoods. For example, both Mary Antin (1881–1949) and Mary MacLane (1881–1929) wrote second life studies that continued the stories of their early lives—Antin's *The Promised Land* (1912) describes with pride the shedding of her Jewish immigrant past, and MacLane's *I, Mary Maclane: A Diary of Human Days* (1917) continues the narcissistic myth of her own creativity.

— Exotic Autobiography Intellectualized —

By the thirties, however, we find literary women writing more about their work, but still, thankfully, within the larger context of their personal life. I say thankfully because while we want to know about their professional life, it is the human, personal element that makes their autobiographies enjoyable to read and meaningful as "life" studies. Sometimes, as readers seeking role models, we wish to know more about the process of their art, their inner doubts and triumphs. But obviously we cannot dictate what is most meaningful to autobiographers, what they want us to know about their lives.

Margaret Anderson (1886–1973), whose sense of herself as a superior person was responsible for many daring ventures, most particularly her founding of the *Little Review* in her twenties, describes episodically and in great detail all her eccentric and innovative personal experiences and experiments in independent living in her first autobiography, *My Thirty Years' War* (1930), a "war," she writes, against doing anything "I . . . don't want to do" and "to do what [I] want to do." In Gertrude Atherton's (1857–1948) *The Adventures of a Novelist* (1932), writing takes second place to her socially prominent friendships and her many travels. Mary Austin (1868–1934) experiments with point of view by mixing first- and third-person narrators in her study of her mystical pursuits in *Earth Horizon* (1932). Mabel Dodge Luhan's (1879–1962) four-volume *Intimate Memories* (1933–37), a lively compendium of anecdotes and portraits, focuses on her spiritual quest for identity.

The best known of these thirties literary autobiographers, Edith Wharton (1862–1937), devotes the first third of *A Backward Glance* (1935) to her youth and the rest to character sketches of her adult friendships—over one hundred pages on Henry James—but tells us nothing about the writing of her successful novels or the recognition that resulted from their publication. Harriet Monroe (1860–1936) is more explicit about her literary efforts, but half of her unfinished autobiography, *A Poet's Life: Seventy Years in a Changing World* (1938), concentrates on the operation of and contributors to *Poetry* magazine, which Monroe founded in 1912 and for which she is most famous. However, Edna Ferber (1887–1968) does a very credible job of integrating her writing career with her personal life in her fine autobiography, *A Peculiar Treasure* (1938).

Although space does not allow a thorough critique of each of these works, I have read enough of them to be able to conclude that most of these autobiographers continue the women's autobiographical tradition. On the whole, they write disjunctive narratives, replete with anecdotes, digressions, flashbacks, and inserted material such as letters and literary samples; while less fragmented than their predecessors, they continue to view their lives as multidimensional, less narrowly focused than male autobiographers. The always prevalent personal context of their autobiographies, of course, also continues the female tradition. The self-consciousness that prevails about their professional achievements is understandable considering that they were still functioning in a social and critical milieu dominated by men and male values. Even though the idea of a woman as a full-time professional gained steady affirmation, one must infer from their works that these autobiographers were still influenced by the popular notion that careers—even literary ones—decrease femininity or interfere with a woman's place in the home.

• • •

It is in such a context that *The Autobiography of Alice B. Toklas* (1933) by Gertrude Stein (1874–1946) appeared. This literary autobiography is a *disguise* autobiography par excellence, a disguise of the self in words rather than in costume, transforming the exotic tradition of the nineteenth-century autobiographies by women who masqueraded as men to a twentieth-century context—the total camouflage of an eccentric personality and an eccentric life-style. By masking her literary voice in that of her friend and lover, Stein attempts to perpetrate the ultimate concealment of the self as protection from judgmental readers. Ironically, it was this pretense at autobiography, this hoax on her readers, suggested by friends to make money, that made Stein famous. Had she not written it, she might not have had the recognition she has today.

Born in the nineteenth century, Gertrude Stein was a woman of her era despite her avant-garde friends and literary experimentation. Although earlier autobiographers merely omitted indiscretions or intimate revelations in order to protect their vulnerability to an unknown audience, they were committed, to some degree at least, to self-revelation. Although Stanton excluded much of her private life and problems within the suffrage movement in order to protect herself and the cause, she does tell us about her childhood, friendships, and other domestic subjects, if not always directly at least by means of personal anecdotes about others. But Stein inverts the autobiographical tradition by writing an ostensibly impersonal autobiography, even more so than Jane Addams's life study, which was, at least, written in the first person and is discursive about her professional work. Not only does Stein use a third-person narrator, Alice

Toklas; not only does she omit almost everything about herself until her life in Paris as an adult—from 1903, when she was twenty-nine, until 1932; but she also camouflages the little that she does present about her personal life.

Such apparent impersonality and the overwhelming distance involved in such an approach seem to place *The Autobiography of Alice B. Toklas* outside the tradition of women's autobiographies and may explain its universal acceptance by autobiographical critics, who see in it an intellectual challenge. Be that as it may, the *Autobiography* does display the usual characteristics of the female tradition.

First, it has an affinity to other women's autobiographies in its use of the anecdotal mode. However, unlike Stanton's autobiography, where anecdotes are integrated into a straightforward narrative, in Stein's life study, anecdotes constitute almost the entire narrative. These anecdotes describe the many artists and writers she befriended while living in Paris before and after World War I—earlier, Picasso, Matisse, Braque, Rousseau, Gris, and Picabia; and later, Hemingway, Wilder, Eliot, Pound, Anderson, Cocteau; and many others—all portrayed humorously in the everyday context of painting, writing, partying, trying to sell their works, and talking and quarreling among themselves about their individual merits and weaknesses.

Half a century after the publication of the *Autobiography,* these anecdotes are still a source of interest and amusement. But Stein does not use these anecdotal portraits the way others like Stanton do, to enlarge, indirectly, her own self-portrait. These anecdotes tell us nothing about Stein's personal life but, instead, function to place her in the center of these giants of twentieth-century art and literature in order to legitimize her as an important and influential person, respected for her opinions and her writings, a genius among geniuses—despite her lack of public recognition.

Another variation of the usual function of anecdotes is Stein's manner of giving bits and pieces at different points in the narrative, never starting or completing an anecdote or portrait at one sitting, so to speak. She repeats previously given information and then adds new details each time the incident is recounted. This incremental repetition creates a degree of suspense, and the reader is usually rewarded when the humor of the incident is finally clear. Stein transforms Picasso's cubist technique into literary planes, presenting new aspects of the same subject with each anecdotal variation. Still, the accumulated details create not in-depth or multidimensional portraits of herself and others but only a flat, unidimensional surface. Each becomes a part of a gallery of abstract still lifes, a static collection in words instead of colors.

Examples of stories that are constructed in this incremental fashion abound. One concerns a party given for Rousseau at Picasso's apartment; another deals with the significance of Toklas's sitting in front of two paintings, one by Derain, the other by Braque, during the first show she attended soon after her arrival in Paris. Another centers around the luncheon of artists in Stein's home in the rue de Fleurus when she placed each painter in front of one of his own compositions, much to everyone's pleasure.

The cumulative effect of these truncated anecdotes is a very fragmented narrative, one that is also nonchronological. Whereas other autobiographers sometimes ignored chronology to complete a portrait, to update a historical event, or to recount the past, Stein's narrative is nonchronological not only within chapters but also from one chapter to another, as the following demonstrates.

Chapter titles	*Chronological order*
1. Before I Came to Paris	3
2. My Arrival in Paris	4
3. Gertrude Stein in Paris, 1903–1907	2
4. Gertrude Stein Before She Came to Paris	1
5. Paris, 1907–1914	4 and 5
6. War	6
7. After the War, 1919–1932	7

This deliberate disorder and fragmentation of chronology reflects not only Stein's scorn for the usual autobiographical mode. It also reflects her consciousness of the chaos of her times, her discontent as an unrecognized writer, and her need to hide her lesbianism from a condemning public.

Catharine Stimpson defines the problem of women at the turn of the century who were liberated intellectually but not sexually as the "feminization of the mind/body problem." For women like Stanton the "solution was to project the ideal woman. She would not abandon sexual functions, particularly maternity, for the mind. Rather, she would add a disciplined and agile intelligence to these traditional functions. The synthesis would be the all-round woman: a sturdy, healthy, interesting wife, mother, and worker."[6]

For women like Stein, "the feminization of the mind/body problem" created confusion over "what women might do with their bodies and what they might say about it, especially in public."[7] For Stein, in her time and with her personality, camouflage was the only way she could write about her life. There was no way for her to coexist or synthesize her dual roles as private lesbian and public writer. Thus, fragmented anecdotes and a discontinuous chronology were necessary to conceal her true self in a genre predicated on self-revelation. And they do not contribute to a rounder or more insightful portrait as they do in Kate Millett's *Flying* (see chapter 12). Instead, they represent Stein's lack of trust and faith in a world that does not accept or allow her to write about her sexual preference. As Richard Bridgman writes: "The verbal crazy-quilts she fashioned from her musings constituted her truest approximation of unity."[8]

It is because of this need to hide her private life with Alice Toklas that the autobiography becomes a pretense at self-portraiture, for she must exclude the only meaningful intimate relationship of her life. She hopes to distract her readers from the absence of this personal element by concentrating on amusing portraits of famous people. Nonetheless, Stein does not entirely exclude her personal life from *The Autobiography of Alice B. Toklas.* Before I describe how she disguises her relationship with Toklas, however, I would like first to describe how she distances her readers from her personal life, especially, her feelings.

For one, she avoids writing about her childhood, summing it up in one paragraph:

> Life in California came to its end when Gertrude Stein was about seventeen years old. The last few years had been lonesome ones and had been passed in an agony of adolescence. After the death of first her mother and then her father she and her sister and one brother left California for the East. They came to Baltimore and stayed with her mother's people. There she began to lose her lonesomeness. She has often described to me how strange it was to her coming from the rather desperate inner life that she had been living for the last few years to the cheerful life of all her aunts and uncles.[9]

Stein seems to be virtually motherless and fatherless, and her brother, whom she adored, imitated, and followed first to college and then to Europe, is mentioned only briefly, and his name, Leo, not at all. Of her loneliness or that "desperate inner life" of her adolescence, she says nothing further.

Second, the subject of death is given strange treatment in the *Autobiography.* Stein says that she and Leo owed their existence to the deaths of two children before them, their parents having resolved to have a total of five children. Perhaps because of this knowledge and the death of her parents when she was an adolescent, she tends to ignore the subject of death or to reveal her feelings indirectly. We guess at her grief at the death of Apollinaire because she mentions it many times, though always objectively and without sentiment. Eve Picasso's death is mentioned in passing. In describing Juan Gris's death, she uses a number of emotional adjectives, but within their flat, mundane contexts, all feeling is repressed.

> Later when Juan died and Gertrude Stein was heart broken Picasso came to the house and spent all day there. I do not know what was said but I do know that at one time Gertrude Stein said to him bitterly, you have no right to mourn, and he said, you have no right to say that to me. You never realised his meaning because you did not have it, she said angrily. You know very well I did, he replied.
>
> The most moving thing Gertrude Stein has ever written is The Life and Death of Juan Gris. It was printed in transition and later on translated in german for his retrospective show in Berlin. (212)

Despite her close contact with death and suffering as a driver of medical supplies to the frontlines during World War I, Stein never mentions the wounded or the dying. After the war, when she observes the trenches, they appear strange to her. She cannot "place" them intellectually with a country's characteristics similar to those she had noticed about war camouflage and the marching rhythms of different countries. The very barrenness of her description seems to signify unstated shock at their desolation. "To any one who did not see it as it was then it is impossible to imagine. It was not terrifying it was strange. We were used to ruined houses and even ruined towns but this was different. It was a landscape. And it belonged to no country" (187). This absence of even the most superficial information about her early life as well as of any emotional response to upsetting experiences is explained as follows:

> Gertrude Stein, in her work, has always been possessed by the intellectual passion for exactitude in the description of inner and outer reality. She has produced a simplification by this concentration, and as a result the destruction of associational emotion in poetry and prose. She knows that beauty, music, decoration, the result of emotion should never be the cause, even events should not be the cause of emotion nor should they be the material of poetry and prose. Nor should emotion itself be the cause of poetry or prose. They should consist of an exact reproduction of either an outer or an inner reality. (211)

Occasionally, Stein expresses feelings through laughter, which seems to be an outlet or safety valve for expressing usually unsociable feelings. Throughout the autobiography we hear her laughing and chuckling, being amused and entertained. She laughs the first time she and her brother Leo go to the art dealer Vollard for some Cézannes when she realizes that he had been showing her half-finished imitations hastily drawn by amateurs in a back room. Another time, she describes Picasso's first dinner visit, when he snatches her bread, saying "this piece of bread is mine. She laughed and he looked sheepish. That was the beginning of their intimacy" (46). When Andrew Green tells her that he would like to make love to Picasso's mistress, if only he knew French; then, he says he would take her away from "that little Picasso. Do you make love with words, laughed Gertrude Stein. He went away before I came to Paris and he came back eighteen years later and he was very dull" (48). When Mabel Dodge suggests that Stein write "portraits of American millionaires which would be a very exciting and lucrative career, Gertrude Stein laughed" (132). *Tender Buttons* (1914) "started off columnists in the newspapers of the whole country on their long campaign of ridicule. I must say that when the columnists are really funny, and they quite often are, Gertrude Stein chuckles and reads them aloud to me" (156).

Like other literary autobiographers, Stein is reticent to discuss her work directly. But she does react with feeling to praise or criticism of her writing efforts. She conspicuously praises people who admire her work and attacks those who criticize or threaten it. Among her consistent admirers were Thornton Wilder, Bernard Faÿ, Virgil Thomson, Mildred Aldrich, and Carl Van Vechten, who became her literary executor and editor. Picasso respected her as a fellow philosopher-genius, and their friendship was a long and close one until Picasso tried his hand at literature, *her* métier. Then her feelings for him cooled.

T. S. Eliot gets contemptuous treatment for his coldness toward her literary efforts. When he demands for his *Criterion* "her very latest thing," she sits down immediately after he leaves "to write a portrait of T. S. Eliot and called it the fifteenth of November, that being this day and so there could be no doubt that it was her latest thing. It was all about wool is wool and silk is silk or wool is woollen and silk is silken. She sent it to T. S. Eliot and he accepted it but naturally he did not print it" (201).

Stein was "overcome with excitement" at Hemingway's idea to publish a section of *The Making of Americans,* which was "the beginning of modern writing . . . and we were very happy" (215). She "always remembered with gratitude that it was Hemingway who first caused to be printed a piece of "The Making of Americans," even after their break when she thought he was "yellow" (216), looked like a modern but smelled of museums (216), and was "fragile"—"whenever he does anything sporting something breaks, his arm, his leg, or his head" (218).

One must infer Stein's deep concern about her work behind these humorous thrusts. One must also infer that same concern by the lengths to which she goes to place in the background all allusions to her writing. There are a number of references to her actual writing, to Toklas's typing of the manuscripts, and to her failures and successes in getting published, but they are interspersed among the anecdotes. The reader must piece together the progression of her publications to see it developing as a significant topic. Like an antiphonally recurring theme, however, the subject of her writing persists until we slowly begin to notice it emerging into fuller view in the last chapter, where she finally declares: "Gertrude Stein was in those days a little bitter, all her unpublished manuscripts, and no hope of publication or serious recognition" (197).

Earlier, when preparing to publish her first book, *Three Lives,* she hides her humiliation behind a laugh when the publisher's representative comes to her in Paris.

> You see, he said, slightly hesitant, the director of the Grafton Press is under the impression that perhaps your knowledge of english. But I am an american, said Gertrude Stein indignantly. Yes yes I understand that perfectly now, he said, but perhaps you have not had much experience in writing. I suppose, she said laughing, you were under the impression that I was imperfectly educated. He blushed. (68)

For the thirty years preceding the publication of the *Autobiography,* Stein had written almost every night from eleven until dawn, undaunted and confident of her genius despite the lack of recognition, which was accorded to those she had nurtured. When her writing schedule was interrupted by the war, she wrote whenever the opportunity presented itself—while waiting for her car to be fixed, while Toklas shopped, even while posing for portraits. By the time she began the autobiography, she had written and published *Three Lives* (1909), *Tender Buttons* (1914), *Geography and Plays* (1922), an abbreviated version of *The Making of Americans* (1925), *Useful Knowledge* (1928), and *Lucy Church Amiably* (1930). When Toklas published the last work in her Plain Edition and efficiently had it displayed in Paris booksellers' windows, this "event gave Gertrude Stein a childish delight amounting almost to ecstasy. . . . she spent all her time in her wanderings about Paris looking at the copies of Lucy Church Amiably in the windows and coming back and telling me about it" (243). It is not surprising that when the publication of *The Autobiography of Alice B. Toklas* made her famous, she was unable to work for a time, so excited was she at finally achieving the recognition she had coveted for so many years.

Like Stanton, Stein seems similarly motivated to keep her professional life in the background. But whereas Stanton struggled to make herself acceptable by trying to cloak her work in the cape of an ordinary woman, Stein strains to amuse her readers so that they will buy her other books and thus establish her as a famous writer. She felt she would then be a public success, not just a private one among a select coterie. "It is . . . a little ironic, even a little sad," writes Elizabeth Sprigge, "that it should be this work, clever though it is, that brought her the glory she had always craved"[10]—ironic because it is unrepresentative of her writing. Stein's need to camouflage her professional work or at least to make it more palatable by emphasizing other aspects of her life places her autobiography among those by so many other professional women.

Less repressed than her feelings about her lonely childhood, her fear of death, or her work is Stein's sense of herself as different from others, especially other women. Although she makes no effort to hide her eccentric personality, conveying even a sense of pride in being a maverick, it is only her socially acceptable eccentricity that she reveals in her autobiography. Stimpson notes: "To think of one's self as special has several functions: to justify loneliness; to glamorize the role of anomaly and to remove it from the realm of social movements and politics; to help scour pollution."[11] It is for the last reason more than the others that Stein defiantly projects an eccentric self-image in her autobiography. She tells us about her experience as an undergraduate, already recognized as exceptional by William James, when she was the only student to have no reaction to an automatic writing experiment. When the experimenter wanted to discount her performance because it skewed his results unrealistically, James responsed: "If Miss Stein gave no response I should say that it was as normal not to give a response as to give one and decidedly the result must not be cut out" (79).

In medical school she tells us that after two years of brilliant work, she became bored and neglected her studies. Nevertheless, her professors passed her because, given her previously impressive performance, they found it hard to believe that she had not done the work. But when one professor refused to overlook her laziness and insisted that she make up an assigned paper, she responded with both contempt and indifference:

> You have no idea how grateful I am to you. I have so much inertia and so little initiative that very possibly if you had not kept me from taking my degree I would have, well, not taken to the practice of medicine, but at any rate to pathological psychology and you don't know how little I like pathological psychology, and how all medicine bores me. The professor was completely taken aback and that was the end of the medical education of Gertrude Stein. (83)

Ironically, Stein follows the above passage with: "She always says she dislikes the abnormal, it is so obvious. She says the normal is so much more simply complicated and interesting" (83).

The *Autobiography* also exemplifies another characteristic of the female tradition in the peripheral view it gives of mainstream political and social events. The world may crumble around her, but from her aesthetic tower, Stein is silent. Though she experienced the human slaughter of World War I firsthand as a driver for the American Fund for French Wounded, from her account the war appears as an occasion for some physical inconveniences and an opportunity to compare cultures. For example, she tells us that she and Toklas are stranded in London as the houseguests of Alfred North Whitehead for six weeks because of the war; after shopping in Paris, her friend Mildred Aldrich has trouble finding a cab to take her back to her house, which overlooks the ongoing Battle of the Marne; Stein notices that the camouflage from each country has its own distinctive pattern; the American doughboys interest her because of their speech patterns and because of her observation that although poor and uneducated, they have a chance to visit Europe. Is Stein merely indifferent to or oblivious of the suffering in her midst, or is she more interested in showing off her wit and superior powers of observation? Women writers typically approach military affairs from the sidelines or from a personal and peripheral perspective; however, Stein's distance seems unusual, perhaps because of her wish or need to disassociate herself and exclude from her life study any excesses of feeling.

All these techniques of omission, camouflage, diverting humor, and conscious detachment serve Stein's two primary objectives: the apparent one, to earn society's recognition of her genius; and the disguised one, to celebrate her friend and lover, Alice Toklas. Stimpson suggests that the reason Stein hid or lost the manuscript of the early novel *Q.E.D.* (published posthumously in 1950 as *Things as They Are*) was "less to suppress public knowledge of her own homosexuality than to protect her private relationship with Toklas."[12] That novel, about an emotional and physical relationship among three women, was based on an actual experience Stein had before moving to Paris. It provoked Edmund Wilson to write in his review of the novel in 1951:

> It is a production of some literary merit and of much psychological interest. The reviewer had occasion some years ago to go through Miss Stein's work chronologically, and he came to the conclusion at that time that the vagueness that began to blur it from about 1910 on and the masking by unexplained metaphors that later made it seem opaque, though partly the result of an effort to emulate modern painting, were partly also due to a need imposed by the problem of writing about relationships between women of a kind that the standards of that era would not have allowed her to describe more explicitly.[13]

Another technique—and the most important—that Stein employed to achieve her twofold intention was using Toklas as the third-person narrator of her autobiography. As in the third-person autobiographies by Henry Adams, Sean O'Casey, and W. B. Yeats, that voice served to distance Stein from her material. "In this way she could confine herself to outward appearances, bar us from intrusive and as she thought meaningless familiarity, and incidentally, too, present herself as the genius she was for her devoted Alice."[14]

Clearly, Toklas's persona allows Stein to praise her friends without appearing sentimental, to criticize those she disliked without attacking them directly, and to brag about herself without appearing egotistical—all without antagonizing her readers. Less perceptible but more significant is Stein's use of Toklas to represent the "acceptable" voice of a traditional female. Toklas's persona is the closest Stein can come to presenting the personal and domestic aspects of a woman's life, which are expected in a woman's life study. Since Stein tells us nothing about herself as a daughter, sister, or lover, Toklas satisfies the reader's expectations of the traditional female component. She likes gardening and needlework, does the cooking and dusting, types Stein's manuscripts, handles her correspondence and appointments, and sits with the wives of geniuses so that her idol can sit with the geniuses themselves—all the normal duties of a wife or servant of a great man. Toklas provides the "wifely" element in their relationship, Stein's other half.

If Stein had written in her own voice about Toklas's wifelike functions, her readers would probably have been shocked or disturbed. But if Toklas chooses to perform these duties, in her own voice, while the genius worked, then the audience may not even notice. Toklas's presence as the narrator legitimized Stein in a world that expected some information stereotypically associated with women in an autobiography by a woman, just as the geniuses Stein gathered around her legitimized her as a professional, if yet unrecognized, writer.

Writing her life story in the voice of her intimate companion serves yet another function. By placing Toklas in the ostensible center of the autobiography and by making her the narrator, Stein pays homage to their—her and Toklas's—personal success story. Stein makes famous the most important person in her life; she makes famous the "wife" of the genius who will one day be famous for her work.

Toklas is the one stable personality throughout the book. Others come and go, writers, painters, editors, and celebrities, but Toklas is always there to support Stein. In the opening chapter of the autobiography, Toklas is described "as a certain type of marriageable young woman,"[15] bored with her life in San Francisco. In the next chapter we learn about her first impression of Stein, one of the three geniuses Toklas immediately recognized when she heard an imaginary bell ring when they met (also Picasso and Whitehead). She is awed by the gallery at the rue de Fleurus, by Picasso and Fernande, who join them for dinner, and even by Stein's cook, Hélène. Toklas is sent to talk with Fernande, the start of her career of sitting with the wives of famous men, while Stein talks with Picasso.

Toklas's awe at her first meeting with Stein is matched by her romantic and lasting impression of Montmartre; there she sees for the first time the real "vie bohème" when Stein takes her to visit Picasso's studio. Later at the famous party for Rousseau, Toklas saves the day and procures the needed food when the caterer reneges on the refreshments. Toklas has begun to live an exciting life now that she has met Stein and has demonstrated her talent for assisting Stein with her work and her domestic affairs.

In 1909, two years after the two women met, Toklas moved into Stein's apartment. By 1913 Leo Stein had left, and the two had sealed their pact for life. At the end of the book, Stein lists Toklas's accomplishments with pride: "I am a pretty good housekeeper and a pretty good gardener and a pretty good needlewoman and a pretty good secretary and a pretty good editor and a pretty good vet for dogs and I have to do them all at once and I found it difficult to add being a pretty good author" (251–52). "Subtly, the book reveals Stein's personal success, the growth of a personal relationship that works."[16]

Stein's need to disguise her relationship with Toklas is not surprising.

During a time when most women had little choice between celibacy and domesticity, it was socially acceptable for women to share homes with one another. Jane Addams lived with another woman. So did M. Carey Thomas, Frances Willard, and Susan B. Anthony. Nevertheless, marriage was still the socially preferred relationship. Unpublished diaries and letters from the nineteenth century are filled with passionate and intense descriptions written by women to one another, sometimes explicit about physical contact but most of the time not.[17] Physical relationships were not common until the beginning of the twentieth century because women were so ignorant of their bodies that they did not often connect sexuality with anything save procreation.

Stimpson describes Stein's motive for disguising and "encoding" her lesbian relationship in her earlier novels *Q.E.D.* and *Fernhurst*, both written between 1903 and 1905, as "the need to write out hidden impulses; the wish to speak to friends without having others overhear; the desire to evade and to confound strangers, aliens, and enemies."[18] By 1932 the disguise was reduced to the "openness" of giving Toklas the role of narrator of Stein's autobiography. Stein did not live to benefit from the struggles of the women "who first exemplified the feminization of the mind/body problem," but she "left for contemporary women the consolation that it could be endured, even transcended."[19]

• • •

In 1937 Stein published a kind of postscript to *The Autobiography of Alice B. Toklas*—*Everybody's Autobiography*, which reads like a travel book about her six-month lecture tour of the United States, taken after the first book made her famous. As unlike the 1933 work as a sequel could be, *Everybody's Autobiography* is predominantly a straightforward chronological narrative with Stein herself the first-person narrator. There is none of the humor of the first book and no portraits of famous people because Stein no longer needs famous people to legitimize her or her work—*she* is now the famous person. In addition, there is only an occasional human interest story or anecdote.

In place of the anecdotes of the first book, this one is strung together by endless abstract and intellectual dissertations; most focus on comparisons between France and America, but also between many other subjects. She compares American and French architecture, street patterns, cars and taxis, road signs, and women and men. She also comments on the differences between painters and writers, nineteenth- and twentieth-century writing, failure and success, armies and dancing, poor people and rich people, public and private schools, speeches and lectures, quickness and slowness, moist food and dry food, the efficiency of planes and armies, mothers and fathers, publicity and audiences, and much more. Some of the comparisons are striking and insightful; others appear trivial, even stupid. One can imagine Stein chuckling to herself as she writes "Well, anyway" or "However" after some of these comparisons, indicating her awareness of their meaninglessness, and also her scorn for popular tastes.

Also unlike *The Autobiography of Alice B. Toklas*, *Everybody's Autobiography* devotes some forty pages to information about Stein's childhood, her brothers and sisters, her mother and father, and her college years—all, however, narrated with her usual detachment. She may feel more confident and therefore less vulnerable about her early life than she had as an unknown writer, but she will not sentimentalize her past. She is merely giving her readers the opportunity to play detective, to calculate how she became a genius—a "portrait of the artist as a young woman."

However, she is not at all detached when she describes unashamedly how it feels to be a celebrity. She is thrilled with her reception on disembarking in New York and with her name in lights on the *New York Times* building, "Gertrude Stein has arrived." Remarks on her pleasure at being a celebrity who can see anyone she wants, at being lionized on college campuses and literary salons, and at being stopped on the street by strangers who give her a friendly "Hello, Miss Stein" appear repeatedly throughout the book.

Finally, unlike the first book, *Everybody's Autobiography* has no female component. Though Toklas accompanies Stein on the trip, the first-person subject is rarely plural. There are occasional brief reminders that Toklas is there, and two of the longest refer to her domesticity.

> I liked the photographers, there is one who came in and said he was sent to do a layout of me. A layout, I said yes he said what is that I said oh he said it is four or five pictures of you doing something. All right I said what do you want me to do. Why he said there is your airplane bag suppose you unpack it, oh I said Miss Toklas always does that oh no I could not do that, well he said there is the telephone suppose you telephone well I said yes but I never do Miss Toklas always does that, well he said what can you do, well I said I can put my hat on and take my hat off and I can put my coat on and I can take it off and I like water I can drink a glass of water all right he said do that so I did that and he photographed while I did that and the next morning there was the layout and I had done it.

The other: "Alice is at present most interested in the curtains in all the English houses when we come to England that is what she finds most exciting that and everything else done by women."[20]

A significant theme in *Everybody's Autobiography* is Stein's concern that fame will change her identity. She needs to reassure herself that she is the same person by repeating that if her little dog knows her, then she must be the same person. But she is not the same person she was in *The Autobiography of Alice B. Toklas.* Writing in Toklas's voice to celebrate her lover, Stein produced a book with a strong female dimension. Even though a conventional female voice, it makes the autobiography a delight to read. In *Everybody's Autobiography,* Stein writes in her own voice as a successful writer who has made it in a man's world. Projecting the image of what she thinks a man is, she burdens her narrative with endless abstract comparisons to impress her readers with her intelligence. As narrated by a successful "male," her second autobiography is intellectual, self-conscious, and dull. By comparison, it points up how much *The Autobiography of Alice B. Toklas* is a part of the women's autobiographical tradition despite its impersonality. Stein gave her lover of twenty-five years immortality by affixing her name to her autobiography, but Toklas, by providing Stein with the female component to her life and her autobiography, gave her immortality through the one work that is still popular today.

· 11 ·

Literary Autobiography Recast: The Oblique Heroism of Lillian Hellman

By the time playwright Lillian Hellman began writing her series of autobiographies in the late sixties, the country was undergoing a major transformation of values and the second women's movement was just beginning. By comparison with the thirties and then with the late sixties through the early eighties, the two previous decades, the forties and fifties, were a dry period for autobiographies, especially by literary women.

The few who did write life studies during this period continued the characteristic of writing about their girlhoods or other personal matters and giving little or no place to their literary work. Lillian Smith (1897–1966) wrote a seminal political/autobiographical account of her experiences of racism in her native South in *Killers of the Dream* (1949). Margaret Anderson's second autobiography, *The Fiery Fountains* (1951), is a more reflective work than her first one, but she does not discuss her writing but focuses instead on her experiences in France, first as a follower of G. I. Gurdjieff, then enduring the slow dying of her intimate companion, Georgette Leblanc, and finally her frightening flight south before the advancing Nazis. Ellen Glasgow's (1873–1945) *The Woman Within* (1954) is a sensitive investigation of Glasgow's inner search for self-clarity, with almost no discussion of her writing career. Mary McCarthy's (1912–) collection of autobiographical essays, *Memories of a Catholic Girlhood* (1957), analyzes her traumatic childhood up to her sixteenth year. And May Sarton's (1912–) *I Knew a Phoenix* (1959), the first of several autobiographical works, presents random "sketches" of her girlhood. Pearl Buck's (1892–1973) *My Several Worlds: A Personal Record* (1954) focuses on the forty happy years she spent in China; while her writing plays an important part in her life, it holds a minor role in her intelligent and compassionate life study.

This was, however, a prolific period for autobiographies by black women, whose life studies constituted a flowering comparable to that by white women during the late nineteenth century; in both cases, it was the greater accessibility of educational opportunities and greater economic freedom that contributed to so much productivity. Not since the Civil War, when Northern abolitionists subsidized the publication of slave narratives, had so many black women written life studies. Now, however, these women were occupied in a wide spectrum of professions. Examples are Jane Edna Hunter's (1882–?) *A Nickel and a Prayer* and the confident and gracious feminist and civil rights activist Mary Church Terrell's (1863–1954) fascinating chronicle *A Colored Woman in a White World,* both published in 1940; Elizabeth Laura Adams's (1909–) *Dark Symphony* and Zora Neale Hurston's *Dust Tracks on a Road,* both published in 1942;[1] Era Bell Thompson's (1905–) *American Daughter* (1946); actress Ethel Waters's (1900–1977) *His Eye Is on the Sparrow* (1951); Helen Caldwell Day's (1926–) two life studies—*Color, Ebony* (1951) and *Not Without Tears* (1954); Ruby Berkley Goodwin's (1903–) idyllic childhood memoir *It's Good to Be Black* (1953); the long-delayed publication of the *Journal of Charlotte Forten* (1953); and opera diva Marian Anderson's (1902–) simple but moving account of her arduous rise to fame, *My Lord, What a Morning!* (1956).

There were also autobiographies by popular singers, who fought both musical and racial conventions to make it to the top, such as Billie Holiday's (1915–59) *Lady Sings the Blues* (1956), Eartha Mae Kitt's (1928–) *Thursday's Child* (1956), and Pearl Bailey's (1918–) *The Raw Pearl* (1968). Tennis champion Althea Gibson (1927–) wrote about her unusual success in *I Always Wanted to Be Somebody* (1958). Writing before the civil rights movement of the sixties had had its dramatic impact in raising awareness of the national scandal of American racism, some of these autobiographers, who had succeeded by dint of exceptional personal courage and professional talent, chose to ignore, play down, or deny racial discrimination. The life studies by Hurston, Goodwin, Anderson, Gibson, and Bailey are cases in point.

The black autobiographers who published in the late sixties and thereafter were generally more outspoken about their pride in their race and in themselves as women. Anne Moody (1940–) wrote about her early and daring civil rights activities in her chronicle *Growing Up in Mississippi* (1968). Of a more poetic temperament, Maya Angelou (1929–) wrote about the traumatic and also strong positive influences of her childhood in the first and best of her several life studies, *I Know Why the Caged Bird Sings* (1969). As different as their autobiographies were in subject matter and mood, both Moody and Angelou were enthusiastically received by both black and white readers, and both established reputations as a result of these works, just as Stein had in 1933, a phenomenon that has become common today for white women as well.

As in previous periods, autobiographies were now being written by women in fields in which they were participating more prominently and with greater respectability. There were autobiographies by athletes, such as Althea Gibson's and Babe Didrikson Zaharias's (1912–56) *The Life I've Lived* (1955). Life studies by actresses and other entertainers, common today, were then just coming into their own after a slow start in the twenties. Besides those by the black women already mentioned, there were ballerina Agnes de Mille's (1909?–) first of four life studies, *Dance to the Piper* (1952), actress Tallulah Bankhead's (1902–68) *Tallulah: My Autobiography* (1952), and folksinger Joan Baez's (1941–) *Daybreak* (1966).

Other autobiographers were engaged in the social or political sphere, many of them in occupations newly entered by these modern-day pioneers. Elizabeth Kenny (1886–1952) wrote about her revolutionary work rehabilitating polio victims, *And They Shall Walk: The Life Story of Sister Elizabeth Kenny* (1943); and Ida Maud Cannon (1877–1960) wrote *On the Social Frontier of Medicine* (1952). Eleanor Roosevelt (1884–1962) covered her years as First Lady and also her independent endeavors after her husband's death in three life studies less personal than her first one, *This Is My Story* (1937): *This I Remember* (1949), *On My Own* (1958), and *Autobiography* (1961), the last including generous excerpts from her first three life studies and a few updated chapters. Radical politics now engaged women in international and predominantly male movements. Dorothy Day (1899–1975), a founder of the radical newspaper *Catholic Worker*, wrote *The Long Loneliness* (1952); IWW agitator Helen Gurley Flynn (1890–1964) penned *I Speak My Own Piece: Autobiography of "The Rebel Girl"* (1955) and *The Alderson Story: My Life as a Political Prisoner* (1963); and Angela Caolomiris (1916–) published *Red Masquerade: Undercover for the F.B.I.* (1950).

• • •

In 1969, when Lillian Hellman (1905–84) published the first of her three life studies,[2] she was already a successful playwright and not a controversial public figure. So, unlike Stanton and Stein (and, as we will see, Millett), she wrote neither to prove herself to the public nor to make herself famous. Also, she was neither a feminist nor a political activist. She was by temperament a woman of the twenties, that generation of women who believed they had won their freedom and needed only to prove by dint of talent and personality that they could make it in a man's world.

And, of course, she had. By 1969 all twelve of her plays, including adaptations, had been produced on Broadway—from 1934 to 1963. She was an independent woman, secure in the public's approval. The reason for undertaking her life study seems to have been primarily to try to make sense of the past for her own personal satisfaction.

However, when Hellman wrote *An Unfinished Woman* (1969), she seems to have had no preconceived idea of what her proper autobiographical mode would be. She wrote: "As I come now to write about them the memories skip about and make no pattern."[3] There is no pattern in the first memoir either. In fact, it is a potpourri of styles, obviously a casual experiment to see which form most suited her personality and skills. Hellman starts with a chronological narrative of her early years. The first fourteen, untitled chapters follow one another chronologically, but internally all of them mix up the chronology with anecdotal flashbacks and flashforwards.

The first two chapters reveal painful and frank recollections of her family and her girlhood, recollections showing such a grasp of her materials that both chapters are capable of standing alone as independent vignettes. Once into young womanhood, however, her memories seem to wander as aimlessly as her own concept of herself. The middle ten chapters seem to have no purpose other than to record many anecdotes about friends and acquaintances. Two chapters on her experiences in the New York publishing world of the twenties (where she goes out of chronology to complete a profile of Horace Liveright) and two on her aimless years in Hollywood convey a sense of helpless torpor during a young womanhood spent waiting for something to happen. She presents a vague and quick vignette of her marriage to and divorce from Arthur Kober and an even more elusive sketch of her meeting and early life with Dashiell Hammett and their return to New York when her writing began in earnest. The reader is left with huge gaps in Hellman's life during the twenties and thirties, but the basic chronology is maintained.

In the next chapter, the eleventh, on her experiences in Spain during the Civil War and in the next five chapters on her trip to Russia during World War II, her narrative skips around. Unsure how to handle a historical panorama, she quotes long sections from her diaries, sometimes inserting in brackets her present reflections or hindsight on her experiences. In the last two chapters on Russia, she begins to get a grasp of her material. Looking back on her trip there in 1944 with the perspective of a return visit in 1967, she is much more capable of integrating the past and the present. Still, it must have become clear to Hellman that sketching an entire country was more difficult for her than writing about individual people. Finally, in the last three chapters of *An Unfinished Woman* she finds her style—in three portraits of people she cared about very dearly: Dorothy Parker, Dashiell Hammett, and Helen Jackson (along with a sketch of Sophronia Mason). None is a complete biography of its subject, but rather each consists of impressionistic and random anecdotes, mostly about the person's last years before death.

Thus, four years later, when Hellman wrote *Pentimento,* she was in complete control of her autobiographical mode. She had learned that her forte was in portraits and vignettes about people—the "silhouettes" that Frances Willard attached as afterthoughts to her life study have become the dominant mode. This second memoir, subtitled *A Book of Portraits,* contains seven skillfully shaped profiles of people she loved—all dead at the time of its writing. Hellman forgoes any attempt at a sustained chronological narrative though the portraits tend to follow one another progressively in time, with some overlapping, and, of course, a great deal of selective omission. Instead of writing about herself directly as she had in one of the early chapters about her girlhood in *An Unfinished Woman,* she presents herself indirectly by means of these miniature biographies. Within each portrait, the time sequence is interrupted constantly by flashbacks and flashforwards, as in the first book, but here she is in complete control of her material; there is no aimlessness but an artistic shaping of each profile. Even when she concentrates on one historical event, as she does in her third memoir, *Scoundrel Time*—her appearance before the House Un-American Activities Committee in 1952—Hellman disrupts the chronology by alluding to events as early as 1929 and as late as 1975, develops cameo portraits of others and herself, and even successfully integrates diary notes with present reflections and insights.

Like other female autobiographers before her, Hellman discovered that the historical or chronological mode was insufficient for expressing her personal vision, that her most comfortable autobiographical method was the vignette or portrait. By means of these entertaining profiles of others, Hellman orchestrates a portrait of herself, one that is never precise or sharp but always elliptical and impressionistic. In her psychologically sophisticated hands, the means of protecting one's vulnerable private self has progressed from Stanton's direct omission and Stein's camouflage to Hellman's subtle exposure.

Unlike most others before her, Hellman expresses no ambivalence or conflict about her personal life in relation to her professional career, just as another successful professional woman, Margaret Sanger, did not. But like other literary women, her writing career takes a back seat to the major personal theme that informs the three memoirs, her unhappiness with an eccentric temperament, which she considers a major flaw in her personality and over which she feels she has little control: It either rages in moods of anger or jealousy where she often does bodily harm to herself; or it goes numb with fear and thus incapacitates her. A true child of psychology, Hellman does not try to conceal her eccentricity but seeks to understand it, to come to terms with it. Her work is an odyssey of personal reconciliation with the self. This overriding concern is the raison d'être behind all the vignettes and portraits in all three life studies. It is the angle or perspective from which she treats all her experiences, whether as a child of six or a woman of sixty.

We can divide Hellman's experiences into three main areas: her childhood self-consciousness about her budding sexuality, her difficult relationships with men, and her peripheral political engagements.

Hellman writes about her childhood with a psychological sophistication that could emerge only after decades of the psychological and sexual revolutions that followed Freud's theories. Her treatment is a major leap forward from Stanton and even Stein. Stanton writes discreetly of the "joys and sorrows" of her childhood and seems generally ignorant of their psychological implications, especially of her father's rejection; Stein refuses to discuss her childhood, considering most psychology a waste of time. Hellman, on the other hand, devotes several chapters to the traumas of her adolescence in both *An Unfinished Woman* and *Pentimento: A Book of Portraits* (1973) and refers to them in many others. Also, unlike her predecessors, she is able to write about her sexuality, especially as it manifested itself in these early years.

Thus, Hellman probes the sources of her eccentric personality. As a child she was angry with her parents for playing off her loyalties toward them. She felt she

> was off balance in a world where . . . two . . . people certainly loved me for myself, but who also liked to use me against each other. I don't think they knew they did that, because most of it was affectionate teasing between them, but somehow I knew early that my father's jokes about how much my mother's family liked money, how her mother had crippled her own children, my grandmother's desire to think of him—and me—as strange vagabonds of no property value, was more than teasing. (*UW*, 5–6)

When Hellman was six, her father lost her mother's money in a business venture, and the family of three moved from New Orleans, where she was born, to New York. Soon thereafter, she began living six months of the year in New York and six months in New Orleans. This seesaw existence between two such diverse social climates further exaggerated her feeling of differentness, fed her discomfort with an unwieldy temper, and convinced her anew that she was a "difficult child."

The major trauma incurred by that move north was her separation from her nanny and best friend, Sophronia Mason, who principally had provided levelheadedness and direction to a growing girl with a passionate and intense nature. In comparing her with her later black housekeeper and friend Helen Jackson, Hellman writes:

> How often Helen had made me angry, but with Sophronia nothing had ever been bad. . . . But the answer there is easy: Sophronia was the anchor for a little girl, the beloved of a young woman, but by the time I had met the other, years had brought acid to a nature that hadn't begun that way—or is that a lie? (*UW*, 203)

On a return trip to New Orleans, the young Hellman decides to challenge the bus segregation laws and forces Sophronia to sit with her in the front of the bus. When they are unceremoniously ejected, Sophronia reprimands her. Years later Hellman realized that "all she meant was that I might blow up my life with impulsiveness or anger or jealousy or all the other things that she thought made a mess, but that day, in my thirteenth year, I shivered at the contempt with which she spoke" (*UW*, 210–11). The separation from Sophronia had a profound psychological effect on the young Hellman, instilling in her a rage against all forms of injustice.

> Oh, Sophronia, it's you I want back always. It's by you I still so often measure, guess, transmute, translate and act. What strange process made a little girl strain so hard to hear the few words that ever came, made the image of you, true or false, last a lifetime? (*UW*, 206–7)

The temper that needed restraint surfaced at an early age. As a child of six or seven, she was aware of her fear of her maternal grandmother, whom everyone in the family feared except her great-uncle Jake. Hellman writes: "Even as a small child I disliked myself for the fear and showed off against it" (*UW*, 1). When she was fifteen, that fearless Uncle Jake brought her a ring on her graduation from high school, which she promptly pawned for some books.

> I went immediately to tell him what I'd done, deciding, I think, that day the break had to come. He stared at me for a long time, and then he laughed and said the

words I later used in *The Little Foxes:* "So you've got spirit after all. Most of the rest of them are made of sugar water." (*UW,* 2)

This combination of fear and defiance of the fear, usually by blundering in a daze into heroic actions, followed Hellman all her life. It manifests itself in two crucial experiences described in the second chapter of *An Unfinished Woman.* Here she shapes a portrait of her prepubescent efforts to deal with her unwieldy temper as it clashed with her sexual jealousy over her father.

The first experience begins symbolically with a description of a fig tree in front of the New Orleans boarding house run by her father's two sisters where the bored eight-year-old, playing hooky, snuggled with a stolen pillow, a book, her lunch, and "a proper nail" for her dress. She retreats to the fig tree with her anger when she sees her father and Fizzy, a boarder, go off in a taxi, proving what she had suspected, that her father is unfaithful to her mother—and to her. There in the tree, while plotting to kill them both, in her rage she throws herself out of the tree and breaks her nose. This earliest vignette of her childhood rage and its physical outlet is typical of Hellman's handling of extreme anger and feelings of impotency all her life. We shall see how frequently Hellman's body takes the brunt of intense feelings for which she has no constructive outlet.

The second experience follows closely on the first. As a lonely child who seemed to be surrounded only by adults with no girlhood friends in New Orleans, she plays with a group of orphans who appeal to her because of their apparent independence. When one of the boys gives her a lock of his hair and then shoves her into the street, she quite rightly assumes that these acts are signs of his affection. She promptly puts the lock in a new watch, which her father had recently given her, perhaps her first act of direct defiance of him for another male. When the watch stops and her indignant father returns it to the jeweler in a fury only to be embarrassed by the discovery of the hair, he makes the mistake of berating her in front of the boarders, including her "rival" Fizzy. At first her rage is transmuted to numbness, but it soon impels her to run away from home. Her break with family confinement is underway.

Wandering for the first time into the whorehouse district of the Latin Quarter, she circles the block uncertainly until the regulars begin to taunt her. Hungry, scared, tired, and feeling sick in a unfamiliar way, she runs from the horror of a man exposing himself, spends hours in a railroad restroom, sleeps outdoors the second night, is awakened by the sight of two rats staring at her, and urinates in terror. Finally, she makes her way to a black rooming house, actually a way station for prostitutes, and gives Sophronia's name as a reference, thus securing a much needed safe place to sleep. Her father, alerted via Sophronia, comes for her and reluctantly apologizes. Then she tells him the news. "Papa, I'll tell you a secret. I've had very bad cramps and I am beginning to bleed. I'm changing life" (*UW,* 23).

This vignette effectively portrays a fourteen-year-old girl struggling with her loyalties to her adored father and with her budding sexuality. It is one of the rare occasions in which Hellman focuses on herself directly, and it is also the only chapter in all her memoirs that is set within a metaphorical context. The mythical fig tree that protects from sexuality, the red purse that she carries on her escapade from home, the experiences wandering around the Latin Quarter, her escape to a black rooming house, and her menstruation—all blend into a portrait of sexual crisis in an adolescent girl. The metaphorical context is a means of controlling fictively a girlhood passage into the world of adults.

In two portraits in *Pentimento*—"Bethe" and "Willy"—Hellman continues to write about her childhood, but there the treatment is less direct, more oblique. In "Bethe" Hellman conveys her maturing sexual sense and her intense feelings about this German woman who was brought to this country to marry and, the family hoped, to tame a no-good cousin of Hellman's. When Bethe is eventually abandoned and then disappears, her life takes on mystery and adventure for the teenage Hellman. As an inquisitive, precocious child, she is thrilled to discover Bethe in the Latin Quarter living with an Italian gangster and then to find herself befriended by this adored and romantic woman. Mixed with her adoration, however, is jealousy. She is outraged when Bethe, Jewish like the rest of the family, claims she has converted to Catholicism. "I said to Bethe before I began to cry, 'You lie because a man tells you to.' "[4] In an aside, Hellman explains her girlhood emotion with the hindsight of the present:

> God help all the children as they move into a time of life they do not understand and must struggle through with precepts they have picked from the garbage cans of older people, clinging with the passion of the lost to odds and ends, that will mess them up for all time, or hating the trash so much they will waste their future on the hatred. (*P,* 18)

When Bethe attempts to placate her by taking her to a restaurant where her Mafia lover sits across the room eyeing them, she thinks: "I was on the edge of acquisition, a state of nervousness which often caused me to move my hands and wrists as if I were entering into a fit" (*P,* 21). And then comes the event that introduces her to her first sense of sexual passion:

> Before any gesture was made, I knew I was seeing what I had never seen before and, since like most only children, all that I saw related to me, I felt a sharp pain as if I were alone in the world and always would be. As she raised her hand to her mouth and then turned the palm toward him, I pushed the heavy paste stuff in front of me so far across the table that it turned and was on the tablecloth. She did not see what I had done because she was waiting for him as he rose from his chair. She went to meet him. When they reached each other, his hand went down her arm and she closed her eyes. As I ran out of the restaurant, I saw her go back to our table. (*P,* 22)

When months later, Bethe's lover is assassinated, Hellman is questioned by the police when she shows up for one of her frequent visits to his storefront cover. "I . . . heard the fear turn into anger. 'Please take your hand off my arm. I don't like to be held down.' He laughed and with that laugh caused a lifelong, often out-of-control hatred of cops, in all circumstances in all countries" (*P,* 28).

Years later and in her twenties, after her marriage to Arthur Kober and when living with Dashiell Hammett, Hellman visits her aunt in New Orleans. When they take her to see Bethe, the intensity of her feelings for this woman who first introduced her to her own sexuality once again affects her physically, causing her to vomit and to become dazed and weak. On another occasion, when Hammett is impatient with her attempt to explain how important Bethe was to their relationship, she writes: "He didn't understand what I meant when I kept repeating that Bethe had had a lot to do with him and me. I got so angry that I left the apartment, drove to Montauk on a snowy day, and came back two days later with the grippe" (*P,* 39).

Concurrent with her first sexual knowledge felt vicariously via her cousin Bethe, Hellman experiences her first sexual crush, on her uncle Willy, who runs guns to South America to "tame" disobedient natives in America's colonial adventures. Hellman's second portrait, "Willy," in *Pentimento,* is about her struggle between her loyalty to blacks because of her love for Sophronia and her passion for her corrupt uncle. Willy barely notices her but occasionally takes her fishing with him. On one trip to the country, she is so thrilled to be with him that though standing in quicksand, she falls into a trance of submission and terror, from which he saves her with great difficulty. In the evening when he goes off to visit his "cajun girl," whom she knows about from her aunt's servants, the teenage Lillian experiences once again the rage of sexual jealousy that plagued her all her life, and she runs off, walking through snake-infested swamps in a stupor.

> I believe that what I felt that night was what I was to feel about myself and other people years later: the humiliation of vanity, the irrational feeling of rejection from a man who, of course, paid me no mind, and had no reason to do so. It is possible to feel many conflicts and not know they are conflicts when you are young: I was at one minute less than nothing and, at another, powerful enough to revenge myself with the murder of Willy. My head and body seemed not to belong together, unable to carry the burden of me. Then, as later, I revenged myself on myself: when the sun came up I left the porch, no longer fearing the swamps. On the way down the road I, who many years later was to get sick at the sight of one in a zoo, stumbled on a snake and didn't care. A few hours after that, a truck gave me a ride into New Orleans. I had been walking in the wrong direction. (*P*, 66)

Looking back on that experience with the hindsight of the present, Hellman, conscious of her girlhood struggle, writes:

> There are many ways of falling in love and one seldom is more interesting or valid than another. . . . I was not ever to fall in love very often, but certainly this was the first time and I would like to think that I learned from it. But the mixture of ecstasy as it clashed with criticism of myself and the man was to be repeated all my life, and the only thing that made the feeling for Uncle Willy different was the pain of that first recognition: not of love, but of the struggles caused by love; the blindness of a young girl trying to make simple sexual desire into something more complex, more poetic, more unreachable. (*P*, 61)

As Hellman moves into adulthood memories, her writing is even more oblique than when describing her childhood. Adult frailties and mistakes are closer at hand and more difficult to face than childhood's pains. Thus, in writing about her mature years, she applies her dramatic artistry to shape portraits that center even more on others and even less on herself, though her own feelings are always conveyed elliptically.

By this means, she is able to write about her eccentric nature as it operates in her adult relationships with men. We do not learn much about her marriage to Arthur Kober when she was only twenty, but we do learn that before she could bring herself to end the marriage, she suffered from trembling fits as she drove home from her play-reviewing job in Hollywood. In "Bethe," she notes that when she went to New Orleans to tell her aunts about her divorce, "It was an unpleasant errand: my parents and my aunts liked my husband, knew that I liked him, and had every right to be puzzled and disturbed about me" (*P*, 33).

Even before she met Dashiell Hammett in Hollywood she knew "I needed a teacher, a cool teacher, who would not be impressed or disturbed by a strange and difficult girl. I was to meet him, but not for another four or five years" (*UW*, 44). That man was Hammett, for whom she wrote one celebratory chapter in *An Unfinished Woman* but whose presence is felt or mentioned in most of the chapters in the two earlier autobiographies and also in *Scoundrel Time* (1976). Hellman is never explicit about their relationship though they lived off and on together for some thirty years. The most she says directly of her feelings for him are in the barest terms:

> I know as little about the nature of romantic love as I knew when I was eighteen, but I do know about the deep pleasure of continuing interest, the excitement of wanting to know what somebody else thinks, will do, will not do, the tricks played and unplayed, the short cord that the years make into rope and, in my case, is there, hanging loose, long after death. (*UW*, 242)

In *Pentimento*, Hellman comments on their unplanned life together:

> We had never . . . made a plan, and yet we had moved a number of times from West Coast to East Coast, bought and sold three houses, been well-heeled and broke, parted, come together, and never had plans or even words for the future. In my case, I think, the mixture came from Bohemia as it bumped into Calvin: in Hammett's it came from never believing in any kind of permanence and a mind that rejected absolutes. (*P*, 171)

Hellman never tells us about Hammett's notorious alcoholism, though allusions are occasionally made to his drinking. Her drinking is also underplayed, but it may account for one of her extreme rages of sexual jealousy against this man who saw her through her first difficult years of playwriting. After the success of *The Children's Hour*, she called him in Hollywood to tell him the good news, but his "secretary" answered.

> On the day I understood about the secretary and three o'clock in the morning I took a plane to Los Angeles. By the time I got to the house in the Pacific Palisades it was night and I had had a good deal to drink. I went immediately to the soda fountain—Hammett had rented the house from Harold Lloyd—smashed it to pieces and flew back to New York on a late night plane. (*P*, 132–33)

The two concluding chapters of *Pentimento* celebrate the nature of their relationship and her enduring feelings for Hammett, who died in 1961 when she was fifty-eight. Both chapters, " 'Turtle' " and "Pentimento," are tender tone poems, creating a mood—primarily by means of elliptical dialogue—rather than a portrait. In the former, she investigates the question of life; the latter is a tentative sketch on the question of death, especially her struggle to accept Hammett's.

In " 'Turtle' " Hammett and Hellman capture and decapitate a snapping turtle that is foraging in their lake. The next morning they find that the body—minus the head—has moved itself from the kitchen to the brush outside. Hammett, the practical one, wants to return the turtle to the kitchen so Helen can make soup out of it, but Hellman says:

> "Let's take it to the lake. It's earned its life."
> "It's dead. It's been dead since yesterday."
> "No. Or maybe it was dead and now it isn't."
> "The resurrection? You're a hard woman for an ex-Catholic." (229)

When Helen wants to know what to do with the turtle, Hammett says: "Make soup." But Hellman says:

> "The next time. The next turtle. Let's bury this one."
> "*You* bury it."
> "You're punishing me," I said. "Why?"
> "I'm trying to understand you."
> "It's that it moved so far. It's that I never before thought about *life*, if you know what I mean."
> "No, I don't," he said.
> "Well, what is life and stuff like that."
> "Stuff like that. At your age." (232)

Finally, she asks him to help her bury the turtle.

> "I don't bury turtles."
> "Will you bury me?"
> "When the time comes, I'll do my best," he said. (232–33)

Hellman buries the turtle by herself, but Hammett pays tribute: "For all the years we lived on the place, and maybe even now, there was a small wooden sign, neatly painted: 'My first turtle is buried here. Miss Religious L. H.' " (234).

In "Pentimento" Hellman describes how every night during her teaching stint at Harvard shortly after Hammett's death, she had trouble sleeping and would often walk to the nursing home at which, it was planned, he would recuperate from his illness. When Jimsie, the friend of her housekeeper, Helen Jackson, follows her as protection, she states, elliptically:

> "Pentimento."
> "What's that mean?" he said.
> I said, "Don't follow me again, Jimsie. I don't like it." (241–42)

When she meets Jimsie years later, he tells her:

> "I loved Helen."
> "Too bad you never told her so. Too late now."
> "I told it to her," he said, "the night I looked up your word, pentimento." (245)

As Hellman explains in her preface to *Pentimento,* these memories, like her staring at the nursing home where Hammett might have been had death not taken him, are her means of "seeing and then seeing again," seeing "what was there for me once, what is there for me now" (1).

Another man in Hellman's life was Arthur Cowan, a brilliant Philadelphia lawyer with very conservative politics who nonetheless financed a number of legal defenses for victims of McCarthyism. More detached in her feelings toward Cowan than she was with Hammett, Hellman is able to concentrate her portrait of this eccentric friend in *Pentimento* more on his quixotic personality and less on her own emotional reactions to him. In contrast to the stabilizing influence that Hammett played in her life, Cowan seems to have been more unpredictable and impulsive than Hellman, which is probably why she was so fascinated with him—a person even more eccentric than herself.

Cowan seems to have had no concept of time or money, and for that reason was always a source of surprise and pleasure to her. When Hammett met him, his usual laconic comment was: "I'm thinking that for the first time in my life I've met a crazy man who is pretending that he is crazy and wondering why you never see danger. Maybe it's what saves you. Let me know when he leaves" (206). Hellman's portrait of Cowan is thus a very chaotic string of anecdotes about him. Despite her confusion about him, and the long intervals between their meetings, her fondness for his eccentricity emerges, and the chapter is witty and entertaining. It ends on a note of anger, however, at the sense of injustice his enigmatic death evokes in her.

> The conflicting details of the accident, why a will disappeared that he certainly wrote and rewrote through the years, the failure even to find out what job he had been doing for what agency, all are to this day unexplained. If his life was puzzling, he entrusted the memory of it to people who have kept it that way. He has disappeared. I do not believe he would have wanted it that way. (215)

The third subject of interest to Hellman is politics—specifically, the significant political events of each of the five decades she covers in her life studies—from the twenties through the sixties. Again each episode is told by means of personal portraits that convey indirectly her own erratic temperament. Her particular perspective, like many of her predecessors, eschews direct historical detail or analysis, relying more on human interest stories about seemingly insignificant people or events. It is here that we often see her bungling into heroism, sometimes out of anger at political or social injustices, other times in a haze of fear.

Hellman's memories of the twenties focus on two unsentimental experiences, very different from the usual flapper image of the decade. First, there is the account of her casual reaction to an abortion she had when she was only nineteen, when she exhibits the same defiance of her fears that she showed her Uncle Jake; there is also the same scorn for pretense and romanticism that will characterize her entire life. Then there is a sad but sympathetic portrait of the once famous and wealthy Horace Liveright, who symbolized a personal brand of publishing that no longer exists. And in an anecdote about a trip she made to Bonn in 1929 to study, she describes her reaction when invited to join the National Socialist Club—"no dues for foreigners if they had no Jewish connections. I said I had no other connections that I knew of . . . and left Bonn the next day and came back to New York" (*UW*, 45).

To Hellman, the thirties meant the Spanish Civil War, especially the devastating effect it had on the people. On her visit to Spain a strange couple stare at her and make meaningless remarks, obviously deranged by the bombings: "I realized they were the first people I had ever seen who were of no age that I could guess because something had happened to their faces" (*UW*, 80). From the ashes of a bombed house she picks family pictures and small china vases as mementoes. She sees starved people savoring each morsel of sardines, crackers, and canned peaches and meets a woman who complains that the bombings do not permit a visit to her hair dresser. The bombings have their effect on Hellman also; she repeatedly vomits, develops a toothache, and one days slips and turns her ankle in a fit of anger at all the bloodshed. But despite a warning that it is too dangerous to keep a recording date at the radio station during the bombing of Madrid, she keeps her appointment. Though absent-minded or sick under stress, she still stumbles her way to heroic achievements.

Another memory from the thirties is Hellman's trip across Germany in 1937 to deliver fifty thousand dollars in ransom money to her friend Julia to help free political prisoners of the Nazis. Though we learn a little about Hellman's childhood friendship with Julia in New York, or rather her adoration of this beautiful and wealthy young woman, Hellman focuses the vignette on the train ride. Julia had given up her inheritance and all her American connections in the twenties to work for the underground against fascism in Europe. Hellman uses flashbacks to convey the information about Julia, including their 1934 meeting in a Viennese hospital where Julia was recuperating from a leg amputation. Hellman underplays her own heroism, dramatizing her successful mission as the accidental result of her aimless and dazed state of fear. At one point, unaware that the money is sewn into the lining of the expensive fur hat provided for the occasion, she begins to leave her coach to be questioned by customs with the hat lying on her seat. Luckily, Julia has planted two women to oversee her journey, and they suggest that she wear the hat because of the chilly weather. After the war, Hellman tries in vain to locate the child Julia bore and sent to London for safekeeping. Like the Cowan piece, this portrait also ends on a note of anger—at Julia's family, who had no interest in her or the child.

Hellman recalls two bumbling though brave experiences during the forties, both occurring in Russia during World War II, the first when she accepts an invitation to visit the Russian front. Terrified of combat, she nevertheless conducts herself graciously, never intruding like the usual journalist by interviewing the general in charge or checking his battle plans. Though she almost jeopardizes their position while focusing binoculars, overall, the general is so impressed by her that he invites her to join him on the army's march to Warsaw; that invitation she politely refuses. On another occasion, a brutally cold trip to Russia by way of Siberia in a small plane, she is so frightened that she breaks her ankle on one of the fuel stops and finally arrives in Moscow with pneumonia.

Hellman's unhappy recollections of the fifties are concentrated in one long vignette, published in *Scoundrel Time* (1976). In the two earlier memoirs, she had alluded very briefly to the Red scare after World War II, particularly to Hammett's refusal to testify about the bail bond fund of which he was a trustee, which resulted in his incarceration in 1951. But in *Scoundrel Time,* Hellman describes her appearance before the House Un-American Activities Committee hearings in 1952. Even here, events are not described in political, social, or historical terms but with personal anecdotes; what she presents is not the intellectual long view but a closeup of personalities. She writes: "I don't want to write about my historical conclusions—it isn't my game. I tell myself that . . . if I stick to what I know, what happened to me, and a few others, I have a chance to write my own history of the time."[5]

In contrast to all her other portraits, where Hellman is celebratory, whether of people or of places, in this book her tone is angry and condemnatory. For the first time, she is able to channel anger, not physically at herself, but where it belongs—at those intellectuals and liberals, some of whom are still alive, who betrayed their friends and their political ideals. In miniature portraits, she indicts Harry Cohn, who wanted her to sign a million-dollar contract that required a loyalty oath; Clifford Odets, who bragged to her about his loyalty to his friends, then turned friendly witness on the stand; and Henry Wallace, who denounced the very communists who had supported his Progressive party.

The actual hearing at which Hellman testified occupies only six pages out of 130. She builds tension and suspense before describing the hearing with anecdotes about those with whom she is still angry. Almost twenty-five years later:

> I am still angry that their reason for disagreeing with McCarthy was too often his crude methods. . . . Many of the anti-Communists were, of course, honest men. But none of them . . . has stepped forward to admit a mistake. It is not necessary in this country; they . . . know that we are a people who do not remember much. (154–55)

As with her other brave actions, Hellman plays down her role at the hearing, crediting Abe Fortas with the strategy of answering questions about herself but not about anyone else. She admits her fear of prison, and when another lawyer suggests that she forgo the above strategy because it is too risky, she responds:

> [Joseph] Rauh, with the best will, had upset me to the point of sickness. I cannot make quick turns . . . have not the mind or the nature to do one thing, maybe wiser, when I am prepared for another. . . . I remember saying to myself, "Just make sure you come out unashamed. That will be enough." (102)

Her fears take their usual toll, however. In the courtroom, she writes, "I felt the sweat on my face and arms and knew that something was going to happen to me, something out of control" (108). When she returns to her hotel room, she vomits for two days. Typically, Hellman undercuts her heroic behavior at the hearing, as she has with every other such memory, by exposing her emotional vulnerability.

Hellman's memoirs of the sixties are represented in several chapters of *An Unfinished Woman* and *Pentimento* in portraits of three young black men. The three run the spectrum of sixties types: Orin is hooked on dope and is indifferent to the civil rights movement; George, a fifteen-year-old, visits the North for surgery to correct dizziness that resulted from a head injury incurred during a civil rights demonstration in Mississippi; and, finally, Jimsie, a brilliant student at Harvard and winner of a Rhodes Scholarship to study astrophysics, gives up a career in science because it would mean helping the military establishment and instead retreats to a farm in Oregon where he supports himself by whittling "rosettes de bois." Hellman's dissatisfaction with his decision emerges in her remark: "I now have some right to disappointment in what the good children of the Sixties have come to" (*ST*, 153).

Hellman's disillusionment with five decades of political bumbling—more critical to human dignity and survival than her own crude reactions would indicate—occupies a prominent place in her three memoirs, as opposed to her plays, which have only a minor part in her recollections. "Theatre" in *Pentimento* presents vignettes of eccentric people she met in the theater, such as Lee Shubert, Tallulah Bankhead, and Paul Muni. It also contains amusing anecdotes about unusual situations, such as the time she helped a director fill tiny matchboxes with rolled condoms to embarrass the host of a pretentious party; or a strange poker game at Lady Asquith's; or scenes of actors bickering over which benefit they should perform for. She tells nothing about how she came to write drama instead of other literary genres, nothing about her writing method or the trial of getting her plays produced, nothing about her evaluation of the plays—only her usual overdrinking or vomiting out of fear on opening night. "Theatre" is the least integrated of the "portraits" in *Pentimento*, probably because she did not really want to write about her work. Prefatory to that chapter, Hellman writes:

> How the pages got there, in their form in their order, is more of a mystery than reason would hope for. That is why I have never wanted to write about the theatre and find the teaching of English literature more rewarding than teaching drama. . . .
>
> There are, of course, other reasons why I have not written about the theatre: I have known for years that part of me struggled too hard within it, and the reasons for that I do not know and they could not, in any case, be of interest to anybody but me. I always knew that I was seldom comfortable with theatre people although I am completely comfortable in a theatre; and I am now at an age when the cutting up of old touches must be carefully watched and any sentence that begins "I remember" lasts too long for my taste, even when I myself say it.
>
> But I have certain pictures, portraits, mementoes of my plays. They are what I have left of the long years, the pleasure in the work and the pains. (125–26)

Spacks notes that Hellman's "accounts of her loves and of her work are oblique, as if neither aspect of experience were vital (although the real meaning of the fact may be that both are too vital to be shared)."[6]

Though Hellman chose to write very little about her writing—so typical of literary women—there are other omissions worth noting. For example, like Stein, she does not consider her Jewish heritage a matter to write about. While Stein is completely silent on the subject, Hellman at least mentions it briefly on two occasions, once in reference to Bethe's conversion to Catholicism and then on her trip to Bonn. Also, though a Southerner, Hellman does not discuss the issue of racism, nor any conflicts or observations raised on her move to the North. Taking an unintellectual approach, she lets her experiences speak for themselves: her childhood loyalty to Sophronia Mason and her effort to integrate the public bus system, her adult relationship with Helen Jackson, and her interaction with the young black men during the sixties.

Hellman also writes very little about her mother. Though she never created a whole portrait of her father, we get glimpses of him throughout the memoirs, and it is clear to readers that both she and Hammett resemble him in many ways. But we rarely see her mother directly, and there are only a few brief comments by others. Hellman writes: "By the time I knew how much I loved my mother and understood that her eccentricities were nothing more than that and could no more be controlled than the blinking of an eye in a high wind, it was, indeed, too late" (*P,* 47). The absence of any clear or adequate portraits of their mothers, as we have seen in Stanton, Stein, and now Hellman—even with her psycholo sophistication—is a regretted omission. Fortunately, this omission h been rectified with the new generation of women more liberated than Hellman.

There is no doubt that Hellman was molded by her generation's advancements in women's rights, as well as by the psychological revolution of the early part of the century. Though she omits areas of her life that would interest modern readers, the portrait she paints of her own personality is quite vivid. Even though it is created indirectly, obliquely, elliptically, primarily by means of portraits of eccentric people like herself or about political experiences that piqued her anger at injustice, we get a clear though impressionistic picture of her in these three autobiographical works. Piece by piece, episodically and anecdotally, as in a jigsaw puzzle, the implied center, the personality of Lillian Hellman, emerges: aimless but defiant, tough but tender, proud but vulnerable, blundering but heroic, frightened but morally strong. Her confidence in herself along with her fears and insecurity create a whole, true picture of this willful woman whose eccentricity was both a gift and a bane. In her sixties she still thought of herself as "unfinished"; in her seventies her memories were sad—*pentimenti.* Then, in 1973, slowly coming to terms with herself, she wrote:

> All my life I believed in the changes I could, and sometimes did, make in a nature I so often didn't like, but now it seems to me that time made alterations and mutations rather than true reforms; and so I am left with so much of the past that I have no right to think it very different from the present. (*P,* 21)

Three years later she wrote: "As I finish writing about this unpleasant part of my life, I tell myself that was then, and there is now, and the years between then and now, and the then and now are one" (*ST,* 155).

In writing her autobiography from the perspective of a psychologically perceptive literary woman, Hellman transformed the women's autobiographical tradition of the personal into a deeper, if oblique, inner analysis. In Kate Millett, we will see the personal become the political.

· 12 ·

cal and Personal ography Integrated:

The Fusion of Kate Millett

Although only five years separated the publication of Hellman's first memoir and Kate Millett's *Flying* (1974), which antedated Hellman's third book by two years, the sensibilities that separate the two women are at least a generation, even a historical era, apart. Hellman was in her sixties and seventies when she wrote her three life studies; Millett was forty and at the height of her creative and political powers when she wrote hers. For Millett and her generation, the writing of autobiography was no longer considered an act of reflection in old age but a process engaged in as one lived one's life. In addition, the civil rights movement had left its stamp and the second women's liberation movement was well under way. It occasioned a massive outpouring of personal statements, the end of women's silence for all time.

Though born in the twentieth century, women of Hellman's era and sensibility continued to write autobiographies, as in the past, in the same disjunctive forms and narratives and with the same emphasis on their personal lives over their public identities. These women had succeeded in a man's world through perseverance and talent, untouched by the movement that was to force the integration of the personal with the public in younger generations of autobiographers. There were the first four volumes of Anaïs Nin's (1903–76) self-absorbed diaries published in 1966, 1967, 1969, and 1974; Margaret Mead's (1901–78) child-focused *Blackberry Winter: My Earlier Years* (1972); Sally Carrighar's (1905–) poignant psychological rendering of her journey from childhood trauma to personal stability, *Home to the Wilderness: A Personal Journey* (1973); and Hannah Tillich's (1896–) tribute to her famous philosopher-husband, *From Time to Time* (1974), a collection of vignettes, portraits, poems, and playlets.

More typical, however, were autobiographies by women who were products of the liberation movements of the sixties and seventies. In addition to Angelou's *I Know Why the Caged Bird Sings* (1969), other autobiographies by black writers published during this time include Lorraine Hansberry's (1930–65) *To Be Young, Gifted, and Black* (1969), an edited collection of autobiographical writings; Nikki Giovanni's (1943–) *Gemini: An Extended Autobiographical Statement of My First Twenty-Five Years of Being a Black Poet* (1971); and Gwendolyn Brooks's (1917–) *Report from Part One* (1972). Shirley Chisholm (1924–), one of the first black elected officials, wrote two autobiographies, *Unbought and Unbossed* (1970) and *The Good Fight* (1973); and lesbian Sharon Isabell's (1942–) *Yesterday's Lessons* (1974) was one of the first life studies to bring lesbians out of the autobiographical closet.

• • •

In this atmosphere of revolutionary change, Kate Millett (1934–) published *Flying* (1974)—when the women's movement for personal and political liberation was in full swing. Four years earlier, in *Sexual Politics*, Millett had identified the sexism at the heart of contemporary society—in the patriarchal system that pervades every area of life, from the board room to the bedroom. Overnight, Millett, an active feminist but unknown to the general public until her doctoral dissertation was published, became a household name. Almost contemporaneous with that success came a public forum at which she admitted her lesbianism to the mass media, which, unfortunately, exploited it to discredit not only her book but the whole women's movement. The implied critique was: How could one trust the views of a woman who loved women, who must, therefore, by definition, hate men, and who must be out to "get" them because she placed the blame for sexism on them rather than on women's "inherent" weakness.

Flying concentrates on the years following the publication of *Sexual Politics* and on the effects Millett's public "coming out" had on her personal life and on the women's movement in general. Thus, its focus on women from the two perspectives of the personal/sexual and the political transforms earlier writers' self-consciousness about their womanhood into a strong assertion of its validity. Whereas Stanton's self-consciousness forced her to protect the women's movement by downplaying her own exceptional talents and Hellman's took the form of discontent with her turbulent heterosexual nature, Millett's is a vivid and positive self-portrait of a woman-identified sexual person. *Flying* is Millett's attempt to clarify for herself and for her readers the complex issue of one's sexual identity and, specifically, Millett's commitment to loving her own sex.

Since it is evident that her eight-year marriage to the sculptor Fumio Yoshimura is a vital part of her life and her politics, it is more accurate to speak of her as a bisexual. At the time she publicly admitted her lesbianism, bisexuality was considered a "copout" by militant feminist lesbians. For Millett, however, bisexuality is not just a matter of physical lovemaking; it is clearly her political solution to patriarchy. In *Sexual Politics* she analyzed *male* sexual politics and identified the cause of sexism as the male patriarchial system. In *Flying* she presents her *female* sexual politics and offers a solution—a bisexual culture or, as she calls it, a "freer sexual culture." All the characteristics typical of women's autobiographies that we find in *Flying* are informed by Millett's vision of a dual or fused sexual culture.

This is evident, for example, in her positive treatment of men, who, she feels, are part of the revolution to destroy the patriarchal system. First, there is her husband, Fumio, who loves her, leads his own creative life, and accepts her woman lovers. Then there are two friends, Paul, who is struggling with his disintegrating marriage; and Fred, who has recently discovered his bisexuality after two decades of marriage. There are the men of the gay liberation movement in London who help to pattern the brain-damaged child of Millett's friends. There is an anonymous man who gives her a ride on the freeway after she runs out of gas because he wanted to do something nice to counter the brutal rape of his seventy-year-old mother. And then there is Van Arsdale, the all-American with know-how who offers her a chartered plane after she misses her scheduled flight to a conference on violence in New York City.

Millett's challenge to separatism—a vital issue to the lesbian movement, newly vocal, out-front, and proud—was just one of the reasons she was considered a rebel, even an "outcast" by the women's movement as a whole. In the early seventies, the National Organization for Women (NOW), representing the majority of feminists in the United States, was aghast when the "philosopher" of the fledgling movement admitted her "deviance" publicly, fearing it would damage NOW's credibility. The minority of lesbians may have been pleased, but the majority of heterosexuals wanted her to be silent. By the late seventies NOW endorsed lesbianism and bisexuality as part of a woman's freedom to choose her sexual partners and to have control over her own biological destiny. But in the interim, Millett opened up a Pandora's box of controversy.

Another reason for Millett's reputation as a rebel was her pacifism. Near the close of *Flying* she discusses the conference on violence and the women's movement. Contrary to the other feminist speakers on the issue, Millett "comes out" once again, this time for nonviolence. She argues: "How do you preserve the purity of revolution when you have already committed crimes in its name?"[1] Change, she says, can come about only by changing the conduct of human life itself. "If we are to succeed, if change is to come there must be mercy. There must finally be love" (629). Such a pacifist stand did little to endear Millett to the women's movement, and it accentuated her feeling of being different from others, a trait she shared with earlier autobiographers.

Another characteristic of *Flying* that is consistent with the female autobiographical tradition is its concentration on areas outside the mainstream of society. While feminists struggle to bring feminism—in Millett's case, bisexuality or bisexual politics—into the mainstream society so that women's experience is not considered peripheral, the women's movement at the time of *Flying* was—and still is—peripheral to the patriarchal culture. Conversely, though Millett refers to some "male" political events, such as the Vietnam War, the atrocities in Bangladesh, and a moon flight, they are the ones that are peripheral to her culture.

Flying also exhibits most of the disjunctive stylistic features we have come to associate with the women's autobiographical tradition. Although each of the book's five parts proceeds chronologically, within each part the narrative is nonlinear and nonprogressive. The time sequence is even more chaotic than Stein's or Hellman's "jungle of memories," with flashbacks within flashbacks, far distant experiences mingling with both more recent and immediate past experiences. There are also flashforwards of varying future times, often mixed into the flashbacks, creating a narrative similar to stream of consciousness. There is, however, a conscious ordering principle to this fragmented narrative—a controlled free association of events and feelings. There is control also of sentence structure, though like Stein's, the writing seems a jungle of fragments. Sentences are truncated, often without grammatical subjects or consisting only of phrases, dependent clauses, or just isolated words. Periodically, there are passages that are chronological, progressive, and strictly grammatical, but many more resemble the kind of shorthand writing characteristic of diaries and notebooks.

Because free association is the dominant mode of this autobiography, fully shaped anecdotes, vignettes, and portraits are rare. When they appear, they constitute the only continuous passages. These islands of linear clarity, such as the dramatic account of the Columbia University riots, the Christopher Street gay liberation march, and the nightclub act of the female impersonator Danny La Rue, provide a welcome relief from the chaotic, free-associative narrative.

The absence of anecdotes in *Flying* is significant because instead of focusing on others, indirectly revealing personal feelings and behavior, Millett focuses directly and intimately on herself. Her aim is not to entertain readers with amusing or interesting stories, which accounts for her earnestness and lack of humor, but to take her audience along with her on a painful voyage of self-discovery. Free association is more appropriate than anecdote for Millett's "search," for defining herself as she writes.

Moreover, Millett uses none of the other typical forms of indirection: omission, camouflage, obliqueness, or understatement. *Flying* is all heart and soul, her affirmation of women's strength. Like Rousseau's *Confessions,* it is an exposé of vulnerable feelings, especially those connected with adult love or sexual relationships. The direct influence on Millett, however, is not Rousseau's work but Doris Lessing's. When the two women met in London, Lessing told her:

> The most curious thing is that the very passages that once caused me the most anxiety, the moments when I thought, no, I cannot put this on paper—are now the passages I'm proud of. That comforts me most out of all I've written. Because through letters and readers I discovered these were the moments when I spoke for other people. So paradoxical. Because at the time they seemed so hopelessly private. (444)

Whereas Lessing's breakthrough was behind a third-person fictional character, Millett breaks new ground in autobiography in her first-person disclosure of intimacies. Millett answered Lessing during this interview:

> But I'm always embarrassed. Have so much to be self-conscious about. Doing it in the first person which seems necessary somehow, much of the point is lost in my case if I didn't put myself on the line. But feeling so vulnerable, my god, a Lesbian. Sure, an experience of human beings. But not described. Not permitted. It has no traditions. No language. No history of agreed values. (444)

The intimacy is evident in three areas that are usually restrained or eliminated entirely from other autobiographies. First, as we have seen in Stanton's *Eighty Years and More,* political figures usually protect their cause or constituency by hiding any weaknesses or factionalism. Millett boldly exposes the confusion and infighting within the women's movement about the issue of lesbianism. She portrays some movement leaders as heavies, others as warm and sincere people. She treats the lesbian leaders honestly, neither glorifying them nor being overly severe. She also deals directly with two other problems within the movement: the overlapping questions of elitism and the conflict between the individual's creative needs and her responsibility to the collective. About elitism, Millett writes:

> It's a double bind; can't quit and can't stay in there either. All the while the movement is sending double signals; you absolutely must preach at our panel, star at our conference—implying fink if you don't . . . and at the same time laying down a wonderfully uptight line about elitism. . . . But I agree with anti-elitism. Despite the countless sermons against elitism I've observed to come from dogmatic adolescents or envious females, each spinning in her own righteous circle, tripping on ambition, making herself famous in her own little pond for her superior insights. (115)

In wrestling with the decision about the credits for her documentary film *Three Women,* Millett must decide how much recognition she will give herself and how much the all-female camera crew. As the person who conceived, financed, directed, and edited the film, should she single herself out in any way from the others for whom the filming became both a consciousness-raising and a collective experience? She opts for the "elitist" credit of filmmaker-director, while continuing her collective commitments by regularly attending her consciousness-raising group and by speaking at demonstrations and conferences.

Actually, the writing of *Flying* is another demonstration of her commitment both to her own creative and personal needs and to the women's movement. The book was motivated by a need to purge herself of her private agony at dealing with sudden fame and notoriety and also by a realization that such self-investigation would have value for others.

> I did realize my scheme was in bad taste, a divulgence superfluous even before one considers its impropriety. . . . One reason I thought it worth doing is because I'm fairly sure that had someone tried to tell me all this I would have been interested. . . . If a feeling of misplaced pride in my own work led me to sign a book before, owning up to this one—despite any masochistic overtones—is also the mandatory acknowledgment of fact, even if it be error.
>
> You may well ask how I expect to assert my privacy by resorting to the outrageous publicity of being one's actual self on paper. There's a possibility of it working if one chooses the terms, to wit: outshouting image-gimmick America through a quietly desperate search for self. And being honest enough. (101, 103)

Certainly, Millett was honest enough.

In addition to allowing herself to appear vulnerable to the public by confronting controversial political issues, Millett also reveals her personal fears, doubts, and weaknesses. She admits her lack of confidence and wonders if she is brave enough to be completely honest. She exposes her desperate need for women's love and also her fear of their rejection. She bickers and competes with her sister and pleads for her mother's acceptance and love. She disparages her speeches and the misplaced adoration of her audiences. She is easily taken in by the excuses of her friends, feels responsible for all the world's ills, and is always being "understanding" and the peacemaker instead of expressing justifiable anger. In short, she portrays herself as she feels: self-effacing, insecure, whining, emotionally helpless, sentimental, and often overly demanding.

Finally, Millett admits and demonstrates strong sexual needs, not stopping with her feelings of attraction but describing in detail the sexual act itself. Were she a man, the reader might find the passages normal, believable, or expected, but for a woman—and a woman loving women—Millett runs the risk of being labeled "promiscuous," "abnormal," or "pornographic."[2]

These literal and lyrical descriptions of the sex act between women had never been described before in autobiography. The leading predecessors for intimate sexual portrayal are, ironically, the three writers whose works Millett deplored in *Sexual Politics:* D. H. Lawrence, Henry Miller, and Norman Mailer. In her literary analysis, Millett attacked their ignorance and disdain of the woman's point of view and their assumption of the male view as universal. In *Flying* she transforms the power politics of competitive male sex into the passionate affairs of love and friendship of women's experiences. She makes no attempt to interpret the male sexual response in the equally lyrical passages of lovemaking with Fumio, which are entirely about her own positive reactions.

Although the other two areas of intimacy—problems within the women's movement and her own fears and doubts—are given substantial attention in *Flying,* they are subsidiary to the sexual theme. Since the book plots Millett's search for her sexual identity and ultimately affirms the bisexual or dual culture, it is the sexual theme that informs the book and dictates what she includes and what she omits. Ironically, what is excluded from *Flying* are the subjects most autobiographies include—the chronicle of her childhood, her early family life, her education, and her early adult life before the onset of her mature work and personal relationships. Unlike Stein, who excludes these out of disdain for the concept of psychological development, Millett omits most aspects of her early life because they are not relevant to the theme of her autobiography. The little that she does include about her childhood, education, religion, and early life before the publication of *Sexual Politics* has been selected specifically for its connection to her sexual growth.

Most of Millett's childhood memories, set within the framework of her Catholic upbringing and schooling, are subsumed under the sexual theme. As a preteen she is almost raped when she accepts a ride from a stranger during a blizzard, mistaking him for a family friend. Afterward, she experiences the trauma of having to hide the incident from her parents and her religious teacher for fear of being blamed for the encounter.

> There's nothing to do but remember. Over and over. This secret. The blue Mercury. His face sort of blurry. The terrible purple thing. Then running. It keeps happening. If I yell no one hears me, the house is empty. Will he find out where I live, get me, tell on me? Face hot, sweating, is it the fever, I wonder. It's a sin and thinking is a sin. How do I stop it from happening? (12)

This and other passages indicate the extent to which she was aware at an early age of her sexual feelings. It is at school, watching the nuns at prayer in the silent chapel, that she experiences her first sexual stirrings. It is at her Catholic high school that she experiences her first crush on a girl. Though she loves her passionately and publicly announces it, she is the one to reject—self-righteously in her fright—her friend's physical overture. It is not until Millett goes to college that she experiences her first physical and serious love affair with a woman.

Millett's heterosexual experiences as a teenager and young woman are treated routinely, including her first affair with a man. The fact that she reveals no anger toward men in this autobiography may be traced to her attitude toward her father. Though she tells us about his alcoholism, his frequent beatings of her and her sisters, and his abandonment of the family when she was thirteen, nonetheless, she still feels the adoration that her face shows in a picture taken with him when she was four. This explains, in part perhaps, her compatibility with the gentle Fumio, with whom she lived monogamously for eight years. There is no question, however, that her affairs with women contemporaneous with *Sexual Politics* and its aftermath take priority in this autobiography.

Although there is a great deal of eroticism in *Flying,* it is all within the context of the intense emotional relationships Millett is working through with her lesbian friends. She is also striving to reconcile problems with her heterosexual female friends. Millett presents a wide spectrum of women to show how they react to her lesbianism. Of the six women who figure prominently in her life study, three are heterosexuals, one is bisexual, and two are lesbians.

First, there is her mother, who was stunned by the public announcement of her daughter's sexual preference and outraged lest she publish a memoir about her lesbian life. Millett confronts the difficult problem that faces all homosexuals—dealing with their parents' rejection of their sexual choice. She makes it very clear that one of her main reasons for writing *Flying* is to try to explain her life to her mother in the hope that she will accept her. Early in the autobiography, Millett writes: "Mother is the heart of the matter. . . .What if she could ever let me be? What even if she'd just climb out of my gut, some triumph of my own delivering myself of her?" (262). Her rebirth requires a long labor. By exposing in this book all that her mother might consider shameful, Millett delivers herself of all fear of exposure. The process of writing the book becomes her rite de passage. Near the end, she writes: "Thinking of my mother, dedicate it to her she will receive me at last who I am" (670). This kind of disclosure of Millett's feelings toward her mother is rare in women's autobiographies. Though more women today are writing about their mothers, the recognition of a shared place as sisters with a common history of oppression is difficult to achieve, probably because it clashes with oedipal forces.

In her relationship with her younger sister, Mallory, Millett bares the rivalry and envy often typical of sisters. Mallory urges her not to write this memoir about her lesbianism for their mother's sake. She calls Millett's love of more than one person at a time both promiscuous and greedy. Cynical, tough, independent, and bitter after a failed marriage, Mallory vacillates between supporting her sister's movement activities and accusing her of being a "Hitler," a "fanatic," and a "star." Though Millett classifies her with "all the younger sisters in the movement who hate me for the media trip, ambitious themselves but purists" (567), in a moment of warmth, she writes:

> We have transcended the circumstances of being sisters. Escaped the family. The feuds. Become friends. It is what we want to be. But we are not yet. The picture is a lie and the truth. . . . The savagery of our love bumping against the inarticulate of the forbidden. How much of lust is there in my impossible affection? How much of revenge in her denial? How much of greed to be each other in each of us? Mallory wants my substance. I want her glamour. The safety of her carefree. And its righteousness. I am helpless before her judging eyes, I am a bug splayed

upon the floor, needing her approval to go on crawling. The one thing she must withhold. Because her eyes had imagined an eagle, Mallory proud and loyal before her greatest disappointment. (572)

Millett has similar difficulties with her filmmaker friend from England. Nell's marriage is on the rocks, but she refuses a lesbian relationship with Millett, who considers such an affair the natural consequences of loving and trusting someone. Like Mallory, Nell is upset by Millett's ability to love more than one person at a time. She also tries to make her relate to Fumio as a wife instead of as a friend she loves. Despite their differences, Nell and Millett remain friends.

Millett's relationships with her sexual female friends are equally fraught with struggle and attempts at resolution. Vita begins her bisexual life with Millett and soon wants to take charge not only of the typing of her correspondence and the manuscript of the autobiography but also to control her life. Throughout the book Millett struggles to understand Vita, who is attempting to make a new life of her own after two decades of marriage and a family. Though the two women become better nonsexual friends than they were lovers, their encounters are still contentious. But Millett, grateful to Vita for her help during a period of depression and a writing block, works at holding the friendship together.

Clearly, however, the central relationship in this book is that between Millett and Celia, the lover who rejected her. Close on the publication of *Sexual Politics,* that rejection contributed to the "vertigo" or madness described at the onset of the autobiography. For Millett, Celia represented a "new life." "I can't explain, it was an idea I loved, a vision she gave me of how to live, but we couldn't. . . . Or maybe it was that Celia was the most delightful person I'd ever met, the greatest joy to be with, the most laughs" (564). It is Millett's love for Celia that makes *Flying* in many respects a love story. Her remorse at her loss, her efforts to restore the relationship, and finally her acceptance of the reality of their nonsexual friendship combine to make her love of Celia a major motif of the autobiography. Millett's working through her emotional dependency on Celia parallels her labors to give up her need for her mother's acceptance.

The transitional pains are relieved by the development of a new love affair with Claire, who appears intermittently throughout the book until the last section, "Landfall," which she dominates. Claire discourages Millett's habits of demeaning herself and "smothering her lovers with adoration." She will not allow Millett to sacrifice her work for their relationship, which in the past placed a burden of guilt on her female lovers. Though ethereal and mystical, Claire, through her integrity and devotion, gives Millett the security she needs to trust herself again and to believe that she is worth a woman's love. She will always love Celia, but she no longer feels enslaved by her passion for her. In Claire she has transcended her fear of rejection to a new kind of love based on mutual independence *and* dependence.

This fusion in her relationship with Claire is only one of many of Millett's efforts to resolve apparent opposites, polarities, ambivalence, or paradox. *Within* the women's autobiographical tradition of fragmentation and multidimensionality, Millett demonstrates a positive fusion or synthesis of the "fragments" of her life. In all her interactions with women, she traces the progression of her feelings from confusion and disorder to those of union or synthesis. With her mother, she will have truth *and* her mother's acceptance of that truth. With Mallory, Nell, and Vita, she retains their friendship despite their many differences in opinion and life-style. With Celia, she realizes her freedom *and* her eternal bond of love for her. With Claire, she achieves her independence *and* continues her dependence.

In the political arena also, Millett fuses seemingly disparate positions: gay liberation combined with women's liberation, the freedom of the artist and the responsibilities of the political leader, the private person and the public figure. In writing this autobiography about finding her self, she also *gives* the book to everyone. Essentially, the reason for the extreme honesty and revelation of her intimate emotional and physical life comes out of her commitment to changing human conduct for that "new life" where patriarchal rule is ended. Her vision of an integrated bisexual world requires her to integrate seemingly disparate elements of her own life, which she sees, therefore, as both personal/sexual *and* political. Her "life" is her sexual politics.

Flying also demonstrates this same fusion in its style. Taking Stein as her model for "saying new things in such novel ways,"[3] Millett sought a new form for her "new life" and created a "new autobiography" from a synthesis of three genre traditions: the historical, the literary/fictional, and the autobiographical.

Millett does not hide her self-consciousness about the style of *Flying* or its new form. In fact, to a large extent, the book is about its own composition, certainly a major motif that runs parallel to the attempts at thematic synthesis. Millett wants the book to document her life as it happens and thus become a new kind of documentary history. At one point, she insists that the book is not literature but a new way of writing about women's experience. In what was originally meant to be a conventional preface but was incorporated after the first hundred pages, Millett writes: "*It had occurred to me to treat my own existence as documentary*" (101; emphasis hers). Throughout the book, this statement is repeated in various ways: "It's a record as I go along doing my thing. Like a documentary. Since I did those three other women in my film, it seemed only fair to subject myself to the same process. It demands I remember everything and be honest" (244). Millett is attempting to synthesize the objective and the subjective in the forms used for communicating, just as she attempts to fuse the boundaries between the sexes and between the personal and the political. Annette Kolodny writes:

> In expanding the *content* of autobiographical narrative, revealing things that have not previously found their way into women's prose, Millett was not only a self-styled political revolutionary intent upon "a transvaluation of values," but a conscious artist attempting an alteration 'of the very *forms of apprehension.*' "[4]

Millett herself writes: "I'm so tired of the old one-dimensional notions of things, the media, even the square historians, they catch nothing at all" (384).

A forerunner of *Flying*'s attempt at destroying the line between the objective and the subjective in nonfiction was Norman Mailer's *Armies of the Night,* an effort to combine history and autobiography. In the journalistic sections of *Flying,* where the narrative is most linear and chronological (her excellent reportage on gay marches and women's conferences), Millett's style most resembles the dramatic writing of *Armies.* But there the resemblance ends, for there is a wide disparity between Mailer's "improvisational" history and Millett's free-associative narrative, between his third-person character named "Mailer" and her first-person narrator, though the aim of the two writers—to fuse the personal and the historical—is similar, as it is with many writers of the "new journalism."

In the process of creating a "new autobiography" to fit the new ways women are living and feeling, Millett adapts not only the methodology of history to her personal narrative but also past literary conventions and techniques. Her knowledge of classical literary tradition is evident in the overall conception of her life study as an odyssey. *Flying* is intended as a modern *Odyssey,* one woman's journey of self-discovery and self-affirmation. In *Flying,* the journey is an inner one, a search into the very core of one's being—one's sexual identity. Millett's metaphorical vehicle of travel is not, however, an ancient ship but the contemporary airplane and automobile. Her academic background is also evident in innumerable allusions to Dante, his *Commedia*—her journey taking her through a similar hell—but especially *La vita nuova*—*Flying* describes the new life Millett is trying to fashion for herself after the "death" of *her* ideal love. Celia is her Beatrice, giving Millett new life by restoring her poetic self to her. A musician by profession and temperament, Celia revives the "Celtic twilight" of Millett's Irish heritage. The freeing of her poetic imagination allows her to write about herself as she feels and talks and to abandon the "academic manner—distant, ironic, mandarin."[5]

Though Millett feels free now to abandon the detached and impersonal style of academic criticism, she has not completely forgotten her intellectual training. She is aware of those literary techniques that can be employed to further her aim of creating a form that both captures the spontaneity of her feelings and results in a crafted work. Thus, she adapts a number of fictional techniques that further this synthesis. Each technique is consciously chosen for each part of the book to render the emotional states described therein.

First, she chose the narrative mode of free association from modern fiction, with its flashbacks and flashforwards, in order to capture the fragmentation of women's experience of reality. No doubt, she incorporated many passages of her notebooks directly into *Flying:*

> Why are there two versions of that first trip to Oxford? Read them both in and choose later. Frantic over a missing link. The order forming itself and then lost again. Should I change a word? Do. And find it less satisfactory. Stick by the original. Have faith in the notebooks' first feel of it. . . . How will I appear? Just fuck it and read it all in. You can always revise later. Already guilty knowing I won't revise enough. (420)

But there is also much evidence that a very conscious process of selection and revision went into the final product.[6] Part One, "Vertigo," takes place entirely in Millett's mind as she free-associates about all the problems that make her feel that she is going mad. This is the most chaotic mixture of past and future associations in the book, and the reader experiences the same "confusion, loss, and disjunction"[7] that Millett does. There is also a great deal of discontinuity in the middle sections of the book, especially whenever she is in New York or London, moving frenetically from one meeting, demonstration, film screening, or friend's house to another. But she also has periods of calm, which are expressed in those linear journalistic anecdotes that provide relief from the chaotic associative narrative. In Part Five there is one last frantic scene when Millett searches for her car in crowded Provincetown, desperate to catch the scheduled flight to the conference on violence. Otherwise, this last part of the book, its most serene section, offers the most linear and chronological narrative of all the five parts. Thus, we see a progression in the narrative style from total discontinuity to relative order, revealing Millett's skill in having the formal elements of the narrative mirror the changing emotional states of her life story.

Another indication of Millett's literary borrowing and craft is in the use of the "flying" image to symbolize her emotional states. Autobiography is not a genre known for its use of metaphor or symbol. Henry Adams, a historian and novelist, is one of the few autobiographers to view his life within a symbolic framework, in his case, the polarity between the medieval Virgin and the contemporary Dynamo. Instead of such precise symbols, Millett uses the flying image to suggest a variety of meanings. We see this first in the symbolic division of the book according to the vehicles of her "movements." In the first three parts, her frantic movements are appropriately expressed in terms of transatlantic flights between England and New York. In Part One she flies from England to New York; Part Two ends with her flying from New York to England; and Part Three ends with her flying back to New York. In the last two parts there is a diminution of tension, and all movement takes place within the United States; here she usually travels by automobile, with a brief trip on a small chartered plane, and, finally, when there is complete calm, by sailboat.

But "flying" also represents madness, unreality, and chaos; escape and adventure; freedom and containment; love and vulnerability; and, finally, sexual ecstasy, transformation, and synthesis. Literally and figuratively, these more subtle images occur in all five parts of the book, but there is a definite progression of emphasis in her flying images—as in her associative narrative—from madness and fragmentation to serenity and synthesis.

In Part One, appropriately called "Vertigo," "flying" signifies madness and unreality. Its first chapter is entitled "Fugue State," and both definitions of *fugue* fit the tormented state of her mind. As in the musical composition, several motifs or problems are juxtaposed contrapuntally in this first section; they are gradually developed through various complex stages until they build up to a remarkable climax. During the initial flight from England to New York, every form of rejection bombards her: the media's attack on *Sexual Politics,* her mother's horror at the revelation of her sexual preference, Celia's rejection of her love, and her own rejection of an academic career for the precarious one of personal expression, represented by the film and this autobiography. Appropriately, as "Fugue State" ends,

Millett's plane lands in a storm. The psychiatric definition of a "fugue" state, one in which the patient suffers from acute anxiety and disorientation as the result of a loss of memory, describes here not a loss of memory but the kind of Dantean purgatory or Laingian hell that Millett undergoes in Part One.

In Part Two, "flying" refers to both "escape" and "adventure." This section does not have a "flying" title, but it is clear that what the title, "The New Life," conceptualizes is still unformed and unresolved. Her friend Vita, who dominates this section, is also seeking a new life to fit her name. She accuses Millett of vacillating between "superwoman and broken wing" (164), either attempting the impossible—the film and this book—or whining like a vulnerable child. She escapes this maze of confusion not with the wings of the lengendary Daedalus but in a contemporary analogue, a plane chartered by the Daedalus company, and lands safely in England.

In Part Three, "Blick. The English Notebook," which refers to the actual notebook she purchased in London and in which she wrote most of the autobiography, she feels free as a bird at first, only to find herself later grounded and caged by her involvement in her friends' problem of patterning their brain-damaged child. That is why this section emphasizes flying images of both freedom and containment. She writes:

> We are all three caged in this house. I flew in, arriving solitary, free as a bird on my wings, and they talked to me, said they were trapped. And now it's all three of us, the rescuer too is stuck. My job was to dig them out. Preposterous meddling. (376)

But it is by "meddling" that she frees herself and Nell and Paul when she engages the men of London's gay liberation movement to help pattern their child.

Part Four captures Millett's state of mind with new emphasis on the flying image—love and vulnerability. The projectile in flight in the title "Trajectory" refers to her life—both the real one and the actual book. The "paths" of both can be "plotted" in several simultaneous dimensions at once throughout the book. Millett divides this part into two "paths," "Ascent" and "Descent"; the former reflects her experiences with her friends and the smooth writing of the book; the latter traces her depression after her confrontations with these friends and her sister and also her insecurity about her upcoming rendezvous with Claire in Provincetown.

In Part Five, "Landfall," Millett "sights land," comes to trust her love for Claire and Claire's love for her. Here the emphasis in the flying images is on sexual ecstasy, transformation, and synthesis. Subtitled "Provincetown," the gay artist colony, this last section portrays her woman-identified love flourishing in peace and calm. When she charters a plane to attend the women's conference on violence, she feels "reborn" because she has at last not let her love for someone interfere with her political responsibilities. When she returns to Provincetown, completely at peace with herself, Millett alternately uses images of the sea and the sky. The sea reflects the serenity she feels with Claire in her sailboat—a modern vehicle of her odyssey's fulfillment. The clear blue sky with gulls circling overhead, diffuse and uncountable but beautiful in their disorder, is the last image she gives us. The last line of the book is "Chaos and serenity together" (678).

Thus, thematically and stylistically, Millett has expanded autobiographical form by fusing the documentary completeness of history with the artistic shaping of literature and the personal truth of autobiography. Her idea of personal truth, however, is a step forward in the autobiographical tradition. Shumaker wisely noted in 1954 that the autobiographer "is likely to explore milieux and vicissitudes concerning which there is no literary tradition."[8] The women's autobiographical tradition gave Millett a context for writing about herself as a multidimensional woman. What she contributed to the tradition is the affirmation of the "fragmented" woman. She is the New Woman, who can fulfill many roles—filmmaker, writer, sculptor, teacher, literary and social critic, political leader, daughter, sister, friend, and lover—and synthesize them into a New Life, a new way of conducting one's life in a utopian "freer sexual culture." Millett is no longer restricted by the solutions that Stanton and Stein opted for in their struggle with the "feminization of the mind/body problem,"[9] for she has transcended that dialectic. She has come a long way from the earliest women autobiographers, who recorded and dramatized "self-realization and self-transcendence through the recognition of another."[10]

Epilogue

In the years since *Flying,* the impetus to write autobiographies has not flagged. In fact, more women than ever before have written and are writing their life studies. The late seventies was a particularly fertile period as a result of a decade of feminist activism and consciousness raising, which gave legitimacy and affirmation to women's lives. Today, autobiographers no longer apologize for writing about themselves; if anything, it has become commonplace to write an autobiography. Writing now as a natural consequence of living—not necessarily with a long life or even a career to the author's credit—many autobiographers are motivated by the same impetus as their nineteenth-century ancestors, to appeal to popular interest—often, today, to make money. But some are writing with the same impulse that has inspired generations of seekers of self-knowledge.

Every conceivable category—some old, some new—has had its contributors, and a number of women have written multiple autobiographies. They have been greeted by a public eager to read about well-known women and about unknowns who are being rediscovered and their life studies reprinted. Autobiographies have been written by women from every possible perspective: widowed women, adopted women, veterans of the Vietnam War, sportswomen, artists, blind women, politicians, the wives of famous (and not-so-famous) men, feminists, teachers, prostitutes, journalists, art collectors, literary critics, singers, women who sailed around the world, sculptors, immigrants, survivors of concentration camps in Europe and internment camps in America, nuns, servants, social workers, activists of all sorts, doctors, factory workers, dancers, and so on. There has also been a large number of life studies by women proud of their ethnic backgrounds who had not written autobiographies with that attitude before: Native American women, Jewish women, Chicanas, and Asian Americans. Also prolific during the late seventies and early eighties have been autobiographies from that once verboten profession, acting, with autobiographers now willing to tell all—if not always about themselves, then certainly about others in the world of "the show business." There have also been many more life studies by writers, and the publication of multivolumes of their letters, journals, and/or diaries, as well as those by earlier writers, is a frequent occurrence.

This spate of autobiographical writing in the last decade and a half has not resulted in works significantly different in characteristics from those in the women's autobiographical tradition that we have documented from antiquity to Millett's *Flying.* What *has* changed over the years has been the subjects the authors discuss—from religious to secular, from an exciting portion of their lives to their whole lives; the self-image they project—from apologetic to ambivalent to self-affirming; and variations on the forms their self-portraits take—from episodic diaries and histories to personal narratives to dramatic portraits and free association. In other words, there has been a gradual progression in sophistication, which has been especially marked in this century, and even more so in recent decades.

Writing an autobiography is a vulnerable occupation, at least if one aims to convey more than facts. Psychologically painful experiences and elusive truths are difficult matters to expose to strangers. And when the autobiographer is a woman, the effort is fraught with even more trepidation.

For women have had a very different history from men in all realms, especially in the realm of promulgating the private self. As far back as Augustine, men who have written autobiographies have done so from the privileged position of social, economic, and political acceptance. For women, such affirmation has been slow in coming. While all autobiographies are in a way a defense of self, in the autobiographers we have discussed here—from Kempe to Cavendish, from Pilkington to Keckley, from Stanton to Millett—we find an even greater effort to rectify what they see as the public's misconception of them, an effort not only to authenticate who they really are but also to prove their worth as human beings.

As a result, most of the autobiographers we have studied, especially before the twentieth century, project a less than confident self-image. Even though in many of the autobiographies we may sense the authors' pride in themselves and their accomplishments, it is usually masked, understated, or presented modestly because of the expected negative response to their "vanity" in writing a life study at all, in believing that their experiences are "worthy" of an autobiography. This pride is evident, with more or less assertion, in several seventeenth- and eighteenth-century British memoirs, a few nineteenth-century American disguise and ex-slave narratives, and a number of the reform autobiographies of the late nineteenth and early twentieth centuries.

Even in recent decades, when more women are writing with the assurance and command usually associated with men's autobiographies, we still find in most women's autobiographies a sense of feeling *other,* of being *different* from the rest of society, even from other women. Even when they are proud of themselves and their achievements, even when they assert a positive self-image, what still emerges is a sense of being mavericks, outcasts, or, at the least, rebels against what society expects of them. They feel they are different from, other than, or outside the male world, a poor fit, indeed, in that world.

This sense of alienation from the male world is very real, but there also exists the positive delineation of a *female* culture, a *women's* world. If our autobiographers rarely focus on "worldly" events—those associated with men—or if they do so peripherally, it is because women are writing about *their* world of family, friends, and issues crucial to women's survival. If they write less about their professional lives, it is because it usually matters less to them than their personal/emotional accomplishments. Even when they emphasize their careers over matters of the heart, it is often with the motive of documenting one more woman's liberation.

Feeling different and other, however, women do not project the "unique" or "special" self-image that is usually found in men's autobiographies; nor do they see their lives as "mythic tales." They do not write in heroic tones about their lives or outline the progress of their souls. They rarely write metaphorically, and they do not see themselves as symbols or mirrors of their era. Like Hellman, they tend to see themselves as "unfinished."

However, contemporary women are more likely to view this sense of being unfinished more positively than earlier generations, who were more easily demoralized by their ambivalence—their divided loyalties between their work and the expected female roles. Today, this struggle continues, but with less self-deprecation. Now it may be condoned as a constructive *process* in becoming a self-affirmed human being.

This process of self-discovery, a less than confident self-image, and a feeling of difference may be one explanation for the forms and narrative style of women's autobiographies. They may begin as chronological narratives, since chronology helps give a sense of order and control over one's life. But it is soon superseded—usually unconsciously—by interruptions to that safe progression with anecdotes, even out of order, and all kinds of insertions—letters, articles, even descriptions by others. That has been women's autobiographical history from earliest times because chronological order does not seem to be sustainable in narratives with selves that are weak in focus, feel ambivalent, or are intent on portraying various and often conflicting roles.

Disjunctive narratives and discontinuous forms are more adequate for mirroring the fragmentation and multidimensionality of women's lives. With the onset of the twentieth century, stylistic choices seem to have become more conscious: Stanton's effort to distract her readers with anecdotes, Stein's scorn of the autobiographical mode with her incremental repetition and jumbled chronology, Hellman's reliance on drama for her portraits, and Millett's free association with its implied embrace of a wide range of life-styles. These disjunctive forms may serve—unconsciously—a protective function, a way of obscuring the lack of a retrospective, coherent, and holistic sense of self; just as the linear, unidimensional life studies by men may—also unconsciously—protect them from their vulnerable inner selves as they delineate what society expects of them, a life centered around a career.

Thirty years ago Richard Lillard listed ten techniques *not* to use when writing an autobiography: flashbacks, anecdotes, reconstructed scenes and dialogue, slabs of undigested diary or journal notes, set pieces on ancestors or parents, details of trips, random memories of youth, name dropping, racing too fast, and covering up—all characteristic of women's autobiographies. Although contemporary critics may disagree with Lillard's criteria—such as Hart, who considered that autobiographies express the "paradox of continuity in discontinuity," and Bruss, who accepted "disrupted narrative sequences and competing foci of attention"—nonetheless, most critics still dismiss or ignore women's autobiographies in their studies. Women's self-portraits are still classified as memoirs or reminiscences because of their episodic and anecdotal nature, their nonprogressive narratives, their fragmented forms, their focus on others, and their lack of heroic self-assertion, all of which are considered obstacles to the shaping of a "true" autobiography.

Clearly, the characteristics, definitions, and criteria outlined for male autobiographies in the Introduction do not fit the substantive and formal characteristics of female autobiographies, whose tradition reflects a strikingly different content and vehicle of expression. In the late seventies and early eighties, there have been more autobiographies by men who center on their personal lives, giving their careers less attention than in the past; and many of these display all the characteristics that Lillard condemned. No doubt, the effects of the women's movement and the human potential movement—which share some mutual goals—as well as the new journalism, have begun to validate for men the expression of concerns and forms similar to women's.

Any theory of autobiography that excludes experimentation—shapes that suit individual personalities—and relies on absolute definitions and forms, dooms the genre to extinction. Fortunately, autobiographers write on, undaunted and unaware of theoreticians. Especially pioneering in innovations are life studies by women from various ethnic backgrounds. Many of these women are creative writers—poets, novelists, and playwrights—long silent in autobiography, who are now "telling their story" in the same aesthetic mode as their other writings. While their works have the characteristics long associated with the women's autobiographical tradition—the focus on the personal within disjunctive narratives—it is their aesthetic mode that shapes the life studies, even when their works are informed by political consciousness. The result today is more autobiographies of enduring literary value.

This is the case with Hellman's autobiographies, which have sometimes been attacked for being "untruthful." By shaping her memoirs in dramatic portraits, Hellman angered that camp of "historical" autobiographical critics that wants—demands—factual honesty in a life study. But her work, like the fictionlike vignettes of Maya Angelou's poignant *I Know Why the Caged Bird Sings,* are shaped by an aesthetic that creates atmosphere, plumbs feelings, and pursues elusive, often psychological, truths. Maxine Hong Kingston's extraordinary *The Woman Warrior: Memoirs of a Girlhood among Ghosts* brings to autobiography a highly atypical sensibility. In combining the mythical world of her Chinese heritage with the realistic world of her adopted American homeland, Kingston has created a "magical chronicle"—which seems a contradiction in terms. It stretches the traditional limits of autobiography, as do the autobiographies by the poets Annie Dillard—the metaphysical nature chronicle *Pilgrim at Tinker Creek*—and Ntozake Shange—the "choreopoem" *For Colored Girls Who Have Considered Suicide / When the Rainbow Is Enuf;* as do also Judy Chicago's *Through the Flower: My Struggle as a Woman Artist* and Kim Chernin's beautifully crafted and sensitive amalgam of autobiography, biography, history, and fiction, *In My Mother's House.*

We see in these recent, especially ethnic, examples of the women's autobiographical tradition a rejection of prescriptive dicta. In their place are greater flexibility and creativity, where subject matter, the author's personality, and the form appropriate to both are inextricably one. In any reevaluation of autobiography, which I see under way, these and other recent writings by women must be recognized as enriching and expanding the genre's possibilities, contributing to a women's tradition whose respected place in the literary history of the genre is long overdue.

Notes

Preface

1. Estelle C. Jelinek, "A Comparison of Women's and Men's Autobiographies," paper presented at the Modern Language Association convention, New York, December 1976.

2. Estelle C. Jelinek, "Women's Autobiography and the Male Tradition," Introduction to *Women's Autobiography: Essays in Criticism* (Bloomington: Indiana University Press, 1980), 1–20.

3. William Matthews, comp., *British Autobiographies: An Annotated Bibliography of British Autobiographies Published or Written before 1951* (Berkeley: University of California Press, 1955); see also the Bibliography for bibliographies of British and American diaries compiled by Matthews. Louis Kaplan, comp., *A Bibliography of American Autobiographies* (Madison: University of Wisconsin Press, 1961). See also Carolyn H. Rhodes, comp., *First Person Female American: A Selected and Annotated Bibliography of the Autobiographies of American Women Living after 1950* (Troy, N.Y.: Whitston Publishing Co., 1980); and Mary Louise Briscoe, Barbara Tobias, and Lynn Z. Bloom, comps., *American Autobiography, 1945–1980: A Bibliography* (Madison: University of Wisconsin Press, 1982); the latter work appeared after I had done the basic research for my book, but it is an invaluable source, with every woman's autobiography asterisked for easy identification.

4. Over the years, I have come to call the traditional definitions and characteristics of autobiography *male* because of the exclusion of women's autobiographies.

5. A few of the many critics who have attributed different characteristics to women are Nancy Chodorow (a female role orientation), Carol Gilligan (a female morality), Lillian Rubin (a female approach in psychotherapy), Vivian Gornick (a female sensibility), Patricia Meyer Spacks (a female imagination), Ellen Moers (a female fictional tradition), Mary Hiatt (a female writing style), Robin Lakoff (a female language), Linda Mizejewski (a female imagery), and, of course, Virginia Woolf, who postulated a female sentence. See the Bibliography for the works of these critics.

Introduction
Autobiographical Criticism: An Overview

1. The present study aims to provide such a study of women's autobiographies.

2. A sampling of these critics include Donald A. Stauffer, *English Biography before 1700* (Cambridge, Mass.: Harvard University Press, 1930); Edward H. O'Neill, *A History of American Biography, 1800–1935* (Philadelphia: University of Pennsylvania Press, 1935); Arthur Melville Clark, *Autobiography: Its Genesis and Phases* (Edinburgh: Folcroft Press, 1935); and E. Stuart Bates, *Inside Out: An Introduction to Autobiography* (New York: Sheridan House, 1937).

3. Until 1980, the Modern Language Association's annual bibliography listed autobiographies under the heading "Biography." The first use of the word *autobiography* was by Robert Southey in his review of Portuguese literature in the *Quarterly Review* in 1809.

4. Edgar Johnson, *One Mighty Torrent: The Drama of Biography* (New York: Stackpole Sons, 1937), 27.

5. Matthews, *British Autobiographies*, and Kaplan, *Bibliography of American Autobiographies.*

6. Wayne Shumaker, *English Autobiography: Its Emergence, Materials, and Form* (Berkeley: University of California Press, 1954).

7. Barrett John Mandel, "The Autobiographer's Art," *Journal of Aesthetics and Art Criticism* 27 (1968):215.

8. Georges Gusdorf, "Conditions and Limits of Autobiography," in *Autobiography: Essays Theoretical and Critical*, ed. and trans. James Olney (Princeton: Princeton University Press, 1980), 43; originally "Conditions et limites de l'autobiographie," in *Formen der Selbstdarstellung*, ed. G. Reichenkron and E. Haase (Berlin: Duncker & Humblot, 1956), 105–23.

9. Roy Pascal, *Design and Truth in Autobiography* (Cambridge, Mass.: Harvard University Press, 1960), chap. 1.

10. Robert F. Sayre, *The Examined Self: Benjamin Franklin, Henry Adams, Henry James* (Princeton: Princeton University Press, 1964).

11. Stephen Spender, "Confessions and Autobiography," in *The Making of a Poem* (London: Hamish Hamilton, 1955).

12. Richard G. Lillard, *American Life in Autobiography: A Descriptive Guide* (Stanford: Stanford University Press, 1956).

13. Stephen A. Shapiro, "The Dark Continent of Literature: Autobiography," *Comparative Literature Studies* 5 (December 1968):436.

14. James M. Cox, "Autobiography and America," *Virginia Quarterly Review* 47 (Spring 1971): 253.

15. Albert E. Stone, "Autobiography and American Culture," *American Studies: An International Newsletter* 12 (Winter 1972):27–28; ten years later Stone's definition continued to serve him well—after a number of fine articles—in his *Autobiographical Occasions and Original Acts: Versions of American Identity from Henry Adams to Nate Shaw* (Philadelphia: University of Pennsylvania Press, 1982); see also Albert E. Stone, ed., *The American Autobiography: A Collection of Critical Essays* (Englewood Cliffs, N.J.: Prentice-Hall, 1981).

16. Francis R. Hart, "Notes for an Anatomy of Modern Autobiography," *New Literary History* 1 (Spring 1970):500.

17. James Olney, *Metaphors of Self: The Meaning of Autobiography* (Princeton: Princeton University Press, 1972).

18. Elizabeth W. Bruss, *Autobiographical Acts: The Changing Situation of a Literary Genre* (Baltimore: Johns Hopkins University Press, 1976), 164.

19. Karl J. Weintraub, *The Value of the Individual: Self and Circumstance in Autobiography* (Chicago: University of Chicago Press, 1978).

20. William C. Spengemann, *The Forms of Autobiography: Episodes in the History of a Literary Genre* (New Haven: Yale University Press, 1980).

21. Avrom Fleishman, *Figures of Autobiography: The Language of Self-Writing in Victorian and Modern England* (Berkeley: University of California Press, 1983), 37–38. Fleishman postulates "six classically influenced Christian motifs or topoi [or] 'figures' . . . [which] are natural childhood, fall and exile, wandering-journey-pilgrimage, the crisis, epiphany and conversion, and renewal and return" (478). Paul deMan, "Autobiography as De-facement," *Modern Language Notes: Comparative Literature* 94, no. 5 (December 1979):919–30. Paul John Eakin, *Fictions in Autobiography: Studies in the Art of Self-Invention* (Princeton: Princeton University Press, 1985).

22. Patricia Meyer Spacks, "Reflecting Women," *Yale Review* 63 (October 1973):26–42; Spacks, *The Female Imagination* (New York: Knopf, 1975); Spacks, *Imagining a Self: Autobiography and Novel in Eighteenth-Century England* (Cambridge, Mass.: Harvard University Press, 1976); Mary G. Mason, "The Other Voice: Autobiographies of Women Writers," in *Autobiography*, ed. Olney, 207–35; and Lynn Z. Bloom, "Promises Fulfilled: Positive Images of Women in Twentieth-Century Autobiographies," in *Feminist Criticism: Essays on Theory, Poetry, and Prose*, ed. Cheryl L. Brown and Karen Olson (Metuchen, N.J.: Scarecrow Press, 1978), 324–38.

23. Matthews, *British Autobiographies*, viii.

24. Gusdorf, "Conditions and Limits," 42.

25. James Olney, "Autobiography and the Cultural Moment," in *Autobiography*, ed. Olney, 3–27; Mason, "The Other Voice," in *Autobiography*, ed. Olney, 207–35.

26. Paul Delany, *British Autobiography in the Seventeenth Century* (New York: Columbia University Press, 1969); Dean Ebner, *Autobiography in Seventeenth-Century England: Theology and the Self* (The Hague: Mouton, 1971); A. O. J. Cockshut, *The Art of Autobiography in Nineteenth- and Twentieth-Century England* (New Haven: Yale University Press, 1984).

27. Daniel B. Shea, Jr., *Spiritual Autobiography in Early America* (Princeton: Princeton University Press, 1968); Mutlu Konuk Blasing, *The Art of Life: Studies in American Autobiographical Literature* (Austin: University of Texas Press, 1977); Thomas Cooley, *Educated Lives: The Rise of Modern Autobiography in America* (Columbus: Ohio State University Press, 1976); G. Thomas Couser, *American Autobiography: The Prophetic Mode* (Amherst: University of Massachusetts Press, 1979).

28. Janet Varner Gunn, *Autobiography: Toward a Poetics of Experience* (Philadelphia: University of Pennsylvania Press, 1982).

1. Earliest Stirrings: The Mystical Voice

1. See Helen Diner, *Mothers and Amazons* (New York: Anchor Books, 1973), 169.

2. See Miriam Lichtheim, *Ancient Egyptian Literature,* vol. 1, *The Old and Middle Kingdoms* (Berkeley: University of California Press, 1973).

3. Ibid., 15–22.

4. See Georg Misch, *A History of Autobiography in Antiquity,* 2 vols. (London: Routledge & Kegan Paul, 1950), 1:chap. 2; W. M. Flinders Petrie, ed., *Egyptian Tales* (New York: Benjamin Blom, 1971); and William Kelly Simpson, ed., *The Literature of Ancient Egypt* (New Haven: Yale University Press, 1972).

5. See John A. Garraty, *The Nature of Biography* (New York: Vintage Books, 1955), 34.

6. Misch, *History of Autobiography,* 1:76.

7. English translation by Eileen Berkun; the Latin is from *The Annals of Tacitus,* ed. Henry Furneaux, vol. 1 (Oxford: Clarendon Press, 1965): "id ego, a scriptoribus annalium non traditum, repperi in commentariis Agrippinae filiae, quae Neronis principis mater vitam suam et casus suorum posteris memoravit."

8. Misch, *History of Autobiography,* 1:259, 268–69.

9. My thanks to Ryoko Winter for her unpublished essay on these tenth-century diaries.

10. Julian of Norwich, *A Shewing of God's Love: The Shorter Version of Sixteen Revelations of Divine Love,* ed. Sister Anna Maria Reynolds (London: Longmans, Green, 1958). The longer version appears in P. Franklin Chambers, *Julian of Norwich: An Introductory Appreciation* (London: Victor Gollancz, 1955). See also the translation in Caroline Spurgeon, *Mysticism in English Literature* (Cambridge: Cambridge University Press, 1913); and a more recent edition: Julian of Norwich, *Showings,* trans. Edmund Colledge and James Walsh (New York: Paulist Press, 1978).

11. See Mary Grimley Mason and Carol Hurd Green, eds., *Journeys: Autobiographical Writings by Women* (Boston: G. K. Hall, 1979), 1–2.

12. Chambers, *Julian,* 41.

13. *The Book of Margery Kempe: A Modernized Version,* ed. W. Butler-Bowden, intro. R. W. Chambers (New York: Devin-Adair Co., 1944).

14. Margaret Bottrall, *Every Man a Phoenix: Studies in Seventeenth-Century Autobiography* (London: John Murray, 1958), 347.

15. Hope Emily Allen, Prefatory Note to *The Book of Margery Kempe,* ed. Sanford Brown Meech (London: Early English Text Society, 1940).

16. Bottrall, *Every Man a Phoenix,* 2.

17. Robert K. Stone, *Middle English Prose Style* (The Hague: Mouton, 1970), 29, quoting R. W. Chambers; see n. 13.

18. Ibid., 12.

19. Shumaker, *English Autobiography,* 16.

20. Pascal, *Design and Truth,* 25.

21. See Ann Haskell, "The Paston Women on Marriage in Fifteenth-Century England," *Viator* 4 (1973):459–71. Virginia Woolf, "The Pastons and Chaucer," in *The Common Reader* (New York: Vintage Books, 1953), notes: "The prattle of children, the lore of the nursery or schoolroom, did not find its way into these elaborate communications. For the most part her letters are the letters of an honest bailiff to his master" (7).

22. See Arthur Ponsonby, *More English Diaries* (London: Methuen & Co., 1927); and Harriet Blodgett, "Englishwomen's Diaries: Historical Backgrounds," *Women's Diaries* 4, no. 1 (1986):1, 3–5.

23. Cellini's autobiography was first published in 1728 and translated into English in 1771. Cardano's was first published in 1643 and translated into English in 1930.

24. Anna Robeson Burr, *The Autobiography: A Critical and Comparative Study* (Boston: Houghton Mifflin, 1909), 243.

25. Pascal, *Design and Truth,* 201.

26. E. Allison Peers, ed., *The Life of Teresa of Jesus* (New York: Doubleday, 1960), 18, 41, 43.

27. See the interesting study by Mason, "The Other Voice," in *Autobiography,* ed. Olney, 207–35. Mason argues that male autobiographies like Augustine's *Confessions,* "where the self is presented as the stage for a battle of opposing forces," do "not accord with the deepest realities of women's life-writing." Discussing Julian, Kempe, Margaret Cavendish, and Anne Bradstreet, Mason argues that "the self-discovery of female identity seems to acknowledge the real presence and recognition of another consciousness, and the disclosure of the female self is linked to the identification of some 'other' " (210).

2. The Seventeenth Century: Psychological Beginnings

1. Most were not printed for public distribution until the nineteenth century; see Cynthia S. Pomerleau, "The Emergence of Women's Autobiography in England," in *Women's Autobiography,* ed. Jelinek, 21–38.

2. See Howard H. Brinton, *Quaker Journals: Varieties of Religious Experience among Friends* (Wallingford, Pa.: Pendle Hill Publications, 1972); Luella Wright, *Literary Life of the Early Friends* (New York: Columbia University Press, 1932); and Owen C. Watkins, *The Puritan Experience* (London: Routledge & Kegan Paul, 1972). See also Metta L. Winter, " 'Heart Watching' through Journal Keeping: A Look at Quaker Diaries and Their Uses," *Women's Diaries: A Quarterly Newsletter* 1, no. 2 (Summer 1983):1–3.

3. Penington's daughter, Gulielma Maria Springett, married William Penn, which may account for the first publication of the autobiography in Philadelphia in 1848.

4. Delany, *British Autobiography,* 158–59. Despite all the "firsts" Delany

ascribes to the six women autobiographers he discusses, he segregates them in a brief chapter ("Female Autobiographers," 158–66) instead of integrating and juxtaposing their works with the less innovative male autobiographers he discusses throughout his study. (Because there is some interesting criticism on seventeenth-century women's autobiographies, I will quote several critics' remarks in these notes.)

5. Delany writes: "In general, female autobiographies have a deeper revelation of sentiments, more subjectivity, and more subtle self-analysis than one finds in comparable works by men" (ibid., 5).

6. Jean Lead, *A Fountain of Gardens Watered by the River of Divine Pleasure, and Springing Up in All Variety of Spiritual Plants* . . . (London: n.p., 1697–1701).

7. See Catherine F. Smith, "Jane Lead: Mysticism and the Woman Cloathed with the Sun," in *Shakespeare's Sisters: Feminist Essays on Women Poets*, ed. Sandra M. Gilbert and Susan Gubar (Bloomington: Indiana University Press, 1979), 3–18.

8. See Joan Goulianos, ed., *By a Woman Writt* (Baltimore: Penguin Books, 1973), 31–53.

9. See Antonia Fraser, *The Weaker Vessel: Women's Lot in Seventeenth-Century England* (New York: Knopf, 1984).

10. Lucy Hutchinson, *Memoirs of the Life of Colonel Hutchinson, with the Fragment of an Autobiography by Mrs. Hutchinson*, ed. and intro. James Sutherland (London: Oxford University Press, 1973), 278–89.

11. *Memoirs of Lady Fanshawe, Wife of the Right Hon. Sir Richard Fanshawe, Bart., Ambassador from Charles the Second to the Court of Madrid in 1665. Written by Herself. To Which Are Added Extracts from the Correspondence of Sir Richard Fanshawe* (London: Henry Colburn, 1829), 1–307; this was its first printing. A more recent edition by John Loftis is in *The Memoirs of Anne, Lady Halkett, and Ann, Lady Fanshawe* (New York: Oxford University Press, 1979).

12. See Delany, *British Autobiography*, 162.

13. See Stauffer, *English Biography*, 156. Shumaker is less impressed with Fanshawe's autobiography than Stauffer, whose interest is more historical than literary. Shumaker considers her memoirs among those that "are intended only for family circulation" and "confine themselves to a compact summary of employments, actions, visits, and social engagements" (*English Autobiography*, 65).

14. Delany sees the "feminine touch" in her "dramatic vignettes which interrupt the orderly exposition" (*British Autobiography*, 161). The anecdotes, he writes, are "enlivened and humanized by the addition of small, but significant, details such as the feminine eye did not scorn to notice and record" (164).

15. *Autobiography of Mary Countess of Warwick*, ed. T. Crofton Croker (London: Percy Society, 1848), 1–38.

16. Her father, Richard Boyle, Lord Coke, wrote *True Remembrances* in 1632; her brother, Robert Boyle, was the author of *An Account of Philaretus During His Minority*. Both were published in *The Life of Robert Boyle* (1734) by Thomas Birch.

17. The half-title page of the Everyman's Library edition (ed. Ernest Rhys) reads: *Margaret, Duchess of Newcastle: Life of the Duke, Memoirs of Her Own Life and Certain Sociable Letters.* The title page reads: "Memoirs of the Duchess," in *The Life of the (1st) Duke of Newcastle and Other Writings of Margaret Duchess* (London and Toronto: J. M. Dent & Sons; New York: E. P. Dutton & Co., n.d.), 187–213. In 1656 *True Relation* was published in *Natures Pictures Drawn by Fancies Pencil to the Life;* in 1667 it was republished in *The Life of William Cavendish.*

18. Virginia Woolf writes in her essay "The Duchess of Newcastle": "Order, continuity, the logical development of her argument are all unknown to her" (*Common Reader,* 74).

19. Delany notes, referring to the *Memoirs* (1618) of Sir Christopher Guise: "This tracing back of adult psychological problems to their roots in childhood experience is uncommon among seventeenth-century autobiographers" (*British Autobiography,* 144), but he neglects to note Cavendish's contribution.

20. Goulianos makes too much of Cavendish's criticism of such women; see *by a Woman writt,* 55.

21. See Angeline Goreau, *The Whole Duty of a Woman: Female Writers in Seventeenth-Century England* (New York: Dial Press, 1985). Shumaker is in error when he writes that David Hume's "Life" (1777) is the first to include a description of a writing career (*English Autobiography,* 25).

22. Delany: "In her ingenuous way she . . . reveal[s] much more about her personality than most autobiographers of her time. Moreover, her revelations show some awareness of subtle differences of temperament. . . . The line of development is unbroken from her work to a modern, subjective autobiography like Rousseau's" (*British Autobiography,* 160).

23. Bottrall calls it a "retrospective narrative, written when she was an elderly woman" (*Every Man a Phoenix,* 149). Halkett's is the only female autobiography discussed by Bottrall (149–60) in her study of seventeenth-century autobiographies.

24. It was published in abbreviated form as a "Life" in a collection of her religious writings in 1701; it was published in full—that is, up to 1656, where the narrative ends abruptly—in 1778. See *The Autobiography of Anne Lady Halkett,* ed. John Gough Nichols (Westminster: Camden Society, 1875), 1–107. (See also the 1979 Loftis edition, n.11 above.) Contrary to what is generally written, it was not published in an abridged form in *Memoirs of Several Ladies of Great Britain* (1752, 1775) by George Ballard (1706–55); Ballard's work is not an anthology of primary autobiographies, but a collection of short biographical sketches that he wrote along with paraphrased summaries of a few autobiographies.

25. Bottrall calls it "a thoroughly feminine document. It is neither reflective nor speculative; it is concerned with persons and actions, not with ideas. . . . [It] contains sufficient material for a full-length novel" (*Every Man a Phoenix,* 149).

26. Delany describes this incident as "a tempest in a tea cup, to which no male autobiographer would give so much importance" (*British Autobiography,* 163).

27. Ibid., 164.

28. Ibid.

29. Delany notes that "in all the secular autobiographies published during the seventeenth century I cannot recall any admission by the author of a serious misdeed or indiscretion" (ibid., 155).

30. Ibid., 164.

31. Shumaker calls Cavendish "eccentric" (*English Autobiography,* 20) probably because, as Goulianos observes, "to emphasize the absurdity with which a woman intellectual was viewed in her time, she often appeared in outlandish costumes" (*by a Woman writt,* 55).

32. Stauffer, *English Biography,* 209. Shumaker gives Cavendish's autobiography its due; her account is "full of psychological significance—and . . . can properly be regarded as a study of character" (*English Autobiography,* 92). He also believes that it antedates nineteenth-century "subjective" (male) autobiography.

3. The Eighteenth Century: Professional Beginnings

1. See Pomerleau, "Emergence of Women's Autobiography," in *Women's Autobiography,* ed. Jelinek, 21–38.

2. Pascal compares the authors to the fictional Moll Flanders (*Design and Truth,* 33); Shumaker calls them "dishonest and libertine" (*English Autobiography,* 24); Felicity Nussbaum, private communication, 1983.

3. *Memoirs of Mrs. Laetitia Pilkington, 1712–1750, Written by Herself, with an Introduction by Iris Barry* (London: George Routledge & Sons, 1928), 3 vols. in 1 (first ed., 3 vols., 1748–54).

4. Shumaker's bias surfaces throughout his otherwise astute discussion of Pilkington's autobiography. After reading her life study, I find his distortion of the facts almost amusing if not incredible. He writes: "Laetitia Pilkington and a few other vituperative women do their malicious best to bring their husbands into disrepute" (*English Autobiography,* 42).

5. Woolf, *Common Reader,* 120–21; see Woolf's spirited and brief but appreciative essay on Pilkington, 120–25.

6. "Pilkington's pride in what she has suffered far exceeds her pride in her authorship" (Spacks, *Imagining a Self,* 73). Spacks also errs in her interpretation of Pilkington's statement that she had many lovers by the time she was thirteen. Her meaning of "lovers" is "suitors," which seems clear from the context. Pilkington was mature for her age and often taken to be much older; her mother, however, refused to countenance male attentions to her daughter until the courtship of the rich (she thought) and pious minister Pilkington.

7. Delany, *British Autobiography,* 155.

8. It was issued in several numbers, then published in London by Phillips in three volumes, each number signed by her to verify its authenticity. See the Bibliography for her complete title.

9. Chapter 81 of Tobias Smollett's *Peregrine Pickle,* 2 vols. (London: J. M. Dent, 1956).

10. Emphasis hers. Vane's emotional appeal may have prompted Shumaker's comment: "Notwithstanding the interlarded sentiment, [it] is mainly *res gestae*" (*English Autobiography,* 65).

11. Walter Allen, Introduction to *Peregrine Pickle,* 1:ix.

12. Shumaker, *English Autobiography,* 23, 24.

13. *A Narrative of the Life of* Mrs. *Charlotte Charke, Daughter of Colley Cibber* (1755) (London: Constable & Co., 1929). The *Narrative* went through two printings in 1755 but was not republished until 1827.

14. Spacks writes that Charke's autobiography is a serious effort to come to terms with "her unaccountably alienated father" and that its "narrative incoherence (a frequent characteristic of early women's autobiographies) reflects her manifest difficulty in coming to terms with herself" (*Imagining a Self,* 75, 76).

15. Matthews, *British Autobiographies,* 241.

16. For an analysis of their autobiographies, see Estelle C. Jelinek, "Disguise Autobiographies: Women Masquerading as Men," *Women's Studies International Forum* (special issue on women's autobiographies) (1986).

17. See Mitzi Meyers, "Wollstonecraft's *Letters Written . . . in Sweden:* Toward Romantic Autobiography," *Studies in Eighteenth-Century Culture* 8 (1979): 165–85.

18. See Donald Stauffer, *The Art of Biography in Eighteenth-Century England* (Princeton: Princeton University Press, 1941).

4. The Nineteenth Century: New Voices

1. Shumaker, *English Autobiography,* 28.

2. *Memoirs of the Late* Mrs. *Robinson, Written by Herself* (London: Cobden-Sanderson, 1930), 1–131.

3. Shumaker errs once again, this time in describing Robinson's work as reading like a gothic novel. Only the first few paragraphs—describing her birth as told to her by her mother—have gothic elements (*English Autobiography,* 93).

4. *Medora Leigh: A History and an Autobiography, with an Introduction and a Commentary on the Charges Brought Against Lord Byron by* Mrs. *Beecher Stowe,* ed. Charles Mackay (London: Richard Bentley, 1869), 122–54.

5. Elizabeth Barrett Browning, *Hitherto Unpublished Poems and Stories, with an Inedited Autobiography,* 2 vols. (Boston: Bibliophile Society, 1914). 1:3–28. Both works were published as "Two Autobiographical Essays by Elizabeth Barrett," in *Browning Institute Studies,* ed. William S. Peterson, no. 2 (New York, 1974), 119–34.

6. Shumaker, *English Autobiography,* 28.

7. See *The Journals of Dorothy Wordsworth,* ed. Mary Moorman (London: Oxford University Press, 1971).

8. See also *The Letters of Mary Wollstonecraft Shelley,* ed. Betty T. Bennett, 2 vols. (Baltimore: Johns Hopkins University Press, 1980–).

9. See Sara Coleridge's (1802–52) *Memoirs and Letters* (1873); and Jane Welsh Carlyle's (1801–66) *Letters and Memorials* (1883) and *New Letters and Memorials of Jane Welsh Carlyle,* ed. Alexander Carlyle (London: John Lane, 1903); Duke University Press is preparing a complete edition of the *Collected Letters of Thomas and Jane Carlyle.*

10. Mary Russell Mitford, *Recollections of a Literary Life and Selections from My Favorite Poets and Prose Writers* (London: Richard Bentley, 1883). Her *Letters* were edited in 2 vols. by A. G. K. L'Etrange (1870).

11. Mitford, *Recollections,* vii. See Elizabeth Winston, "The Autobiographer and Her Readers: From Apology to Affirmation," in Jelinek, ed., *Women's Autobiography,* 93–111.

12. Charlotte Elizabeth, *Personal Recollections* (New York: Charles Scribner, 1858). The name *Tonna* does not appear anywhere in the book, not even on the title page.

13. First published serially as "Letters from the Rocky Mountains" in the genteel English weekly *Leisure Hour* in 1878; it was published in 1879 under its present title by John Murray in London and by G. P. Putnam Sons in New York. A modern edition was published in 1982 by Virago Press in London, with an introduction by Pat Barr.

14. Victoria Alexandrina Maria Louisa Stuart Wortley, who became the Honorable Lady Welby-Gregory, was important in the history of semiotics, wrote *Links and Clues* and *What Is Meaning?* and was an influential correspondent of Charles Sanders Peirce between 1903 and 1911.

15. Harriet Martineau, *Harriet Martineau's Autobiography,* ed. Maria Weston Chapman, 2 vols. (Boston: James R. Osgood, 1877).

16. See Mitzi Meyers, "*Harriet Martineau's Autobiography:* The Making of a Female Philosopher," in Jelinek, ed., *Women's Autobiography,* 53–70.

17. Shumaker argues that at the point where she describes acquiring a literary reputation, Martineau's narrative breaks down, revealing a "new self-confidence and even vindictiveness of character" (*English Autobiography,* 90; Shumaker does not explain his statement, frequently the case when he disparages female autobiographers). Ellen Moers interprets Martineau's self-confidence as a stoicism in reaction to the romanticism she saw in the works of Mary Wollstonecraft (*Literary Women* [New York: Doubleday, 1975], 20).

18. Annie Besant, *An Autobiography* (London: T. Fisher Unwin, 1908).

19. Frances Power Cobbe, *The Life of . . . ,* 2 vols. (Boston: Houghton Mifflin, 1894), 1:1–330, 2:331–648.

20. *The Autobiography and Letters of Mrs. M. O. W. Oliphant,* arranged and edited by Mrs. Harry Coghill (New York: Dodd, Mead & Co., 1899), 3–150. Unfortunately, the editor arranged the installments in the chronological order of

the events rather than in the order of their writing, presumably for the sake of historical clarity rather than autobiographical authenticity.

21. Spacks, *Imagining a Self,* 78.

5. Seventeenth and Eighteenth Centuries: Traditional Beginnings

1. See Kenneth A. Lockridge, *Literacy in Colonial New England* (New York: Norton, 1974), esp. 38–42. Also see Nancy F. Cott, *The Bonds of Womanhood: "Woman's Sphere" in New England, 1780–1835* (New Haven: Yale University Press, 1977), chap. 3.

2. Eve Merriam, ed., *Growing Up Female in America* (New York: Dell, 1971), 11.

3. William Matthews, comp., *American Diaries: An Annotated Bibliography of American Diaries Written prior to the Year 1861* (Berkeley: University of California Press, 1945); William Matthews, comp., *American Diaries in Manuscript, 1580–1954: A Descriptive Bibliography* (Athens: University of Georgia Press, 1974).

4. Laura Arksey, Nancy Pries, and Marcia Reed, comps., *American Diaries: An Annotated Bibliography of Published American Diaries and Journals,* vol. 1, *Diaries Written from 1492 to 1844* (Detroit: Gale Research Company, 1983). My totals based on Matthews's 1945 compilation of published diaries are as follows, with my totals from Arksey, Pries, and Reed given in parentheses:

	Women		*Men*	
(1492–1628)		(0)		(11)
Colonial Period, 1629–1774	30	(31)	700	(827)
Early Republic, 1775–1829	75	(90)	850	(1,354)
Age of Expansion, 1830–60	60		550	
(1826–44)		(107)		(450)

5. Briscoe, Tobias, and Bloom, *American Autobiography, 1945–1980;* it should be noted that this work includes many reprints of books published before 1945, as well as husband-wife autobiographies, some letters and journals, as-told-to narratives, some autobiographical novels, and even rare editions of the same book, so my rough total of 1,107 autobiographies by women for the period 1945–80 must be considered a *low* one-fourth.

6. Kenneth B. Murdock, *Literature and Theology in Colonial New England* (Cambridge, Mass.: Harvard University Press, 1949), 100.

7. Matthews, *American Diaries.* Shepard's diary was edited by Adeline E. H. Slicer as "A Puritan Maiden's Diary" and first published in *New England Magazine* 11 (1894–95):20–25; Coit's was published in *Mehetabel Chandler Coit: Her Book* (Norwich, Conn.: Bulletin Print., 1895), 5–12.

8. In Merriam, *Growing Up Female,* 35–36. The original can be found in

A Girl's Life Eighty Years Ago: Selections from the Letters of Eliza Southgate Browne (New York: Scribner's, 1888).

9. For Byrd: Helen Batchelor, "Some Portraits of Women in Private Communication," paper presented at the Modern Language Association convention, New York, December 1976. For Livingston, see excerpts from her diary in Steven E. Kagle, *American Diary Literature, 1620–1799* (Boston: Twayne Publishers, 1979), 92–97. For Fish, see Joy Day Buel and Richard Buel, Jr., *The Way of Duty: A Woman and Her Family in Revolutionary America* (New York: Norton, 1985).

10. Sarah Kemble Knight, *The Journal of Madam Knight,* intro. George Parker Winship (New York: Peter Smith, 1935).

11. Matthews, *American Diaries,* considers the journal "remarkable, . . . one of the best feminine diaries extant."

12. For excerpts from some of these diaries and others for this period, see Elizabeth Evans, *Weathering the Storm: Women of the American Revolution* (New York: Scribner's, 1975).

13. Albert Cook Myers, ed., Introduction to *Sally Wister's Journal: A True Narrative, Being a Quaker Maiden's Account of Her Experiences with Officers of the Continental Army, 1777–1778* (Philadelphia: Ferris & Leach Publishers, 1902), 8.

14. See Carol Edkins, "Quest for Community: Spiritual Autobiographies of Eighteenth-Century Quaker and Puritan Women in America," in *Women's Autobiography,* ed. Jelinek, 39–52.

15. Murdock, *Literature and Theology,* 101.

16. Elizabeth White, *The Experiences of God's Gracious Dealings with Mrs. Elizabeth White: As They Were Written Under Her Own Hand, and Found in Her Closet After Her Decease, December 5, 1669* (Boston: S. Kneeland, 1741), 21 pp.

17. Daniel B. Shea, Jr., *Spiritual Autobiography in Early America* (Princeton: Princeton University Press, 1968), 185.

18. The editor was John Harvard Ellis; see *The Works of Anne Bradstreet,* ed. Jeannine Hensley (Cambridge, Mass.: Harvard University Press, 1967), 241.

19. See Edmund S. Morgan, *The Puritan Family: Religion and Domestic Relations in Seventeenth-Century New England* (New York: Harper & Row, 1966).

20. Mason, "The Other Voice," considers Bradstreet's account, along with Julian's, Kempe's, and Cavendish's, "not only important beginnings in the history of women's autobiography in English as a distinct mode of interior disclosure but also something like a set of paradigms for life-writing by women right down to our time" (209–10).

21. I read the 1831 edition, *Some Account of the Early Part of the Life of Elizabeth Ashbridge, Who Died, in the Service of the Truth, at the House of Robert Lecky, in the County of Carlow, Ireland, the 16th of 5th Month, 1755, Written by Herself* (Providence, R.I.: H. K. Brown), 60 pp.

22. Shea, *Spiritual Autobiography,* 34.

23. See Roy Harvey Pearce, "The Significance of the Captivity Narrative," *American Literature* 19 (March 1947):1–20.

24. John Smith's was the very first account, which was included in his *General History of Virginia* (1624).

25. This is the title of the second edition, printed in London. The first edition, printed in New England, also in 1682, was entitled *The Soveraignty and Goodness of God, Together with the Faithfulness of His Promises Displayed: Being a Narrative of the Captivity and Restauration of* Mrs. *Mary Rowlandson,* but this edition is not extant. See Frederick Lewis Weis, Preface to *The Narrative of the Captivity and Restoration of Mrs. Mary Rowlandson* (Boston: Houghton Mifflin, 1930).

26. Printed by William Bradford in Philadelphia under the title *A Journal of the Captivity of Jean Lowry and Her Children, Giving an Account of Her Being Taken by the Indians, the 1st of April 1756, from William McCord's, in Rocky-Spring Settlement in Pennsylvania, with an Account of the Hardships She Suffered, etc.*, 31 pp.

27. Pearce, "Significance of the Captivity Narrative."

28. See Annette Kolodny's excellent discussion of Jemison's work, in *The Land before Her: Fantasy and Experience of the American Frontiers, 1630–1860* (Chapel Hill: University of North Carolina Press, 1984).

29. Fanny Kelly, My *Captivity Among the Sioux Indians,* intro. Jules Zaner (Secaucus, N.J.: Citadel Press, 1962), ca. 290 pp.; it went through several editions between 1871 and 1873. For a study of the changing emphasis on Indians in captivity narratives, see Glenda Riley, *Women and Indians on the Frontier, 1825–1915* (Albuquerque: University of New Mexico Press, 1984).

6. Early Nineteenth Century: Stirrings of Adventure and Defiance

1. Thomas Cooley, *Educated Lives: The Rise of Modern Autobiography in America* (Columbus: Ohio State University Press, 1976), 7. Cooley does not discuss women's autobiographies; he devotes chapters to Henry Adams, Mark Twain, W. D. Howells, and Henry James, with Lincoln Steffens, Sherwood Anderson, and Gertrude Stein sharing the last chapter.

2. Arksey, Pries, and Reed, *American Diaries,* 71.

3. This brief title appears on the pamphlet manuscript that I obtained from the New York Public Library. However, the complete title reads: *Memoirs of Mrs. Elizabeth Fisher, of the City of New York, Daughter of the Rev. Harry Munro, Who Was a Chaplain in the British Army, During the American Revolution—Giving a Particular Account of a Variety of Domestic Misfortunes, and Also of Her Trial, and Cruel Condemnation to the State's Prison for Six Years, at the Instance of Her Brother Peter Jay Munro.*

4. The complete title reads: *The Female Prisoner: A Narrative of the Life and Singular Adventures of Josephine Amelia Perkins, a Young Woman Who . . . for the Three Years Last Past . . . Has Been Unhappily Addicted to a Criminal Propensity, More Singular and Surprising in Its Nature (for One of Her Sex) Than Can Be Found*

on Record; in the Commission of Which She Has Been Four Several Times Detected, Twice Pardoned on Account of Her Sex, Once for Reason of Supposed Insanity, and the Fourth and Last Time, Convicted and Sentenced to Two Years' Imprisonment in Madison County Jail, Kentucky. Ammended Is a Well-Written Address to Parents and Children—all this in twenty-four pages!

5. Kinney's is a rare account by a woman accused of murder, but her treatment was typical of that accorded middle-class women whose independent character was the subject of suspicion on the death of a husband. See Mary S. Hartman, *Victorian Murderesses: A True History of Thirteen Respectable French and English Women Accused of Unspeakable Crimes* (New York: Schocken Books, 1977).

6. Metcalf's work was published in Chicago by Ottaway & Colbert, 1876, 75 pp.; Agnew's in Cincinnati by R. Clarke & Co., 1886, 196 pp.; and Lathrop's in New York by Bryant Publishing Co., 1890, 339 pp.

7. The complete title reads: *The Awful Disclosures of Maria Monk, as Exhibited in a Narrative of Her Sufferings During a Residence of Five Years as a Novice, and Two Years as a Black Nun, in the Hotel Dieu Nunnery at Montreal* (London: R. Groombridge, 1836), 221 pp. The authorship is attributed to the Reverend J. J. Slocum.

8. See Ray Allen Billington, *The Protestant Crusade, 1800–1860* (New York: Macmillan, 1938); and Mary Ewens, *The Role of the Nun in Nineteenth-Century America* (New York: Arno Press, 1978).

9. See the Bibliography for Bunkley's complete title.

10. Subsequently published as the *Trials and Persecution of Miss Edith O'Gorman, Otherwise Sister Teresa de Chantal of St. Joseph's Convent, Hudson City, N.J., Written by Herself* (Hartford: Connecticut Publishing Co., 1884), 242 pp. The publishers appended to O'Gorman's autobiography excerpts from a French work, *The History of Auricular Confession* (1848) by Count C. P. de Lasteyrie. Titled "Debauchery and Irregularities Introduced by Means of Confession into the Nunneries of Tuscany," the excerpts were followed by an ad of several pages for *Romanism as It Is: An Exposition of the Roman Catholic System for the Use of the American People, etc.*, by the Reverend Samuel W. Barnum. The publishers obviously saw this entire volume as a substantial attack on Catholicism.

11. See Jelinek, "Disguise Autobiographies."

12. The National Union Catalog lists *The Female Marine* under the name Lucy Brewer, giving the aliases Louisa Baker and Eliza Bowen, plus her married name Lucy Brewer West. Kaplan's *Bibliography of American Autobiographies* errs in listing her under the name Eliza Bowen Webb. The twenty-four-page 1816 edition published in Portsmouth, N.H., gives the following title page copy: *An Affecting Narrative of Louisa Baker, a Native of Massachusetts, Who in Early Life Having Been Shamefully Seduced, Deserted Her Parents, and Enlisted in Disguise, on Board an American Frigate as a Marine, Where, in Two or Three Engagements, She Displayed the Most Heroic Fortitude, and Was Honorably Discharged Therefrom, a Few Months Since, Without a Discovery of Her Sex Being Made.* See also the edition by Alexander

Medlicott, Jr., *The Female Marine or Adventures of Miss Lucy Brewer* (New York: Da Capo Press, 1966), 101 pp., which reprints both versions.

13. See John Laffin, *Women in Battle* (London: Abelard-Schuman, 1967); and Ménie Muriel Dowie, *Women Adventurers* (London: T. F. Unwin, 1893).

14. In the original, Paul's account occupied twenty-four pages. It was published in Boston by N. Coverly, Jr., in 1816 and by M. Brewster in 1819. The publisher of Stephens's work describes Paul's account as follows: "Annexed is the still more surprising exploits of Almira Paul, who garbed as a male in the capacity of cook, &c., served on board several English and American vessels for the space of three years, without betraying her sex."

15. See the Bibliography for Stephens's complete title.

16. Leonora Siddons, *The Female Warrior: An Interesting Narrative of the Sufferings and Singular and Surprising Adventures of . . . Written by Herself* (New York: E. E. Barclay, 1844), 23 pp.

17. *The Life and Sufferings of Miss Emma Cole, Being a Faithful Narrative of Her Life. Written by Herself* (Boston: M. Auerlius, 1844), 36 pp.

7. Mid–Nineteenth Century: Breaking the Bonds

1. Sidonie Smith, *Where I'm Bound: Patterns of Slavery and Freedom in Black American Autobiography* (Westport, Conn.: Greenwood Press, 1974), 7.

2. See John W. Blassingame, "Using the Testimony of Ex-Slaves: Approaches and Problems," in *The Slave's Narrative,* ed. Charles T. Davis and Henry Louis Gates, Jr. (New York: Oxford University Press, 1985), 78–98, esp. 82.

3. Kaplan cites the work as an autobiography. Born about 1797, Truth (d. 1883), whose previous name was Isabella Baumfree (or van Wagener), was a slave in New York until that state passed its emancipation laws in 1827. Her life is one of extraordinary dedication to the cause of women and to the emancipation of the slaves, but unfortunately she did not leave us an autobiography. Along with the *Narrative* (1850), a sequel by Gilbert called *Book of Life* (1875)—a compilation of documents, letters, articles, and testimonials—was published by Frances W. Titus; both have been reprinted in *Narrative of Sojourner Truth* (New York: Arno Press, *New York Times* American Negro History and Literature series, 1968).

4. Both Stephen Butterfield, *Black Autobiography in America* (Amherst: University of Massachusetts Press, 1974), 6; and Frances Smith Foster, *Witnessing Slavery: The Development of Ante-Bellum Slave Narratives* (Westport, Conn.: Greenwood Press, 1979), 144, assert that it was ghostwritten. It is not mentioned in *The Slave's Narrative,* ed. Davis and Gates.

5. Griffiths's name is not mentioned anywhere in the front matter of the book, including the title page, and the narrator refers to herself only as "Ann" throughout the book. Variants on Mattie Griffiths's name are Martha, Griffith, Griffin, and Browne.

6. Linda Brent, *Incidents in the Life of a Slave Girl, Written by Herself,* ed. L. Maria Child (Boston: By the Author, 1861), 301 pp. The authenticity of this autobiography is unquestionably established in Jean Fagan Yellin, "Text and Contexts of Harriet Jacobs' *Incidents in the Life of a Slave Girl: Written by Herself,*" in *The Slave's Narrative,* ed. Davis and Gates, 262–82.

7. Yellin (ibid.) uses Jacobs's correspondence to document the consistency in her style with the autobiography. She also cites a letter from Child to Jacobs, explaining her "editing":

> I have very little occasion to alter the language, which is wonderfully good, for one whose opportunities for education have been so limited. The events are interesting, and well told; the remarks are also good, and to the purpose. But I am copying a great deal of it, for the purpose of transposing sentences and pages, so as to bring the story into continuous *order,* and the remarks into *appropriate* places. I think you will see that this renders the story much more clear and entertaining. (267; italics hers)

8. Elizabeth Keckley, *Behind the Scenes; or, Thirty Years a Slave and Four Years in the White House* (New York: n.p., 1868), 18–331.

9. Susie King Taylor, *Reminiscences of My Life in Camp, with the 33D United States Colored Troops Late 1st S.C. Volunteers* (Boston: By the Author, 1902), 76 pp.

10. See Norman R. Yetman, *Life under the "Peculiar Institution": Selections from the Slave Narrative Collection* (New York: Holt, Rinehart & Winston, 1970), which discusses and analyzes the interviews with ex-slaves in the WPA collection; and Federal Writers' Project, *Slave Narratives: A Folk History of Slavery in the United States from Interviews with Former Slaves* (Washington, D.C.: Federal Writers' Project, 1941). See also George P. Rawick, ed., *The American Slave: A Composite Autobiography,* 16 vols. (Westport, Conn.: Greenwood Press, 1975–); and Dorothy Sterling, ed., *We Are Your Sisters: Black Women in the Nineteenth Century* (New York: W. W. Norton, 1984).

11. Frances Anne Kemble, *Journal of a Residence on a Georgian Plantation in 1838–1839,* ed. John A. Scott (New York: New American Library, 1961), 344 pp.

12. Janet Wilson James, Introduction to *Notable American Women, 1607–1950,* ed. Edward T. James, Janet Wilson James, and Paul S. Boyer (Cambridge, Mass.: Harvard University Press, 1971), xxiii.

13. Mary Ann Webster Loughborough, *My Cave Life in Vicksburg* (New York: Appleton & Co., 1864), 9–146.

14. Chesnut's diaries, about one-third of the original manuscript, were first published nineteen years after her death in 1905 by D. Appleton. In 1949 Houghton Mifflin published a volume twice as large as the first edition under the same title, *A Diary from Dixie,* with a foreword by Edmund Wilson—excerpted from his chapter "Three Confederate Ladies," in *Patriotic Gore: Studies in the Literature of the American Civil War* (1962), ed. Ben Ames Williams. The most recent edition is C. Vann Woodward, *Mary Chesnut's Civil War* (New Haven: Yale University

Press, 1981). Calling the original title, *A Diary from Dixie,* deceptive and trivializing, Woodward considers the work "a masterpiece," "a work of art," and "a classic," one that combines diary, autobiography, history, and fictional shaping; see also C. Vann Woodward, "Mary Chesnut in Search of Her Genre," *Yale Review* 73 (January 1984):199–299.

15. Mary Jane Moffat and Charlotte Painter, eds., *Revelations: Diaries of Women* (New York: Vintage Books, 1974), 270–71.

8. Late Nineteenth Century: Pioneering in Literature, the Land, and Social Reform

1. For a study of early novelists, see Mary Kelley, *Private Woman, Public State: Literary Domesticity in Nineteenth-Century America* (New York: Oxford University Press, 1984).

2. Despite its inclusion in Kaplan's *Bibliography of American Autobiographies,* Woolson's *Old Stone House* (1873) is a children's novel, written under the pen name Anne March.

3. Margaret Fuller Ossoli, *Memoirs of Margaret Fuller Ossoli,* 2 vols. (Boston: Phillips, Sampson, & Co., 1852), 1:11–57. See also *The Letters of Margaret Fuller,* ed. Robert N. Hudspeth, 3 vols. (Ithaca: Cornell University Press, 1983–85); and Bell G. Chevigny, *The Woman and the Myth: Margaret Fuller's Life and Writings* (Bloomington: Indiana University Press, 1976).

4. Catharine Maria Sedgwick, "Recollections of Childhood," in *Life and Letters,* ed. Mary E. Dewey (New York: Harper & Bros., 1872), 13–78.

5. Lucy Larcom, *A New England Girlhood: Outlined from Memory* (Boston: Houghton Mifflin, 1889), 274 pp.

6. I am indebted, in this and the next paragraph, to Rose Lynn Norman for her study, "Autobiographies of American Women Writers before 1914," Ph.D. diss., University of Tennessee, 1979.

7. Anna Cora Mowatt, *Autobiography of an Actress; or, Eight Years on the Stage* (Boston: Ticknor, Reed, & Fields, 1854), 448 pp.; Olive Logan, *Before the Footlights and Behind the Scenes: A Book About "The Show Business" . . .* (Philadelphia: Parmelee & Co., 1870), 612 pp., reprinted in 1871 as *The Mimic World.*

8. Rose Lynn Norman, personal communication, 1978.

9. An early exception is Caroline M. Kirkland's (1801–64) *A New Home—Who'll Follow? or, Glimpses of Western Life, by Mrs. Mary Clavers, An Actual Settler* (1839), a novelistic rendering of what is essentially Kirkland's autobiography. Two others were published early in the twentieth century by Elinore Pruitt Stewart (1876–1933)—*Letters of a Woman Homesteader* (1914) and *Letters on an Elk Hunt: By a Woman Homesteader* (1915).

10. For a fascinating and distinguished study of women's participation in this migration, particularly their contribution to its mythic and realistic render-

ings, see Kolodny, *Land before Her.* See also John Mack Faragher, *Women and Men on the Overland Trail* (New Haven: Yale University Press, 1979); and Nancy Wilson Ross, *Westward the Women* (San Francisco: North Point Press, 1985).

11. See also *First White Women over the Rockies: Diaries, Letters, and Biographical Sketches of the Six Women of the Oregon Mission Who Made the Overland Journey in 1836 and 1838,* intro. and ed. Clifford Merrill Drury, 3 vols. (Glendale, Ca.: A. H. Clark Co., 1963–66). The six women, besides Narcissa Prentiss Whitman, are Eliza Hart Spalding (1807–51), Mary Augusta Dix Gray (1810–81), Sarah Gilbert Smith (1813–55), Mary Richardson Walker (1811–97), and Myra Fairbanks Eells (1805–78).

12. Compiled by T. C. Elliott for the Oregon Historical Society, Portland, 1937. It was originally published as *A Journey Across the Plains in 1836;* the *Journal of Narcissa Whitman* was also published, in 1891.

13. See Cathy Luchetti, with Carol Olwell, *Women of the West* (St. George, Utah: Antelope Island Press, 1982), a collection of diaries by eleven women; and *Women's Diaries of the Westward Journey,* ed. Lillian Schlissel (New York: Schocken Books, 1982). Schlissel notes that over 800 such diaries and day journals have been published or cataloged in archives. See also *Pioneer Women: Voices from the Kansas Frontier,* ed. Joanna L. Stratton, intro. Arthur M. Schlesinger, Jr. (New York: Simon & Schuster, 1981).

14. See, for example, Margaret Von Horn Dwight, *A Journey to Ohio in 1810,* ed. Max Farrand (New Haven: Yale University Press, 1912); Sarah J. Cummins, *Autobiography and Reminiscences* (Walla Walla, Wash.: Walla Walla Bulletin, 1914); Frances M. A. Roe, *Army Letters from an Officer's Wife* (1872) (New York: Arno Press, 1979; Omaha: University of Nebraska Press, 1982); Nannie Tiffany Alderson (1860–1947), with Helena Huntington Smith, *A Bride Goes West* (1942) (Omaha: University of Nebraska Press, 1982); Anne Ellis (1875–1938), *The Life of an Ordinary Woman* (1929) (Omaha: University of Nebraska Press, 1982); and Mary McNair Matthews, *Ten Years in Nevada, or Life on the Pacific Coast* (Omaha: University of Nebraska Press, 1985).

15. The original title of Tillson's work was *Reminiscences of Early Life in Illinois by Our Mother.*

16. See excerpts in Merriam, *Growing Up Female,* 137–57.

17. Ibid., 86, 96, 100. See also Mitchell's *Life, Letters, and Journals,* comp. Phebe Mitchell Kendall (Boston: Lee & Shepard, 1896; rpt. 1979).

18. Frances E. Willard, *Glimpses of Fifty Years: The Autobiography of an American Woman* (Chicago: H. J. Smith & Co., 1889), 704 pp.

19. See the Bibliography for Livermore's complete title.

20. The titles are worth noting: "What Shall We Do with Our Daughters?" "The Boy of To-Day," "Concerning Husbands and Wives," "The Battle of Life," "Does the Liquor Traffic Pay?" and "Has the Night of Death No Morning?"

21. See Sacvan Bercovitch, "Emerson the Prophet: Romanticism, Puritanism, and Auto-American-Biography," in *Emerson: Prophecy, Metamorphosis, and Influence,* ed. David Levin (New York: Columbia University Press, 1975), 16.

22. See Cox, "Autobiography and America."

23. Gerda Lerner, *The Female Experience: An American Documentary* (Indianapolis: Bobbs-Merrill, 1977), xxiv–xxv.

9. Traditional Autobiography Liberated: The Ordinary and Superwoman Elizabeth Cady Stanton

1. *Eighty Years and More: Reminiscences, 1815–1897* (New York: Schocken Books, 1971), xxiii; subsequent page references, given in the text, are from this edition.

2. Elisabeth Griffin's biography, *In Her Own Right: The Life of Elizabeth Cady Stanton* (New York: Oxford University Press, 1984), presents Stanton's personal life as less successful than she depicts it in her autobiography. See this biography for other contradictory facts about Stanton's life.

3. Emmeline Pankhurst recounts a similar experience in her autobiography *My Own Story* (1914). When just a child, she overhears her father say: "What a pity she wasn't born a lad" (6). Even though Pankhurst's parents supported women's suffrage and she attended her first women's suffrage meeting at fourteen, she still knew that society considered men superior to women.

4. Alma Lutz, in *Notable American Women, 1607–1950,* ed. James, James, and Boyer.

5. Ellen Dubois (*Feminism and Suffrage* [Ithaca: Cornell University Press, 1978]), who has specialized in Stanton's life and work, notes that nothing among Stanton's papers indicates her feelings about her mother.

6. Catharine Stimpson, "Thy Neighbor's Wife, Thy Neighbor's Servants: Women's Liberation and Black Civil Rights," in *Woman in Sexist Society,* ed. Vivian Gornick and Barbara K. Moran (New York: Basic Books, 1971), 625.

7. Lutz, in *Notable American Women,* ed. James, James, and Boyer.

10. Exotic Autobiography Intellectualized: The Legitimation of Gertrude Stein

1. See Candace Falk, *Love, Anarchy, and Emma Goldman* (New York: Holt, Rinehart, & Winston, 1984).

2. Patricia Meyer Spacks, "Selves in Hiding," in *Women's Autobiography,* ed. Jelinek, 113, 114. For a discussion of the positive self-image in the autobiographies of several twentieth-century women, see Bloom, "Promises Fulfilled: Positive Images of Women in Twentieth-Century Autobiography," *Feminist Criticism,* ed. Brown and Olson, 324–38.

3. See Anne M. Butler, *Daughters of Joy, Sisters of Misery: Prostitutes in the American West, 1865–1890* (Urbana: University of Illinois Press, 1985).

4. Jean Rhys, *Smile Please: An Unfinished Autobiography* (New York: Harper & Row, 1979).

5. See Elizabeth Winston, "The Autobiographer and Her Readers: From Apology to Affirmation," in *Women's Autobiography,* ed. Jelinek, 93–94.

6. Catharine R. Stimpson, "The Mind, the Body, and Gertrude Stein," *Critical Inquiry* 3 (Spring 1977):490.

7. Ibid., 505, 491.

8. Richard Bridgman, *Gertrude Stein in Pieces* (New York: Oxford University Press, 1970), 347.

9. Gertrude Stein, *The Autobiography of Alice B. Toklas* (New York: Vintage Books, 1960), 75; subsequent page references, given in the text, are from this edition.

10. Elizabeth Sprigge, *Gertrude Stein: Her Life and Work* (New York: Harper & Brothers, 1957), 174.

11. Stimpson, "The Mind, the Body," 497.

12. Ibid., 504.

13. "Gertrude Stein as a Young Woman," *New Yorker,* 15 September 1951, 115.

14. Pascal, *Design and Truth,* 56.

15. Lisa H. Smith, paper presented at National Endowment for the Humanities seminar in American autobiography at Dartmouth College, 9 December 1975.

16. Ibid.

17. Carroll Smith-Rosenberg, "The Female World of Love and Ritual: Relations between Women in Nineteenth-Century America," *Signs* 1 (Autumn 1975):1–29.

18. Stimpson, "The Mind, the Body," 497.

19. Ibid., 505.

20. Gertrude Stein, *Everybody's Autobiography* (New York: Vintage Books, 1973), 218–19, 136.

11. Literary Autobiography Recast: The Oblique Heroism of Lillian Hellman

1. Hurston's 1942 autobiography has been reissued in an excellent new edition (1985) by Robert Hemenway, which restores many sections of the work that publishers found objectionable—her views on American imperialism and racism and on other issues too controversial for her forties' readers.

2. I will not be discussing Hellman's quasi-autobiographical work, *Maybe* (1980), because it is less a memoir than a philosophical search for the "truth" of memory.

3. Lillian Hellman, *An Unfinished Woman: A Memoir* (New York: Bantam Books, 1970), 226; subsequent page references, given in the text as *UW,* are from this edition.

4. Lillian Hellman, *Pentimento: A Book of Portraits* (New York: New Amer-

ican Library, 1973), 21; subsequent page references, given in the text as *P,* are from this edition.

5. Lillian Hellman, *Scoundrel Time* (Boston: Little, Brown, 1976), 41; subsequent page references, given in the text as *ST,* are from this edition.

6. Spacks, *Female Imagination,* 298.

12. Political and Personal Autobiography Integrated: The Fusion of Kate Millett

1. Kate Millett, *Flying* (New York: Ballantine Books, 1974), 628; subsequent page references, given in the text, are from this edition.

2. See Elinor Langer, "Confessing," *Ms.*, December 1974, pp. 69–71, 108.

3. Kate Millett, 1972 Preface to *The Prostitution Papers* (New York: Ballantine Books, 1976), 41.

4. Annette Kolodny, "The Lady's Not for Spurning: Kate Millett and the Critics," *Contemporary Literature* 17 (Autumn 1976):560–61; emphasis Kolodny's.

5. Millett, 1972 Preface, *Prostitution Papers,* 24.

6. In her 1976 Introduction to *The Prostitution Papers,* she tells us that it took her two years to polish and revise *Flying.*

7. Kolodny, "Lady's Not for Spurning," 545.

8. Shumaker, *English Autobiography,* 135–36.

9. See Stimpson, "The Mind, the Body," 489–506.

10. Mason, "The Other Voice," 235.

Bibliography

Autobiographical Works

ADAMS, HANNAH. *A Memoir of Miss Hannah Adams, Written by Herself, with Additional Notices, by a Friend.* Boston: Gray & Bowen, 1832.

ADDAMS, JANE. *Twenty Years at Hull-House.* New York: New American Library, 1961.

AHURI. "The Tale of Ahuri." In *Egyptian Tales. Translated from the Papyri. XVIIIth to XIXth Dynasty,* edited by W. M. Flinders Petrie. 2d ser. New York: Benjamin Blom, 1971.

ANDERSON, MARGARET C. *My Thirty Years' War.* New York: Covici, 1930.

———. *The Fiery Fountains.* New York: Hermitage House, 1951.

———. *The Strange Necessity.* New York: Horizon Press, 1969.

ANDERSON, MARIAN. *My Lord, What a Morning!* New York: Viking Press, 1956.

ANGELOU, MAYA. *I Know Why the Caged Bird Sings.* New York: Bantam Books, 1969.

———. *Gather Together in My Name.* New York: Bantam Books, 1975.

———. *Singin' and Swingin' and Gettin' Merry like Christmas.* New York: Random House, 1976.

———. *The Heart of a Woman.* New York: Random House, 1981.

ASHBRIDGE, ELIZABETH. *Some Account of the Early Part of the Life of Elizabeth Ashbridge, Who Died, in the Service of the Truth, at the House of Robert Lecky, in the County of Carlow, Ireland, the 16th of 5th Month, 1755. Written by Herself.* Providence, R.I.: H. K. Brown, 1831.

ATHERTON, GERTRUDE. *The Adventures of a Novelist.* New York: Liveright, 1932.

AUSTIN, MARY. *Earth Horizon: Autobiography.* Boston: Houghton Mifflin, 1932.

BAEZ, JOAN. *Daybreak: An Autobiography.* New York: Avon Books, 1968.

BAILEY, PEARL. *The Raw Pearl.* New York: Pocket Books, 1970.

BENGIS, ESTHER. *I Am a Rabbi's Wife.* Lakewood, N.J.: By the Author, 1935.

BESANT, ANNIE. *An Autobiography.* London: T. Fisher Unwin, 1908.

BIRD, ISABELLA L. *A Lady's Life in the Rocky Mountains.* Introduction by Daniel J. Boorstin. Norman: University of Oklahoma Press, 1960.

BRADSTREET, ANNE. "To My Dear Children." In *The Works of Anne Bradstreet,* edited by Jeannine Hensley. Cambridge, Mass.: Harvard University Press, 1967.

BRENT, LINDA. See Jacobs, Harriet.

BREWER, LUCY. *An Affecting Narrative of Louisa Baker, a Native of Massachusetts, Who in Early Life Having Been Shamefully Seduced, Deserted Her Parents, and Enlisted in Disguise, on Board an American Frigate as a Marine, Where, in Two or Three Engagements, She Displayed the Most Heroic Fortitude, and Was Honorably Discharged Therefrom, a Few Months Since, Without a Discovery of Her Sex Being Made.* Portsmouth, N.H.: Printed for the Purchaser, 1816. 24 pp.

———. *The Female Marine, or Adventures of Miss Lucy Brewer.* Edited with an introduction by Alexander Medlicott, Jr. New York: Da Capo Press, 1966.

BROWNE, ELIZABETH SOUTHGATE. *A Girl's Life Eighty Years Ago: Selections from the Letters of Eliza Southgate Browne.* New York: Scribner's, 1888.

BROWNING, ELIZABETH BARRETT. *Hitherto Unpublished Poems and Stories, with an Inedited Autobiography.* 2 vols. Boston: Bibliophile Society, 1914.

———. "Two Autobiographical Essays by Elizabeth Barrett." In *Browning Institute Studies,* edited by William S. Peterson, no. 2, pp. 119–34. New York, 1974.

BUCK, PEARL. *My Several Worlds: A Personal Record.* New York: John Day Co., 1954.

BUNKLEY, JOSEPHINE M. *Miss Bunkley's Book: The Testimony of an Escaped Novice from the Sisterhood of St. Joseph, Emmettsburg, Maryland, the Mother-House of the Sisters of Charity in the United States.* New York: Harper & Bros., 1855.

BURTON, ANNIE L. *Memories of Childhood's Slavery Days.* Boston: n.p., 1909.

BURTON, LADY ISABEL. *The Romance of Isabel Lady Burton: The Story of Her Life, Told in Part by Herself and in Part by W. H. Wilkins, with Portraits and Illustrations.* 2 vols. London: Hutchinson & Co., 1897.

CALISHER, HORTENSE. *Herself.* New York: Dell, 1972.

CARRIGHAR, SALLY. *Home to the Wilderness: A Personal Journal.* Baltimore: Penguin Books, 1974.

CAVENDISH, MARGARET. "Memoirs of the Duchess." In *The Life of the (1st) Duke of Newcastle and Other Writings of Margaret Duchess.* London and Toronto: J. M. Dent & Sons; New York: E. P. Dutton & Co., n.d.

CHARKE, CHARLOTTE. *A Narrative of the Life of Mrs. Charlotte Charke, Daughter of Colley Cibber.* London: Constable & Co., 1929.

CHESNUT, MARY. *Mary Chesnut's Civil War.* Edited by C. Vann Woodward. New Haven: Yale University Press, 1981.

CHISHOLM, SHIRLEY. *Unbought and Unbossed.* Boston: Houghton Mifflin, 1970.

———. *The Good Fight.* New York: Harper & Row, 1973.

COBBE, FRANCES POWER. *The Life of Frances Power Cobbe.* 2 vols. Boston: Houghton Mifflin, 1894.

COLE, EMMA. *The Life and Sufferings of Miss Emma Cole, Being a Faithful Narrative of Her Life. Written by Herself.* Boston: M. Aurelius, 1844.

COLETTE. *Earthly Paradise: An Autobiography.* Compiled by Robert Phelps. Translated by Herma Briffault, Derek Coltman, et al. New York: Farrar,

Straus, & Giroux, 1966.

CUMMINS, MARGARET. *Leaves from My Port Folio, Original and Selected Together with a Religious Narrative.* St. Louis: Wm. E. Foote, 1860.

DAVIES, CHRISTIAN CAVENAUGH. *The Life and Adventures of Mrs. Christian Davies. Commonly Call'd Mother Ross; Who, in Several Campaigns Under King William and the Late Duke of Marlborough, in the Quality of a Foot-Soldier and Dragoon, Gave Many Signal Proofs of an Unparallell'd Courage and Personal Bravery. Taken from Her Own Mouth When a Pensioner of Chelsea-Hospital and Known to Be True by Many Who Were Engaged in Those Great Scenes of Action.* London: R. Montagu, 1740. 191 pp.

DAVIS, ANGELA. *With My Mind on Freedom: An Autobiography.* New York: Bantam Books, 1975.

DAY, DOROTHY. *The Long Loneliness.* New York: Harper & Brothers, 1952.

DAY, HELEN CALDWELL. *Color, Ebony.* New York: Sheed & Ward, 1951.

DILLARD, ANNIE. *Pilgrim at Tinker Creek.* New York: Harper's Magazine Press, 1974.

DUNCAN, ISADORA. *My Life.* London: Sphere Books, 1969.

ELDRIDGE, ELLEANOR. See Greene, Frances Whipple.

ELLIS, ANNE. *"Plain Anne Ellis": More about the Life of an Ordinary Woman.* Boston: Houghton Mifflin, 1931.

EMMONS, ELISABETH. *A Sketch of the Life of Elisabeth Emmons, or The Female Sailor.* Boston: Graves & Bartlett, 1841.

FANSHAWE, ANN. *The Memoirs of Anne, Lady Halkett, and Ann, Lady Fanshawe.* New York: Oxford University Press, 1979.

FERBER, EDNA. *A Peculiar Treasure.* New York: Doubleday, 1939.

FIELD, JOANNA. *A Life of One's Own.* Los Angeles: J. P. Tarcher, 1981.

FISHER, ELIZABETH. *Memoirs of Mrs. Elizabeth Fisher.* New York Public Library pamphlet collection. No date, no publisher.

FLYNN, ELIZABETH GURLEY. *The Rebel Girl: An Autobiography: My First Life (1906–1926).* New York: International Publishers, 1973. Originally published by *Masses & Mainstream* under the title *I Speak My Own Piece: Autobiography of "The Rebel Girl"* (1955).

FRANK, ANNE. *The Diary of a Young Girl.* Translated by B. M. Mooyaart-Doubleday. Introduction by Eleanor Roosevelt. New York: Modern Library, 1952.

FULLER, MARGARET. See Ossoli, Margaret Fuller.

GILMAN, CHARLOTTE PERKINS. *The Living of Charlotte Perkins Gilman: An Autobiography.* Foreword by Zona Gale. New York: Harper & Row, 1975.

GIOVANNI, NIKKI. *Gemini: An Extended Autobiographical Statement of My First Twenty-Five Years of Being a Black Poet.* New York: Viking, 1971.

GLASGOW, ELLEN. *The Woman Within.* New York: Harcourt, Brace, 1954.

GOLDMAN, EMMA. *Living My Life.* 2 vols. New York: Dover, 1970.

GOODWIN, RUBY BERKLEY. *It's Good to Be Black.* New York: Doubleday & Co., 1953.

GREENE, FRANCES WHIPPLE. *Memoirs of Elleanor Eldridge.* Providence, R.I.: B. T. Albro, 1838.

GRIFFITHS, MATTIE (MARTHA). *Autobiography of a Female Slave.* New York: Redfield, 1857.

HALKETT, ANNE. *The Autobiography of Anne Lady Halkett.* Edited by John Gough Nichols. Westminster: Camden Society, 1875.

HANSBERRY, LORRAINE. *To Be Young, Gifted, and Black.* Englewood Cliffs, N.J.: Prentice-Hall, 1969.

HELLMAN, LILLIAN. *An Unfinished Woman: A Memoir.* New York: Bantam Books, 1970.

———. *Pentimento: A Book of Portraits.* New York: New American Library, 1973.

———. *Scoundrel Time.* Introduction by Garry Wills. Boston: Little, Brown, 1976.

———. *Maybe: A Story.* Boston: Little, Brown, 1980.

HERBST, JOSEPHINE. "The Starched Blue Sky of Spain." *Noble Savage* 1 (1960):76–117.

———. "A Year of Disgrace." *Noble Savage* 3 (1961):128–60.

———. "Yesterday's Road." *New American Review* 3 (1968):84–104.

HOLIDAY, BILLIE. *Lady Sings the Blues.* New York: Lancer Books, 1972.

HURSTON, ZORA NEALE. *Dust Tracks on a Road: An Autobiography.* Edited by Robert E. Hemenway. 2d ed. Champaign: University of Illinois Press, 1985.

HUTCHINSON, LUCY. *Memoirs of the Life of Colonel Hutchinson, with the Fragment of an Autobiography by Mrs. Hutchinson.* Edited with an introduction by James Sutherland. London: Oxford University Press, 1973.

ISABELL, SHARON. *Yesterday's Lessons.* Oakland, Ca.: Women's Press Collective, 1974.

[JACKSON, MATHILDA]. *The Story of Mattie J. Jackson; . . . A True Story, Written and Arranged by Dr. L. S. Thompson, . . . as Given by Mattie.* Lawrence, Mass.: n.p., 1866.

JACOBS, HARRIET. *Incidents in the Life of a Slave Girl, Written by Herself.* Edited by L. Maria Child. Boston: By the Author, 1861.

JAMES, ZILLA FITZ. *The Female Bandit of the South-West; or the Horrible, Mysterious, and Awful Disclosures in the Life of the Creole Murderess, Zilla Fitz James, Paramour and Accomplice of Green H. Long, the Treble Murderer, for the Space of Six Years. An Autobiographical Narrative.* Edited by Rev. A. Richards, Little Rock, Ark.: A. R. Orton, 1851. 31 pp.

JULIAN OF NORWICH. *Revelations of Divine Love.* In *Juliana of Norwich: An Introductory Appreciation.* Edited by P. Franklin Chambers. London: Victor Gollancz, 1955.

KECKLEY, ELIZABETH. *Behind the Scenes; or, Thirty Years a Slave and Four Years in the White House.* New York: n.p., 1868.

KELLER, HELEN. *The Story of My Life.* Introduction by Robert Russell. New York: Scholastic Book Services, 1967.

KELLY, FANNY. *My Captivity Among the Sioux Indians.* Introduction by Jules Zaner. Secaucus, N.J.: Citadel Press, 1962.

KEMBLE, FRANCES ANNE. *Journal of a Residence on a Georgia Plantation in 1838–1839.* Edited by John A. Scott. New York: New American Library, 1961.

KEMPE, MARGERY. *The Book of Margery Kempe: A Modernized Version.* Edited by W. Butler-Bowden. Introduction by R. W. Chambers. New York: Devin-Adair Co., 1944.

KINGSTON, MAXINE HONG. *The Woman Warrior: Memoirs of a Girlhood among Ghosts.* New York: Vintage, 1975.

———. *China Men.* New York: Alfred A. Knopf, 1977.

KINNEY, HANNAH. *A Review of the Principal Events of the Last Ten Years in the Life of Mrs. Hannah Kinney: Together with Some Comments upon the Late Trial, Written by Herself.* Boston: n.p., 1841.

KNIGHT, SARAH KEMBLE. *The Journal of Madam Knight.* Introduction by George Parker Winship. New York: Peter Smith, 1935.

LARCOM, LUCY. *A New England Girlhood, Outlined from Memory.* Boston: Houghton Mifflin, 1889.

LAWRENCE, DOROTHY. *Sapper Dorothy Lawrence: The Only English Woman Soldier, Late Royal Engineers, 51st Division, 79th Tunnelling Company, B.E.F.* London and New York: John Lane, 1919. 191 pp.

LEAD, JANE. *A Fountain of Gardens Watered by the River of Divine Pleasure, and Springing Up in All Variety of Spiritual Plants. . . .* London: n.p., 1697–1701.

LEE, JARENA. *Religious Experience and Journal of Mrs. Jarena Lee, Giving an Account of Her Call to Preach the Gospel.* Philadelphia: n.p., 1849.

LEIGH, MEDORA. *Medora Leigh: A History and an Autobiography, with an Introduction and a Commentary on the Charges Brought Against Lord Byron by Mrs. Beecher Stowe.* Edited by Charles Mackay. London: Richard Bentley, 1869.

LIVERMORE, MARY A. *The Story of My Life; or the Sunshine and Shadow of Seventy Years, by Mary A. Livermore, Teacher, Author, Wife, Mother, Army Nurse, Soldier's Friend, Lecturer, and Reformer. A Narrative of Her Early Life and Struggles for Education, Three Years' Experiences on a Southern Plantation Among White Masters and Black Slaves, Her Courtship, Marriage, Domestic Life, etc. with Hitherto Unrecorded Incidents and Recollections of Three Years' Experiences as an Army Nurse in the Great Civil War, and Reminiscences of Twenty-Five Years' Experiences on the Lecture Platform, Including Thrilling, Pathetic, and Humorous Incidents of Platform Life; to Which Is Added Six of Her Most Popular Lectures. Superbly Illustrated with Portraits and One Hundred and Twenty Engravings from Designs by Eminent Artists, Made Expressly for This Work. Sold Only to Subscribers.* Hartford, Conn.: A. D. Worthington & Co., 1897.

LOBDELL, LUCY ANN. *Narrative of Lucy Ann Lobdell, the Female Hunter of Delaware Counties, N.Y.* New York: Published for the Authoress, 1855. Pp. 3–47.

LOGAN, OLIVE. *Before the Footlights and Behind the Scenes: A Book About "The*

Show Business." . . . Philadelphia: Parmelee & Co., 1870.

LOUGHBOROUGH, MARY ANN WEBSTER. *My Cave Life in Vicksburg.* New York: Appleton & Co., 1864.

LOWRY, JEAN. *A Journal of the Captivity of Jean Lowry.* Edited by Wilcomb E. Washburn. Vol. 8 of *The Garland Library of Narratives of North American Indian Captivities,* Edited by Wilcomb E. Washburn. New York and London: Garland Publishing Co., 1978.

McCARTHY, MARY. *Memories of a Catholic Girlhood.* New York: Harcourt Brace Jovanovich, 1957.

MacLAINE, SHIRLEY. *"Don't Fall Off the Mountain."* New York: Bantam Books, 1971.

———. *You Can Get There from Here.* New York: W. W. Norton, 1975.

———. *Out on a Limb.* New York: Bantam Books, 1983.

MARTINEAU, HARRIET. *Harriet Martineau's Autobiography.* Edited by Maria Weston Chapman. 2 vols. Boston: James R. Osgood, 1877.

MEAD, MARGARET. *Blackberry Winter: My Earlier Years.* New York: Simon & Schuster, 1972.

MILLETT, KATE. *Flying.* New York: Ballantine Books, 1974.

MITFORD, MARY RUSSELL. *Recollections of a Literary Life, and Selections from My Favorite Poets and Prose Writers.* London: Richard Bentley, 1883.

MONROE, HARRIET. *A Poet's Life: Seventy Years in a Changing World.* New York: Macmillan, 1938.

MOODY, ANNE. *Coming of Age in Mississippi.* New York: Dell, 1968.

MOORE, MADELINE. *The Female Officer, or the Wonderful, Startling, and Thrilling Adventures of Madeline Moore, Who to Be Near Her Lover, Procured a Male Disguise, and Joined the Late Expedition to Cuba, Was Elected Lieutenant, and Fought in the Battle of Cardenas, Under the Renowned General Lopez, an Accurate Description of Battle, and Her Own Perilous Adventures and Hair-Breadth Escapes, as Well as Those of Her Lover, and a Great Deal More of Like Nature, Are Described with a Graphic Power That Will Fairly Make One's Blood Tingle with Excitement. The Reader May Rely upon This Narrative, as Being Strictly Authentic.* New York: Published for the Author, 1851. Pp. 5–48.

MORTON, ROSALIE. *A Woman Surgeon: The Life and Work of Rosalie Slaughter Morton.* New York: Frederick A. Stokes Co., 1937.

MOUNTAIN WOLF WOMAN. *Sister of Crashing Thunder: The Autobiography of a Winnebago Indian.* Edited by Nancy Oestreich Lurie. Foreword by Ruth Underhill. Ann Arbor: University of Michigan Press, 1961.

MOWATT, ANNA CORA. *Autobiography of an Actress; or, Eight Years on the Stage.* Boston: Ticknor, Reed, & Fields, 1854.

NIN, ANAÏS. *The Diary of Anaïs Nin.* Edited by Gunther Stuhlmann. 7 vols. New York: Harcourt Brace Jovanovich, 1978.

———. *The Early Diary of Anaïs Nin.* 4 vols. New York: Harcourt Brace Jovanovich, 1978–85.

O'GORMAN, EDITH. *Convent Life Unveiled.* Hartford: Connecticut Publishing

Co., 1884.

OLIPHANT, MARGARET. *The Autobiography and Letters of Mrs. Margaret Oliphant.* Edited by Mrs. Harry Coghill. Introduction by Qu.D. Leavis. Leicester: Leicester University Press, 1974. Facsimile of 1899 ed.

OSSOLI, MARGARET FULLER. *Memoirs of Margaret Fuller Ossoli.* 2 vols. Boston: Phillips, Sampson, & Co., 1852.

PAUL, ALMIRA. *The Surprising Adventures of Almira Paul, a Young Woman, Who, Garbed as a Male, Has . . . Actually Served as a Common Sailor, on Board of English and American Armed Vessels Without a Discovery of Her Sex Being Made.* Appended to *The Cabin Boy Wife; or, Singular and Surprising Adventures of Mrs. Ellen Stephens. . . .* New York: C. E. Daniels, 1840.

PENINGTON, MARY. *A Brief Account of My Exercises from My Childhood.* Philadelphia: n.p., 1848.

PHILLIPS, TERESIA CONSTANTIA. *An Apology for the Conduct of Mrs. Teresia Constantia Phillips, More Particularly That Part of It Which Relates to Her Marriage with an Eminent Dutch Merchant, the Whole Authenticated by Faithful Copies of His Letters, and of the Settlement Which He Made upon Her to Induce Her to Suffer (Without Any Real Opposition on Her Part) a Sentence to Be Pronounced Against Their Marriage; Together with Such Other Original Papers, Filed in the Cause, as Are Necessary to Illustrate That Remarkable Story.* 3 vols. in 1. London: By the Author, 1748–49.

PILKINGTON, LAETITIA. *Memoirs of Mrs. Laetitia Pilkington, 1712–1750, Written by Herself.* Introduction by Iris Barry. 3 vols. in 1. London: George Routledge & Sons, 1928.

PRINCE, NANCY. *Narrative of the Life and Travels of Mrs. Nancy Prince.* 2d ed. Boston: n.p., 1853; 3d ed., 1856.

RICH, MARY BOYLE. *Autobiography of Mary Countess of Warwick.* Edited by T. Crofton Croker. London: Percy Society, 1848.

RITCHIE, ANNA CORA. See Mowatt, Anna Cora.

ROBINSON, MARY DARBY. *Memoirs of the Late Mrs. Robinson, Written by Herself.* London: Cobden-Sanderson, 1930.

ROOSEVELT, ELEANOR. *The Autobiography of Eleanor Roosevelt.* New York: Harper & Row, 1961.

ROWLANDSON, MARY WHITE. *The Narrative of the Captivity and Restoration of Mrs. Mary Rowlandson.* Boston: Houghton Mifflin, 1930.

SACKVILLE-WEST, VITA. Journal. In *Portrait of a Marriage* by Nigel Nicolson. New York: Bantam Books, 1974.

SANGER, MARGARET. *Margaret Sanger: An Autobiography.* New York: Dover Publications, 1971.

SAPPHO OF LESBOS. *Her Work Restored. A Metrical English Version of Her Poems, with Conjectural Restorations by Beram Saklatvala.* London: Charles Kilton, 1968.

SARTON, MAY. *I Knew a Phoenix: Sketches for an Autobiography.* New York: W. W. Norton, 1959.

———. *Journal of a Solitude.* New York: W. W. Norton, 1973.

SCUDDER, JANET. *Modeling My Life.* New York: Harcourt, Brace & Co., 1925.

SCUDDER, VIDA DUTTON. *On Journey.* New York: E. P. Dutton & Co., 1937.

SEDGWICK, CATHARINE MARIA. "Recollections of Childhood." In *Life and Letters,* edited by Mary E. Dewey. New York: Harper & Bros., 1872.

SHELLEY, MARY WOLLSTONECRAFT. *The Letters of Mary Wollstonecraft Shelley.* Edited by Betty T. Bennett. 2 vols. Baltimore: Johns Hopkins University Press, 1980–.

SIDDONS, LEONORA. *The Female Warrior: An Interesting Narrative of the Sufferings and Singular and Surprising Adventures of Leonora Siddons, Written by Herself.* New York: E. E. Barclay, 1844.

SIGOURNEY, LYDIA H. *Letters of Life.* New York: D. Appleton & Co., 1866.

SMITH, AMANDA. *An Autobiography: The Story of the Lord's Dealings with Mrs. Amanda Smith, the Colored Evangelist: Containing an Account of Her Life Work of Faith, and Her Travels in America, England, Scotland, India, and Africa, as an Independent Missionary.* Chicago: n.p., 1893.

SMITH, LILLIAN. *Killers of the Dream.* New York: Doubleday, 1961.

SNELL, HANNAH. *The Female Soldier, or, the Surprising Life and Adventures of Hannah Snell . . . Who Took upon Herself the Name of James Gray; and Being Deserted by Her Husband, Put on Mens Apparel, and Travelled to Coventry in Quest of Him Where She Enlisted in Col. Guise's Regiment of Foot-Soldiers . . . also a Full and True Account of Her Enlisting Afterwards into Fraser's Regiment of Marines . . Together with an Account of What Happened to Her in the Voyage to England, in the Eltham Man of War.* London: R. Walker, 1750. 42 pp.

SOUTHGATE, ELIZABETH. See Browne, Elizabeth Southgate.

STANTON, ELIZABETH CADY. *Eighty Years and More: Reminiscences, 1815–1897.* Introduction by Gail Parker. New York: Schocken Books, 1973.

STEIN, GERTRUDE. *The Autobiography of Alice B. Toklas.* New York: Vintage, 1960.

———. *Everybody's Autobiography.* New York: Vintage, 1973.

STEPHENS, ELLEN. *The Cabin Boy Wife; or, Singular and Surprising Adventures of Mrs. Ellen Stephens, Who, Having Been Compelled to Marry Against Her Will, After Experiencing Much Cruel Treatment, Was Deserted by Her Husband, and in Pursuit of Whom (and Her Infant Child), Dressed in Male Attire, and Obtaining a Berth on One of the Steamers, on the Mississippi River, as Cabin Boy, in That Capacity Made Several Passages Up and Down the River in 1839 and '40, Without Her Sex Being Known or Suspected.* New York: C. E. Daniels, 1840.

TARBELL, IDA MINERVA. *All in the Day's Work: An Autobiography.* New York: Macmillan, 1939.

TAYLOR, SUSIE KING. *Reminiscences of My Life in Camp, with the 33D United States Colored Troups Late 1st S.C. Volunteers.* Boston: By the Author, 1902.

TERESA, ST. *The Life of Teresa of Jesus.* Translated and edited by E. Allison Peers. New York: Doubleday, 1960.

TERHUNE, MARY VIRGINIA HAWES. *Marion Harland's Autobiography: The*

Story of a Long Life. New York: Harper & Brothers, 1910.

TERRELL, MARY CHURCH. *A Colored Woman in a White World.* New York: Arno Press, 1980.

TILLICH, HANNAH. *From Time to Time.* New York: Stein & Day, 1973.

TILLSON, CHRISTIANA HOLMES. *A Woman's Story of Pioneer Illinois.* Chicago: R. R. Donnelley & Sons, 1919.

TOKLAS, ALICE B. *What Is Remembered.* New York: Holt, Rinehart & Winston, 1963.

TONNA, CHARLOTTE ELIZABETH. *Personal Recollections.* New York: Charles Scribner, 1858.

TRUITT, ANNE. *Daybook: The Journal of an Artist.* New York: Pantheon Books, 1982.

VANE, FRANCES ANNE. "Memoirs of a Lady of Quality." In *Peregrine Pickle,* by Tobias Smollett, chap. 81. London: J. M. Dent, 1956.

VELAZQUEZ, LORETA JANETA. *The Woman in Battle: A Narrative of the Exploits, Adventures, and Travels of Madame Loreta Janeta Velazquez, Otherwise Known as Lieutenant Harry T. Buford, Confederate States Army, in Which Is Given Full Descriptions of the Numerous Battles in Which She Participated as a Confederate Officer; of Her Perilous Performances as a Spy, as a Bearer of Despatches, as a Secret-Service Agent, and as a Blockade-Runner; of Her Adventures Behind the Scenes at Washington, Including the Bond Swindle; of Her Career as a Bounty and Substitute Broker in New York; of Her Travels in Europe and South America; Her Mining Adventures on the Pacific Slope; Her Residence Among the Mormons; Her Love Affairs, Courtships, Marriages, etc., etc.* Edited by C. J. Worthington, Hartford, Conn.: T. Belknap, 1876. 606 pp.

VIVA. *Superstar.* New York: Lancer Books, 1970.

VORSE, MARY HEATON. *A Footnote to Folly: Reminiscences of Mary Heaton Vorse.* New York: Farrar & Rinehart, 1935.

WALD, LILLIAN D. *The House on Henry Street.* New York: Dover Publications, 1971.

WATERS, ETHEL. *His Eye Is on the Sparrow.* New York: Jove Publications, 1972.

WELLS, IDA B. *Crusade for Justice: The Autobiography of Ida B. Wells.* Edited by Alfreda M. Duster. Chicago: University of Chicago Press, 1970.

WHARTON, EDITH. *A Backward Glance.* New York: Appleton-Century Co., 1934.

WHITE, ELIZABETH. *The Experiences of God's Gracious Dealings with Mrs. Elizabeth White: As They Were Written Under Her Own Hand, and Found in Her Closet After Her Decease, December 5, 1669.* Boston: S. Kneeland, 1741.

WHITELEY, OPAL. *The Story of Opal: The Journal of an Understanding Heart.* Boston: Atlantic Monthly Press, 1920.

WHITMAN, NARCISSA. In *First White Women over the Rockies: Diaries, Letters, and Biographical Sketches of the Six Women of the Oregon Mission Who Made the Overland Journey in 1836 and 1838.* Introduced and edited by Clifford Merrill Drury. 3 vols. Glendale, Ca.: A. H. Clark Co., 1963–66.

WILLARD, FRANCES E. *Glimpses of Fifty Years: The Autobiography of an American Woman.* Chicago, Philadelphia, Kansas City, Oakland, Ca.: H. J. Smith & Co., for the Women's Temperance Publication Association, 1889.

WISTER, SARAH. *Sally Wister's Journal; A True Narrative; Being a Quaker Maiden's Account of Her Experiences with Officers of the Continental Army, 1777–1778.* Edited by Albert Cook Myers. Philadelphia: Ferris & Leach Publishers, 1902.

WOOLF, VIRGINIA. *A Writer's Diary.* Edited by Leonard Woolf. New York: Harcourt Brace Jovanovich, 1973.

———. *The Diary of Virginia Woolf.* Edited by Anne Oliver Bell. 5 vols. New York: Harcourt Brace Jovanovich, 1984.

WORTLEY, VICTORIA. *A Young Traveller's Journal.* London: John Murray, 1879.

Critical Works

ABEL, ELIZABETH, ed. *Writing and Sexual Difference.* Chicago: University of Chicago Press, 1982.

ADAMS, TIMOTHY DOW. "The Contemporary American Mock-Autobiography." *Clio* 8, no. 3 (Spring 1979):417–28.

ADDIS, PATRICIA K. *Through a Woman's I: An Annotated Bibliography of American Women's Autobiographical Writings, 1946–1976.* Metuchen, N.J.: Scarecrow Press, 1983.

ARKSEY, LAURA, PRIES, NANCY, and REED, MARCIA, comps. *American Diaries: An Annotated Bibliography of Published American Diaries.* Vol. 1, *Diaries Written from 1492 to 1844.* Detroit: Gale Research Co., 1983.

BACHSCHEIDER, PAUL R., NUSSBAUM, FELICITY A., and ANDERSON, PHILIP B., comps. *Annotated Bibliography of Critical Studies of Women and Literature, 1660–1800.* New York: Garland Publishing Co., 1977.

BALLARD, GEORGE. *Memoirs of Several Ladies of Great Britain, Who Have Been Celebrated for Their Writings or Skill in the Learned Languages, Arts, and Sciences.* Oxford: W. Jackson, 1752.

BANES, RUTH A. "The Exemplary Self: Autobiography in Eighteenth-Century America." *Biography* 5, no. 3 (Summer 1982):226–39.

BARTON, REBECCA CHALMERS. *Witnesses for Freedom: Negro Americans in Autobiography.* New York: Harper, 1948. Reprint. Oakdale, N.Y.: Dowling College Press, 1976.

BATES, E. STUART. *Inside Out: An Introduction to Autobiography.* New York: Sheridan House, 1937.

BATTS, JOHN STUART. *British Manuscript Diaries of the Nineteenth Century: An Annotated History.* Totawa, N.J.: Rowman & Littlefield, 1976.

BAYLISS, JOHN F. *Black Slave Narratives.* New York: Macmillan, 1970.

BERCOVITCH, SACVAN. "Emerson the Prophet: Romanticism, Puritanism, and

Auto-American-Biography." In *Emerson: Prophecy, Metamorphosis, and Influence,* edited by David Levin, pp. 1–27. New York: Columbia University Press, 1975.

———. *The Puritan Origins of the American Self.* New Haven: Yale University Press, 1975.

BERGER, JOSEF, and BERGER, DOROTHY, eds. *Small Voices.* New York: P. S. Eriksson, 1967.

BILLSON, MARCUS. "The Memoir: New Perspectives on a Forgotten Genre." *Genre* 10 (Summer 1977):259–82.

BLASING, MUTLU KONUK. *The Art of Life: Studies in American Autobiographical Literature.* Austin: University of Texas Press, 1977.

BLOOM, LYNN Z. "Promises Fulfilled: Positive Images of Women in Twentieth-Century Autobiographies." In *Feminist Criticism: Essays on Theory, Poetry, and Prose,* edited by Cheryl L. Brown and Karen Olson, pp. 324–38. Metuchen, N.J.: Scarecrow Press, 1978.

BONTEMPS, ARNA, ed. *Great Slave Narratives.* Boston: Beacon Press, 1969.

BOTTRALL, MARGARET. *Every Man a Phoenix: Studies in Seventeenth-Century Autobiography.* London: John Murray, 1958.

BOTTRALL, MARGARET, ed. *Personal Records: A Gallery of Self-Portraits.* New York: John Day, 1961.

BRIDGMAN, RICHARD. *Gertrude Stein in Pieces.* New York: Oxford University Press, 1970.

BRIGNANO, RUSSELL C., comp. *Black Americans in Autobiography: An Annotated Bibliography of Autobiographies and Autobiographical Books Written since the Civil War.* Durham, N.C.: Duke University Press, 1974.

BRISCOE, MARY LOUISE. "Political Autobiography." *American Notes and Queries* 16 (September 1977):6–8 (entire issue devoted to women's autobiographies).

BRISCOE, MARY LOUISE, TOBIAS, BARBARA, and BLOOM, LYNN Z., comps. *American Autobiography, 1945–1980: A Bibliography.* Madison: University of Wisconsin Press, 1982.

BROWNSTEIN, RACHEL M. *Becoming a Heroine: Reading about Women in Novels.* New York: Viking Press, 1982.

BRUMBLE, H. DAVID III, comp. *An Annotated Bibliography of American Indian and Eskimo Autobiographies.* Lincoln: University of Nebraska Press, 1981.

BRUSS, ELIZABETH W. *Autobiographical Acts: The Changing Situation of a Literary Genre.* Baltimore: Johns Hopkins University Press, 1976.

BUCKLEY, JEROME HAMILTON. *The Turning Key: Autobiography and the Subjective Impulse since 1800.* Cambridge, Mass.: Harvard University Press, 1984.

BURR, ANNA ROBESON. *The Autobiography: A Critical and Comparative Study.* Boston: Houghton Mifflin, 1909.

BUTTERFIELD, STEPHEN. *Black Autobiography in America.* Amherst: University of Massachusetts Press, 1974.

Bibliography

BUTTURFF, DOUGLAS, and EPSTEIN, EDMUND L., eds. *Women's Language and Style.* Akron, Ohio: L & S Books, 1978.

CHODOROW, NANCY. "Family Structure and Feminine Personality." In *Woman, Culture, and Society,* edited by M. Z. Rosaldo and L. Lamphere, pp. 43–66. Stanford: Stanford University Press, 1974.

CLARK, ARTHUR MELVILLE. *Autobiography: Its Genesis and Phases.* Edinburgh: Folcroft Press, 1935.

COCKSHUT, A. O. J. *The Art of Autobiography in Nineteenth- and Twentieth-Century England.* New Haven: Yale University Press, 1984.

COLE, JOHNNETTA B. "Black Women in America: An Annotated Bibliography." *Black Scholar* 3 (December 1971):42–53.

COOLEY, THOMAS. *Educated Lives: The Rise of Modern Autobiography in America.* Columbus: Ohio State University Press, 1976.

COTT, NANCY F. *The Bonds of Womanhood: "Woman's Sphere" in New England, 1780–1835.* New Haven: Yale University Press, 1977.

COUSER, G. THOMAS. *American Autobiography: The Prophetic Mode.* Amherst: University of Massachusetts Press, 1979.

CULLEY, MARGO, ed. *A Day at a Time: The Diary Literature of American Women: From 1764 to the Present.* New York: Feminist Press, 1986.

DAVIS, CHARLES T., and GATES, HENRY LOUIS, JR., eds. *The Slave's Narrative.* New York: Oxford University Press, 1985.

DELANY, PAUL. *British Autobiography in the Seventeenth Century.* New York: Columbia University Press; London: Routledge & Kegan Paul, 1969.

DELANY, SHEILA. *Writing Woman: Women Writers and Women in Literature: Medieval to Modern.* New York: Schocken Books, 1983.

deMAN, PAUL. "Autobiography as De-facement." *Modern Language Notes: Comparative Literature* 94, no.5 (December 1979):919–30.

DIAMOND, ARLYN, and EDWARDS, LEE R., eds. *The Authority of Experience: Essays in Feminist Criticism.* Amherst: University of Massachusetts Press, 1977.

DINER, HELEN. *Mothers and Amazons: The First Feminine History of Culture.* Edited and translated by John Philip Lundin. Introduction by Brigitte Berger. New York: Anchor Books, 1973.

DONOVAN, JOSEPHINE, ed. *Feminist Literary Criticism: Explorations in Theory.* Lexington: University Press of Kentucky, 1975.

DOUGLAS, ANN. *The Feminization of American Culture.* New York: Alfred A. Knopf, 1977.

DOWIE, MÉNIE MURIEL. *Women Adventurers.* London: T. F. Unwin, 1893.

EAKIN, PAUL JOHN. *Fictions in Autobiography: Studies in the Art of Self-Invention.* Princeton: Princeton University Press, 1985.

EBNER, DEAN. *Autobiography in Seventeenth-Century England: Theology and the Self.* The Hague: Mouton, 1971.

EDKINS, CAROL. "Quest for Community: Spiritual Autobiographies of Eighteenth-Century Quaker and Puritan Women in America." In *Women's Autobiography: Essays in Criticism,* edited by Estelle C. Jelinek, pp. 39–52. Bloomington: Indiana University Press, 1980.

EDWARDS, LEE R. "The Labors of Psyche: Toward a Theory of Female Heroism." *Critical Inquiry* 6 (Autumn 1979):33–49.

ELLMANN, MARY. *Thinking about Women.* New York: Harcourt Brace Jovanovich, 1968.

ERIKSON, ERIK H. *Childhood and Society.* New York: W. W. Norton, 1950.

EVANS, ELIZABETH. *Weathering the Storm: Women of the American Revolution.* New York: Charles Scribner's Sons, 1975.

EWENS, MARY. *The Role of the Nun in Nineteenth-Century America.* New York: Arno Press, 1978.

FLEISHMAN, AVROM. *Figures of Autobiography: The Language of Self-Writing in Victorian and Modern England.* Berkeley: University of California Press, 1983.

FINDLEY, SANDRA, and HOBBY, ELAINE. "Seventeenth-Century Women's Autobiography." In *1642: Literature and Power in the Seventeenth Century,* edited by Francis Barker et al., pp. 11–36. Colchester: University of Essex, Department of Literature, 1981.

FORBES, HARRIETTE M. *New England Diaries: 1602–1800: A Descriptive Catalogue of Diaries, Orderly Books, and Sea Journals.* New York: Russell & Russell, 1967.

FOSTER, FRANCES SMITH. *Witnessing Slavery: The Development of Ante-Bellum Slave Narratives.* Westport, Conn.: Greenwood Press, 1979.

FOTHERGILL, ROBERT A. *Private Chronicles: A Study of English Diaries.* London: Oxford University Press, 1974.

FRASER, ANTONIA. *The Weaker Vessel: Women's Lot in Seventeenth-Century England.* New York: Alfred A. Knopf, 1984.

FURNEAUX, HENRY, ed. *The Annals of Tacitus.* 2d ed. Vol. 1. Oxford: Clarendon Press, 1965.

GILBERT, SANDRA M., and GUBAR, SUSAN. *The Madwoman in the Attic: The Woman Writer in the Nineteenth-Century Literary Imagination.* New Haven: Yale University Press, 1979.

GILLIGAN, CAROL. *In a Different Voice: Psychological Theory and Women's Development.* Cambridge, Mass.: Harvard University Press, 1982.

GOODWATER, LEANNA, comp. *Women in Antiquity: An Annotated Bibliography.* Metuchen, N.J.: Scarecrow Press, 1975.

GORNICK, VIVIAN. "Toward a Definition of the Female Sensibility." *Village Voice,* 31 May 1973, pp. 21–22.

GOULIANOS, JOAN, ed. *By a Woman Writt: Literature from Six Centuries by and about Women.* Baltimore: Penguin Books, 1973.

GUNN, JANET VARNER. *Autobiography: Toward a Poetics of Experience.* Philadelphia: University of Pennsylvania Press, 1982.

GUSDORF, GEORGES. "Conditions and Limits of Autobiography." In *Autobiography: Essays Theoretical and Critical,* edited and translated by James Olney, pp. 28–48. Princeton: Princeton University Press, 1980. Originally appeared as "Conditions et limites de l'autobiographie." In *Formen der Selbstdarstellung: Analekten zu einer Geschichte des literarischen Selbstportraits,* edited by Günther Reichenkron and Erich Haase, pp. 105–23. Berlin: Duncker & Humblot, 1956.

HART, FRANCIS R. "Notes for an Anatomy of Modern Autobiography." *New Literary History* 1 (Spring 1970):485–511.

———. "History Talking to Itself: Public Personality in Recent Memoir." *New Literary History* 11 (Autumn 1979):193–210.

HASKELL, ANN S. "The Paston Women on Marriage in Fifteenth-Century England." *Viator* 4 (1973):459–71.

HEILBRUN, CAROLYN G. *Toward a Recognition of Androgyny.* New York: Harper & Row, 1973.

HIATT, MARY. *The Way Women Write.* New York: Teachers College Press, 1977.

HOFFMANN, LEONORE, and CULLEY, MARGO, eds. *Women's Personal Narratives: Essays in Criticism and Pedagogy.* New York: Modern Language Association, 1985.

HOWARTH, WILLIAM L. "Some Principles of Autobiography." *New Literary History* 5 (Winter 1974):363–81.

IRELAND, NORMA OLIN, ed. *Index to Women of the World: From Ancient to Modern Times: Biographies and Portraits.* Westwood, Mass.: F. W. Faxon, 1970.

JAMES, EDWARD T., JAMES, JANET WILSON, and BOYER, PAUL S., eds. *Notable American Women, 1607–1950: A Biographical Dictionary.* 3 vols. Cambridge, Mass.: Harvard University Press, 1971.

JELINEK, ESTELLE C. "Women's Autobiography and the Male Tradition." Introduction to *Women's Autobiography: Essays in Criticism,* pp. 1–20. Bloomington: Indiana University Press, 1980.

———. "Disguise Autobiographies: Women Masquerading as Men." *Women's Studies International Forum* (special issue on women's autobiographies) (1986).

JOHNSON, EDGAR. *One Mighty Torrent: The Drama of Biography.* New York: Stackpole Sons, 1937.

JONES, MARCIA BELL. "Self-Images: A Study of Female Autobiography Written in England from 1600–1800." Ph.D. dissertation, University of North Carolina at Chapel Hill, 1978.

KAGLE, STEVEN E. *American Diary Literature: 1620–1799.* Boston: Twayne Publishers, 1979.

KAPLAN, LOUIS, comp. *A Bibliography of American Autobiographies.* Madison: University of Wisconsin Press, 1961.

KAZIN, ALFRED. "Autobiography as Narrative." *Michigan Quarterly Review* 3 (Fall 1964):210–16.

KELLEY, MARY, ed. *Woman's Being, Woman's Place: Female Identity and Vocation in American History.* Boston: G. K. Hall, 1979.

KOLODNY, ANNETTE. "The Lady's Not for Spurning: Kate Millett and the Critics." *Contemporary Literature* 17 (Autumn 1976):541–62.

———. *The Land before Her: Fantasy and Experience of the American Frontiers, 1630–1860.* Chapel Hill: University of North Carolina Press, 1984.

LAFFIN, JOHN. *Women in Battle.* London: Abelard-Schuman, 1967.

LAKOFF, ROBIN. *Language and Woman's Place.* New York: Harper & Row, 1975.

LANDOW, GEORGE P., ed. *Approaches to Victorian Autobiography.* Athens: Ohio University Press, 1979.

LANGER, ELINOR. *Josephine Herbst: The Story She Could Never Tell.* Boston: Atlantic-Little Brown, 1984.

LEJEUNE, PHILIPPE. *L'Autobiographie en France.* Paris: Armand Colin, 1971.

LERNER, GERDA. *The Female Experience: An American Documentary.* Indianapolis: Bobbs-Merrill, 1977.

LILLARD, RICHARD G. *American Life in Autobiography: A Descriptive Guide.* Stanford: Stanford University Press, 1956.

LOCKRIDGE, KENNETH A. *Literacy in Colonial New England: An Enquiry into the Social Context of Literacy in the Early Modern West.* New York: W. W. Norton, 1974.

LOEWENBERG, BERT JAMES, and BOGIN, RUTH, eds. *Black Women in Nineteenth-Century American Life: Their Words, Their Thought, Their Feelings.* University Park: Pennsylvania State University Press, 1976.

LUCHETTI, CATHY, with OLWELL, CAROL. *Women of the West.* St. George, Utah: Antelope Island Press, 1982.

McCONNELL-GINET, SALLY, BORKER, RUTH, and FURMAN, NELLY, eds. *Women and Language in Literature and Society.* New York: Praeger, 1980.

MANDEL, BARRETT JOHN. "The Autobiographer's Art." *Journal of Aesthetics and Art Criticism* 27 (1968):215–26.

———. "Basting the Image with a Certain Liquor: Death in Autobiography." *Soundings* 57 (1974):175–88.

MARKS, ELAINE. " 'I Am My Own Heroine': Some Thoughts about Women and Autobiography in France." *Female Studies* 9 (1975):1–10.

MASON, MARY G. "The Other Voice: Autobiographies of Women Writers." In *Autobiography: Essays Theoretical and Critical,* edited by James Olney, pp. 207–35. Princeton: Princeton University Press, 1980.

MASON, MARY GRIMLEY, and GREEN, CAROL HURD, eds. *Journeys: Autobiographical Writings by Women.* Boston: G. K. Hall, 1979.

MATTHEWS, WILLIAM, comp. *American Diaries: An Annotated Bibliography of American Diaries Written prior to the Year 1861.* Berkeley: University of California Press, 1945.

———. *British Diaries: An Annotated Bibliography of British Diaries Written between 1442 and 1942.* Berkeley: University of California Press, 1950.

———. *British Autobiographies: An Annotated Bibliography of British Autobiographies Published or Written before 1951.* Berkeley: University of California Press, 1955.

———. "Seventeenth-Century Autobiography." In *Autobiography, Biography, and the Novel,* pp. 3–28. Berkeley: University of California Press, 1973.

———. *American Diaries in Manuscript, 1580–1954: A Descriptive Bibliography.* Athens: University of Georgia Press, 1974.

MAY, ROBERT. *Sex and Fantasy: Patterns of Male and Female Development.* New York: W. W. Norton, 1980.

MAZLISH, BRUCE. "Autobiography and Psycho-Analysis: Between Truth and Self-Deception." *Encounter* 35 (October 1970):28–37.

MERRIAM, EVE. *Growing Up Female in America: Ten Lives.* New York: Dell, 1971.

MEYERS, MITZI. "Wollstonecraft's *Letters Written . . . in Sweden*: Toward Romantic Autobiography." *Studies in Eighteenth-Century Culture* 8 (1979):165–85.

———. "*Harriet Martineau's Autobiography:* The Making of a Female Philosopher." In *Women's Autobiography: Essays in Criticism,* edited by Estelle C. Jelinek, pp. 53–70. Bloomington: Indiana University Press, 1980.

MILLETT, KATE. *Sexual Politics.* New York: Doubleday, 1970.

———. *The Prostitution Papers: "A Quartet for Female Voices."* New York: Ballantine Books, 1976.

MISCH, GEORG. *A History of Autobiography in Antiquity.* Translated by E. W. Dickes. 2 vols. 1907. Reprint. London: Routledge & Kegan Paul, 1950.

MIZEJEWSKI, LINDA. "Sappho to Sexton: Woman Uncontained." *College English* 35 (December 1973):340–45.

MOERS, ELLEN. *Literary Women: The Great Writers.* New York: Doubleday, 1975.

MOFFAT, MARY JANE, and PAINTER, CHARLOTTE, eds. *Revelations: Diaries of Women.* New York: Vintage Books, 1974.

MORGAN, EDMUND S. *The Puritan Family: Religion and Domestic Relations in Seventeenth-Century New England.* New York: Harper & Row, 1966.

MORRIS, JOHN. *Versions of the Self: Studies in English Autobiography from John Bunyan to John Stuart Mill.* New York: Columbia University Press, 1966.

MURDOCK, KENNETH B. *Literature and Theology in Colonial New England.* Cambridge, Mass.: Harvard University Press, 1949.

Narratives of Captivity among the Indians of North America: A List of Books and Manuscripts on This Subject in the Edward E. Ayer Collection of the Newberry Library. Chicago: Newberry Library, 1961.

NORMAN, ROSE LYNN. "Autobiographies of American Women Writers before 1914." Ph.D. dissertation, University of Tennessee, 1979.

NYE, RUSSEL B., and GRABO, NORMAN S., eds. *American Thought and Writing.* Vol. 1, *The Colonial Period.* Boston: Houghton Mifflin, 1965.

O'BRIEN, LYNN W. *Plains Indian Autobiographies.* Boise, Idaho: Boise State College, 1973.

OLNEY, JAMES. *Metaphors of Self: The Meaning of Autobiography.* Princeton: Princeton University Press, 1972.

———. "Autobiography and the Cultural Moment: A Thematic, Historical, and Bibliographical Introduction." In *Autobiography: Essays Theoretical and Criti-*

cal, pp. 3–27. Princeton: Princeton University Press, 1980.

OMORI, ANNIE SHEPELY, and DOI KOCHI, trans. *Diaries of Court Ladies of Old Japan.* Introduction by Amy Lowell. Tokyo: Kenkyusha, 1935.

O'NEILL, EDWARD H. *A History of American Biography, 1800–1935.* Philadelphia: University of Pennsylvania Press, 1935.

OSBORN, JAMES, M. *The Beginnings of Autobiography in England.* Los Angeles: University of California, William Andrews Clark Memorial Library, 1960.

PASCAL, ROY. *Design and Truth in Autobiography.* Cambridge, Mass.: Harvard University Press, 1960.

PEARCE, ROY HARVEY. "The Significance of the Captivity Narrative." *American Literature* 19 (March 1947):1–20.

PILLING, JOHN. *Autobiography and Imagination: Studies in Self-Scrutiny.* London: Routledge & Kegan Paul, 1981.

POMERLEAU, CYNTHIA S. "The Emergence of Women's Autobiography in England." In *Women's Autobiography: Essays in Criticism,* edited by Estelle C. Jelinek, pp. 21–38. Bloomington: Indiana University Press, 1980.

PONSONBY, ARTHUR. *English Diaries.* London: Methuen & Co., 1923.

———. *More English Diaries.* London: Methuen & Co., 1927.

RHODES, CAROLYN H. *First Person Female American: A Selected and Annotated Bibliography of the Autobiographies of American Women Living after 1950.* Troy, N.Y.: Whitston Publishing Co., 1980.

RICHARD, BETTY. "Review Essay: Women and Writing: A Decade of Scholarship and Criticism." *Papers on Language and Literature* 18 (1982):91–111.

RILEY, GLENDA. *Women and Indians on the Frontier.* Albuquerque: University of New Mexico, 1984.

ROSENBERG, MARIE BAROVIC, and BERGSTROM, LEN V. *Women and Society: A Critical Review of the Literature with a Selected Annotated Bibliography.* Beverly Hills: Sage Publications, 1975.

ROSENFELD, ALVIN H. "Inventing the Jew: Notes on Jewish Autobiography." In *The American Autobiography: A Collection of Critical Essays,* edited by Albert E. Stone, pp. 133–56. Englewood Cliffs, N.J.: Prentice-Hall, 1981.

RUBIN, LILLIAN. *Intimate Strangers.* New York: Harper & Row, 1983.

SAYRE, ROBERT F. *The Examined Self: Benjamin Franklin, Henry Adams, Henry James.* Princeton: Princeton University Press, 1964.

———. "Autobiography and the Making of America." In *Autobiography: Essays Theoretical and Critical,* edited by James Olney, pp. 146–68. Princeton: Princeton University Press, 1981.

———. "The Proper Study: Autobiographies in American Studies." In *The American Autobiography: A Collection of Critical Essays,* edited by Albert E. Stone, pp. 11–30. Englewood Cliffs, N.J.: Prentice-Hall, 1981.

SCHLISSEL, LILLIAN. "Women's Diaries on the Western Frontier." *American Studies* 18 (Spring 1977):87–100.

SCHLISSEL, LILLIAN, ed. *Women's Diaries of the Westward Journey.* New York:

Schocken Books, 1982.

SCHMIDT, JAN ZLOTNIK. "The Other: A Study of the Persona in Several Contemporary Women's Autobiographies." *CEA Critic* 43 (November 1980):24–31.

SCHULTZ, ELIZABETH. "To Be Black and Blue: The Blues Genre in Black American Autobiography." *Kansas Quarterly* 7 (1975):81–96.

SHAPIRO, STEPHEN A. "The Dark Continent of Literature: Autobiography." *Comparative Literature Studies* 5 (December 1968):421–52.

SHEA, DANIEL B., JR. *Spiritual Autobiography in Early America.* Princeton: Princeton University Press, 1968.

SHOWALTER, ELAINE. *A Literature of Their Own: British Women Novelists from Brontë to Lessing.* Princeton: Princeton University Press, 1977.

SHUMAKER, WAYNE. *English Autobiography: Its Emergence, Materials, and Form.* Berkeley: University of California Press, 1954.

SICHERMAN, BARBARA, and GREEN, CAROL HURD, eds. *Notable American Women: The Modern Period.* Cambridge, Mass.: Harvard University Press, 1980.

SIMPSON, WILLIAM KELLY, ed. *The Literature of Ancient Egypt: An Anthology of Stories, Instructions, and Poetry.* Translated by R. O. Faulkner, Edward F. Wente, Jr., and William Kelly Simpson. Introduction by William Kelly Simpson. New Haven: Yale University Press, 1972.

SMITH, CATHERINE F. "Jane Lead: Mysticism and the Woman Cloathed with the Sun." In *Shakespeare's Sisters: Feminist Essays on Women Poets,* edited by Sandra M. Gilbert and Susan Gubar, pp. 3–18. Bloomington: Indiana University Press, 1979.

SMITH, SIDONIE. *Where I'm Bound: Patterns of Slavery and Freedom in Black American Autobiography.* Westport, Conn.: Greenwood Press, 1974.

SMITH-ROSENBERG, CARROLL. "The Female World of Love and Ritual: Relations between Women in Nineteenth-Century America." *Signs* 1 (Autumn 1975):1–29.

SPACKS, PATRICIA MEYER. "Reflecting Women." *Yale Review* 63 (October 1973):26–42.

———. *The Female Imagination.* New York: Alfred A. Knopf, 1975.

———. *Imagining a Self: Autobiography and Novel in Eighteenth-Century England.* Cambridge, Mass.: Harvard University Press, 1976.

———. "Self as Subject: A Female Language." In *In/Sights: Self-Portraits by Women,* edited with an introduction by Joyce Tenneson Cohen, pp. 110–14. Boston: David R. Godine, 1978.

———. "Selves in Hiding." In *Women's Autobiography: Essays in Criticism,* edited by Estelle C. Jelinek, pp. 112–32. Bloomington: Indiana University Press, 1980.

———. "Stages of Self—Notes on Autobiography and the Life Cycle." In *The American Autobiography: A Collection of Critical Essays,* edited by Albert E. Stone, pp. 44–60. Englewood Cliffs, N.J.: Prentice-Hall, 1981.

SPENDER, STEPHEN. "Confessions and Autobiography." In *The Making of a Poem.* London: Hamish Hamilton, 1955.

SPENGEMANN, WILLIAM C. *The Forms of Autobiography: Episodes in the History of a Literary Genre.* New Haven: Yale University Press, 1980.

SPENGEMANN, WILLIAM C., and LUNDQUIST, L. R. "Autobiography and the American Myth." *American Quarterly* 17 (Fall 1965):501–19.

SPURGEON, CAROLINE. *Mysticism in English Literature.* Cambridge: Cambridge University Press, 1913.

STARLING, MARION WILSON. *The Slave Narrative: Its Place in American History.* Boston: G. K. Hall, 1981.

STAROBINSKI, JEAN. "The Style of Autobiography." In *Literary Style: A Symposium,* edited by Seymour Chatman, pp. 285–94. New York: Oxford University Press, 1971.

STAUFFER, DONALD A. *English Biography before 1700.* Cambridge, Mass.: Harvard University Press, 1930.

———. *The Art of Biography in Eighteenth-Century England.* Princeton: Princeton University Press, 1941.

STERLING, DOROTHY. *Black Foremothers: Three Lives.* Old Westbury, N.Y.: Feminist Press; New York: McGraw-Hill, 1979.

STERLING, DOROTHY, ed. *We Are Your Sisters: Black Women in the Nineteenth Century.* New York: W. W. Norton, 1984.

STIMPSON, CATHARINE R. "The Mind, the Body, and Gertrude Stein." *Critical Inquiry* 3 (Spring 1977):489–506.

STONE, ALBERT E. "Autobiography and American Culture." *American Studies: An International Newsletter* 12 (Winter 1972):22–36.

———. "The Sea and the Self: Travel as Experience and Metaphor in Early American Autobiography." *Genre* 7 (September 1974):279–306.

———. "American Autobiographies as Individual Stories and Cultural Narratives." Introduction to *The American Autobiography: A Collection of Critical Essays,* pp. 1–9. Englewood Cliffs, N.J.: Prentice-Hall, 1981.

———. *Autobiographical Occasions and Original Acts: Versions of American Identity from Henry Adams to Nate Shaw.* Philadelphia: University of Pennsylvania Press, 1982.

STONE, ALBERT E., ed. *The American Autobiography: A Collection of Critical Essays.* Englewood Cliffs, N.J.: Prentice-Hall, 1981.

STONE, ROBERT KARL. *Middle English Prose Style: Margery Kempe and Julian of Norwich.* The Hague: Mouton, 1970.

STRATTON, JOANNA L., ed. *Pioneer Women: Voices from the Kansas Frontier.* Introduction by Arthur M. Schlesinger, Jr. New York: Simon & Schuster, 1981.

SUTHERLAND, DONALD. *Gertrude Stein: A Biography of Her Work.* New Haven: Yale University Press, 1951.

WEINTRAUB, KARL J. "Autobiography and Historical Consciousness." *Critical Inquiry* 1 (June 1975):821–48.

———. *The Value of the Individual: Self and Circumstance in Autobiography.* Chicago: University of Chicago Press, 1978.

WETHERED, H. N. *The Curious Art of Autobiography: From Benvenuto Cellini to Rudyard Kipling.* London: Christopher Johnson, 1956.

WINSTON, ELIZABETH. "The Autobiographer and Her Readers: From Apology to Affirmation." In *Women's Autobiography: Essays in Criticism,* edited by Estelle C. Jelinek, pp. 93–111. Bloomington: Indiana University Press, 1980.

WINTER, METTA L. " 'Heart Watching' through Journal Keeping: A Look at Quaker Diaries and Their Uses." *Women's Diaries: A Quarterly Newsletter* 1 (Spring 1983):1–3.

WOODWARD, C. VANN. "Mary Chesnut in Search of Her Genre." *Yale Review* 73 (January 1984):199–209.

WOOLF, VIRGINIA. *A Room of One's Own.* New York: Harcourt, Brace & World, 1929.

———. *The Common Reader.* New York: Vintage Books, 1953.

———. *The Second Common Reader.* New York: Vintage Books, 1960.

YELLIN, JEAN FAGAN. "Text and Contexts of Harriet Jacobs' *Incidents in the Life of a Slave Girl: Written by Herself.*" In *The Slave's Narrative,* edited by Charles T. Davis and Henry Louis Gates, Jr., pp. 262–82. New York: Oxford University Press, 1985.

YETMAN, NORMAN R., ed. *Life under the "Peculiar Institution": Selections from the Slave Narrative Collection.* New York: Holt, Rinehart, & Winston, 1970.

Index

— Index —

Index

Index

About the Author

Estelle C. Jelinek grew up in Philadelphia and studied at the University of Pennsylvania and the State University of New York, Buffalo, where she earned her Ph.D. in English in 1977. She is the recipient of a National Endowment for the Humanities fellowship (1975–76) in American autobiography and has taught literature at San Francisco State University and various other colleges in the Bay area. She is the editor of *Women's Autobiography: Essays in Criticism* (1980) and has published critical articles in such journals as *Women's Studies International Forum,* the *Women's Review of Books,* and *College English.* She lives in Berkeley, California, where she devotes herself full-time to writing and editing.